Humanities Data in R

Quantitative Methods in the Humanities and Social Sciences

Editorial Board
Thomas DeFanti, Anthony Grafton, Thomas E. Levy, Lev Manovich,
Alyn Rockwood

Quantitative Methods in the Humanities and Social Sciences is a book series designed to foster research-based conversation with all parts of the university campus from buildings of ivy-covered stone to technologically savvy walls of glass. Scholarship from international researchers and the esteemed editorial board represents the far-reaching applications of computational analysis, statistical models, computer-based programs, and other quantitative methods. Methods are integrated in a dialogue that is sensitive to the broader context of humanistic study and social science research. Scholars, including among others historians, archaeologists, classicists and linguists, promote this interdisciplinary approach. These texts teach new methodological approaches for contemporary research. Each volume exposes readers to a particular research method. Researchers and students then benefit from exposure to subtleties of the larger project or corpus of work in which the quantitative methods come to fruition.

More information about this series http://www.springer.com/series/11748

Taylor Arnold • Lauren Tilton

Humanities Data in R

Exploring Networks, Geospatial Data, Images, and Text

Taylor Arnold
Yale University
New Haven, CT, USA

Lauren Tilton
Yale University
New Haven, CT, USA

ISSN 2199-0956   ISSN 2199-0964 (electronic)
Quantitative Methods in the Humanities and Social Sciences
ISBN 978-3-319-20701-8   ISBN 978-3-319-20702-5 (eBook)
DOI 10.1007/978-3-319-20702-5

Library of Congress Control Number: 2015945113

Springer Cham Heidelberg New York Dordrecht London
© Springer International Publishing Switzerland 2015
This work is subject to copyright. All rights are reserved by the Publisher, whether the whole or part of the material is concerned, specifically the rights of translation, reprinting, reuse of illustrations, recitation, broadcasting, reproduction on microfilms or in any other physical way, and transmission or information storage and retrieval, electronic adaptation, computer software, or by similar or dissimilar methodology now known or hereafter developed.
The use of general descriptive names, registered names, trademarks, service marks, etc. in this publication does not imply, even in the absence of a specific statement, that such names are exempt from the relevant protective laws and regulations and therefore free for general use.
The publisher, the authors and the editors are safe to assume that the advice and information in this book are believed to be true and accurate at the date of publication. Neither the publisher nor the authors or the editors give a warranty, express or implied, with respect to the material contained herein or for any errors or omissions that may have been made.

Printed on acid-free paper

Springer International Publishing AG Switzerland is part of Springer Science+Business Media (www.springer.com)

Preface

There has been a rapid increase in the application of computational methods to humanities data in recent years. Numerous workshops, lectures, bootcamps, blogs, and texts have arisen to provide an introduction to these techniques. Many of these are very well presented and have enabled humanists with minimal technical background to quickly produce an impressive array of novel applications and scholarship.

The goal of this text is to complement rather than duplicate this extant body of work. We aim to address two distinct groups of readers: students in a one- or two-semester introductory course on digital methods in the humanities and intermediate users looking for a self-study text to solidify and extend their basic working knowledge of both computational methods and R. While entirely self-contained, the text moves at a pace that may be difficult for complete beginners without supplementary materials such as additional R tutorials or the support and structure of a formal classroom.

A particular challenge of applying computational methods in the humanities is that data is often unstructured and complex. Typical examples include large text corpora, archives of digital images, and geospatially enriched databases. Each of these require customized techniques for visualization and analysis, none of which are commonly taught in introductory texts in statistics. As such, this text is structured around the four basic data types commonly encountered in digital humanities: networks, geospatial data, images, and text. Dedicated chapters present techniques specific to each of these data types, preceded by an introduction to the general principles of exploratory data analysis. The result is a single text that brings together several disparate methodologies, preparing students and scholars to integrate computational methods into their own work.

A Note to Instructors

We have made this text as modular as possible without being overly repetitive. An instructor should be able to teach any permutation or subset of the individual chapters by filling in only small gaps in the material with additional background information as the need arises. It is also possible to teach the material with an emphasis on only the core computational concepts, with the code snippets and specific R syntax presented at a later point. One particular approach that we recommend for a single semester course is to start with Chap. 6, a relatively accessible introduction to network analysis, followed by a quick study of the basic syntax and plotting commands in R presented in Chaps. 2–4, with the remainder of the semester spent on whichever topics from Chaps. 7–10 are of most relevance and interest. A two-semester course should allow for sufficient time to work through all of the later chapters, as well as covering the introductory exploratory data analysis material in more detail.

The modularity of each chapter also allows them to be used as a basis for independent workshops. If one is willing to either focus only on the core concepts or require a basic working knowledge of R as a prerequisite, we have found that each chapter can be taught in a single day, with 2–3 days being ideal. With a week-long workshop, it is possible to weave in some additional introductory programming material to teach the basics of R alongside the broader computational concepts.

Supplementary Materials

We make extensive use of example datasets through this text. Particular care was taken to use data in the public domain, or otherwise freely and openly accessible. Whenever possible, subsets of larger archives were used instead of smaller one-off datasets. This approach has the dual benefit that these larger sets are often of independent interest, as well as providing an easy source of additional data for use in course projects, lectures, and further study. These datasets are available (or linked to) from the text's website:

```
http://humanitiesdata.org/
```

Complete code snippets from the text, further references, and additional links and notes are also included in that site and will continue to be updated.

Our Background

Applying computational techniques to humanities data should ultimately yield new scholarly questions and knowledge. We feel that the best way to accomplish these tasks is through the interdisciplinary collaboration between technical experts and humanists. With one of us (Lauren Tilton) a scholar of American Studies and the other (Taylor Arnold) a statistician, our primary fields of study respond well to this need.

We came to see the value of interdisciplinary work firsthand in the Fall of 2010. We had the good fortune of crossing paths and realized we shared mutual interests in data and the humanities. We soon embarked on our first project together, visualizing and analyzing 170,000 photographs from the Great Depression and World War II.[1] To look at each photograph for 5 s would take over 200 h. Neither possible nor desirable, computational techniques offered another set of techniques to read, explore, and analyze the entire collection. We came to view the methods and algorithms made possible through computation as a part of our methodological toolbox just like the theorists such as Judith Butler, Jerome Friedman, Michel Foucault, and John Tukey who undergird our scholarly inquiry. Visualization and algorithmic approaches held the potential to reveal latent information about the collection at different scales including at the level of the individual photograph and the collection.[2] We also hoped to see new questions and scholarship about the collection surface, thanks to an interdisciplinary approach.

Accordingly, the book is written in the way we believe some of the best interdisciplinary scholarship is approached. It is a merger of expertise in order to find ways to build a bridge across disciplines while acknowledging that each field is key to the bridge's foundation. For those with a background in social science and science, the idea of collaboration and co-authorship is fundamental. On the other hand, single author scholarship remains central to the humanities. Therefore, we see this book as a testament to the need to acknowledge the collaboration necessary in interdisciplinary work, particularly in digital humanities.

Acknowledgments

It would not have been possible to write this text without the collaboration and support offered by our many colleagues, friends, and family. In particular, we would like to thank those who agreed to read and comment on the early drafts of this text: Carol Chiodo, Jay Emerson, Alex Gil, Jason Heppler, Matthew Jockers, Mike Kane, Lev Manovich, Laura Wexler, Jeri Wieringa, and two anonymous readers.

New Haven, CT, USA   Taylor Arnold
July 2015   Lauren Tilton

---

[1] The project continues under the name *Photogrammar*, available at: photogrammar.yale.edu.

[2] See our more technical paper at: https://github.com/statsmaths/dhq-paper.

Contents

Part I Basics

1 Set-Up **3**
    1.1   Introduction 3
    1.2   Structure of This Book 4
    1.3   Obtaining R 5
    1.4   Supplemental Materials 5
    1.5   Getting Help with R 5
    References 6

2 A Short Introduction to R **7**
    2.1   Introduction 7
    2.2   Calculator and Objects 7
    2.3   Numeric Vectors 9
    2.4   Logical Vectors 11
    2.5   Subsetting 12
    2.6   Character Vectors 14
    2.7   Matrices and Data Frames 16
    2.8   Data I/O 19
    2.9   Advanced Subsetting 22
    References 24

3 EDA I: Continuous and Categorical Data **25**
    3.1   Introduction 25
    3.2   Tables 26

	3.3	Histogram	29
	3.4	Quantiles	31
	3.5	Binning	35
	3.6	Control Flow	37
	3.7	Combining Plots	40
	3.8	Aggregation	42
	3.9	Applying Functions	44
		References	46
4	**EDA II: Multivariate Analysis**		**47**
	4.1	Introduction	47
	4.2	Scatter Plots	47
	4.3	Text	50
	4.4	Points	53
	4.5	Line Plots	54
	4.6	Scatter Plot Matrix	58
	4.7	Correlation Matrix	60
5	**EDA III: Advanced Graphics**		**63**
	5.1	Introduction	63
	5.2	Output Formats	63
	5.3	Color	65
	5.4	Legends	70
	5.5	Randomness	71
	5.6	Additional Parameters	76
	5.7	Alternative Methods	77
		References	78

Part II Humanities Data Types

6	**Networks**		**81**
	6.1	Introduction	81
	6.2	A Basic Graph	81
	6.3	Citation Networks	84
	6.4	Graph Centrality	87
	6.5	Graph Communities	90
	6.6	Further Extensions	92
		References	93
7	**Geospatial Data**		**95**
	7.1	Introduction	95
	7.2	From Scatter Plots to Maps	96
	7.3	Map Projections and Input Formats	100
	7.4	Enriching Tabular Data with Geospatial Data	105
	7.5	Enriching Geospatial Data with Tabular Data	107

Contents

	7.6 Further Extensions 110
	References 110

8 Image Data **113**
   8.1 Introduction 113
   8.2 Basic Image I/O 113
   8.3 Day/Night Photographic Corpus 117
   8.4 Principal Component Analysis 120
   8.5 K-Means 123
   8.6 Scatter Plot of Raster Graphics 126
   8.7 Extensions 127
   References 129

9 Natural Language Processing **131**
   9.1 Introduction 131
   9.2 Tokenization and Sentence Splitting 132
   9.3 Lemmatization and Part of Speech Tagging 134
   9.4 Dependencies 138
   9.5 Named Entity Recognition 143
   9.6 Coreference 145
   9.7 Case Study: Sherlock Holmes Main Characters .. 148
   9.8 Other Languages 150
   9.9 Conclusions and Extensions 152
   References 153

10 Text Analysis **157**
   10.1 Introduction 157
   10.2 Term Frequency: Inverse Document Frequency .. 157
   10.3 Topic Models 162
   10.4 Stylometric Analysis 167
   10.5 Further Methods and Extensions 174
   References 175

Part III   Appendix

11 R Packages **179**
   11.1 Installing from Within R 179
   11.2 rJava 181
   11.3 coreNLP 181
   11.4 sessionInfo 182

12 100 Basic Programming Exercises **183**

13 100 Basic Programming Solutions **193**

About the Authors

Taylor Arnold is a Senior Scientist at AT&T Labs Research and Lecturer of Statistics at Yale University. His research focuses on statistical computing, numerical linear algebra, and machine learning. He is the technical director of Photogrammar (`photogrammar.yale.edu`).

Lauren Tilton is a Doctoral Candidate in American Studies at Yale University. Her interests include documentary media, twentieth-century history, and visual culture. She is an active member of the digital humanities community, serving as the humanities director of Photogrammar and co-principal investigator of the Participatory Media project.

Part I
Basics

Chapter 1
Set-Up

Abstract In this chapter, an introduction to the text as a whole and the basics for getting set-up with the R programming language are given.

1.1 Introduction

Exploratory data analysis (EDA), initially described in John Tukey's classic text by the same name, is a general approach to examining data through visualizations and broad summary statistics [6].[1] It prioritizes studying data directly in order to generate hypotheses and ascertain general trends prior to, and often in lieu of, formal statistical modeling. The growth in both data volume and complexity has further increased the need for a careful application of these exploratory techniques. In the intervening 40 years, techniques for EDA have enjoyed great popularity within statistics, computer science, and many other data-driven fields and professions.

Concurrent with Tukey's development of EDA, Rick Becker, John Chambers, and Allan Wilks of Bell Labs began developing software designed specifically for statistical computing.[2] By 1980, the "S" language was released for general distribution outside Labs. It was followed by a popular series of books and updates, including "New S" and "S-Plus" [1, 2, 3, 5]. In the early 1990s, Ross Ihaka and Robert Gentleman produced a fully open-source implementation of S called "R".[3] Their implementation has become the de-facto tool in the field of statistics and is often cited as being amongst the Top-20 used programming languages in the world.[4]

---

[1] An enjoyable and highly recommended biography of Tukey by David Brillinger (a student of his) was recently published by the *Annals of Statistics* [4].

[2] John Tukey in fact split his time between Bell Labs and Princeton during this time.

[3] It is called "R" for it is both the "next letter in the alphabet" and the shared initial in the Authors' names.

[4] See www.tiobe.com/index.php/tiobe_index for one such ranking. Exact rankings of programming language use are, however, impossible to produce to everyone's satisfaction, and results often lead to fairly heated debate. Our point is simply to point out that R is not strictly a tool for a small niche of academic research, but is in fact used quite broadly.

© Springer International Publishing Switzerland 2015
T. Arnold, L. Tilton, *Humanities Data in R*, Quantitative Methods
in the Humanities and Social Sciences, DOI 10.1007/978-3-319-20702-5_1

There is a clear and strong link between EDA and S/R.[5] Each owes a great deal of gratitude to the other for their continued popularity. Without the interactive console and flexible graphics engine of a language such as R, modern data analysis techniques would be largely intractable. Conversely, without the tools of EDA, R would likely still have been a welcome simplification to programming in lower-level languages, but would have played a far less pivotal role in the development of applied statistics.

The historical context of these two topics underscores the motivation for studying both concurrently. In addition, we see this book as contributing to efforts to bring new communities to learn from and to help shape data analysis by offering other fields of study to engage with. It is an attempt to provide an introduction for students and scholars in the humanities and the humanistic social sciences to both EDA and R. It also shows how data analysis with humanities data can be a powerful method for humanistic inquiry.

1.2 Structure of This Book

The book is written in two parts. The first half is an overview of R and EDA. Chapter 2 provides a very basic and straightforward introduction to the language itself. Chapters 3–5 give an introduction to the tools of data analysis by way of worked examples using the rich demographic data from the United States American Community Survey and the French 2012 Presidential Election. Since concepts and analysis build off work in previous chapters, these introductory chapters are meant to be read sequentially. Chapter 12 provides 100 short programming questions for further practice, with example solutions in Chap. 13.

The second half introduces key areas of analysis for humanities data. Each chapter introduces a type of analysis and how it can be applied to humanities data sets along with practice problems and extensions. While some concepts are referenced between chapters, each is intended to stand on its own (with the exception of Chaps. 9 and 10, which should be read as a pair).

For those new to the concepts covered in this book, we recommend skimming the chapters in the second half that interest you before walking through the first half. The code may look daunting, but do not fret. The second half provides examples and reasons why these methods and forms of analysis are informative and exciting. We find it easier to learn how to code and explore data when we know what scholarly questions and modes of inquiry excite us.

---

[5] We will refer to the language simply as R for the remainder of this text for simplicity and to conform to the majority of other references; this is meant in no way as a lack of appreciation for the historical importance of the original "S".

1.3 Obtaining R

The majority of readers will eventually want to follow along with the code and examples given through the text. The first step in doing so is to obtain a working copy of R. The Comprehensive R Archive Network, or CRAN, is the official home of the R language and supplies download instructions according to a user's operating system (i.e., Mac, Windows, Linux):

```
http://cran.r-project.org/
```

A popular alternative, particularly for users with limited to no programming background, is offered by RStudio:

```
http://www.rstudio.com/
```

The company offers commercial support but provides a single-user version of the software at no cost. Other download options exist for advanced users, up-to and including a custom build from the source code. We make no assumptions throughout this text regarding which operating system or method of obtaining or accessing R readers have chosen. In the rare cases where differences exist based on these options, they will be explicitly addressed.

A major selling point of R is its extensive collection of user-contributed add-ons, called packages. The details of these packages and how to install them are described in detail in Chap. 11.

1.4 Supplemental Materials

In addition to the R software, walking through the examples in this text requires access to the datasets we explore. Care has been taken to ensure that these are all contained in the public domain so as to make it easy for us to redistribute to readers. The materials and download instructions can be found here:

```
http://humanitiesdata.org/
```

For convenience, a complete copy of the code from the book is also provided to make replicating (and extending) our results as easy as possible.

1.5 Getting Help with R

Learning to program is hard and invariably questions and issues will arise in the process (even the most experienced users require help with surprisingly high frequency). The first source of help should be the internal R help documentation, which we describe in detail in Chap. 2. When these fail to address a question, a web search will often turn up the desired result.

When further help is required, the R mailing lists, `http://www.r-project.org/mail.html`, and the third-party question and answer site, `stackoverflow.com/`, provide mechanisms for submitting questions to a broad community of R users. Both will also frequently show up as highly ranking results when running generic web searches for R help.

References

[1] Richard A Becker and John M Chambers. *S: an interactive environment for data analysis and graphics.* CRC Press, 1984.

[2] Richard A Becker and John M Chambers. *Extending the S system.* Wadsworth Advanced Books and Software, 1985.

[3] Richard A Becker, John M Chambers, and Allan Reeve Wilks. The new s language: A programming environment for data analysis and graphics, 1988.

[4] David R Brillinger. John W. Tukey: his life and professional contributions. *Annals of Statistics*, pages 1535–1575, 2002.

[5] John M Chambers and Trevor J Hastie. *Statistical models in S.* CRC Press, Inc., 1991.

[6] John W Tukey. Exploratory data analysis. *Reading, Ma*, 231:32, 1977.

Chapter 2
A Short Introduction to R

Abstract In this chapter, a basic introduction to working with objects in R is given. We provide the minimal working knowledge to work through the remainder of Part I. Basic computations on vectors, matrices, and data frames are shown. Particular attention is given to R's subsetting mechanism as it is often a source of confusion for new users.

2.1 Introduction

Here we provide an introduction to the core features of the R programming language. It is meant to provide enough of a background to proceed through Part I. It is not exhaustive, with some important features, such as random variable generation and control flow functions, presented as they are necessary. This chapter should provide the right depth for getting started. Practice problems are also given in Chap. 12 (with solutions in Chap. 13). Anyone comfortable with other scripting languages will most likely find a quick read sufficient. Accordingly, we assume that readers have already managed to download and set up R as described in Chap. 1.

For readers looking for a dense and complete introduction, we recommend the freely available manual "An Introduction to R" [2]. On the other hand, readers looking for a slower introduction to the language may prefer first working through Matthew Jockers's "Text Analysis with R for Students of Literature" [1].

2.2 Calculator and Objects

The R console can be used as a simple calculator. Typing in a mathematical expression and hitting enter prints out the result.

```
> 1 + 2
[1] 3
```

The familiar order of operation rules worked as expected and many mathematical functions such as the square root, sqrt, can also be applied.

```
> 1 / (2 + 17) - 1.5 + sqrt(2)
[1] -0.03315486
```

The result of a mathematical expression can be assigned to an object in R using the <- operator.

```
> x <- 1 + 2
```

When assignment is used, the result is no longer printed in the console window. If we want to see the result, we type the variable name x to print out its value.

```
> x
[1] 3
```

We can apply further manipulations to the constructed objects; for example, here we divide the value of x by 2.

```
> x/2
[1] 1.5
> x
[1] 3
```

The result 1.5 prints to the console; however, notice that the actual value of x has not changed. If we want to save the output it has to be reassigned to a variable (this does not have to be a new variable; x <- x/2 is allowed). Here we construct an object named y.

```
> y <- x/2
> y
[1] 1.5
```

At this point the object named x has a value of 3 and the object named y has a value of 1.5.

Every object in R belongs to a *class* describing the type of object it represents. To determine an object's class, we use a function called class[1]; this function has one input parameter named x. Accordingly, this input can be explicitly called (class(x=y)) or implicitly (class(y)).

```
> class(x=y)
[1] "numeric"
> class(y)
[1] "numeric"
```

---

[1] Functions are reusable code. Functions have a set of assumptions built in and can be accessed by placing a ? before the function name. Type ?class() in the R console. Note the usage information. It provides information about the functions' inputs. This particular function has one input parameter named x. Scroll down and inspect the documentation about the function. It may seem overwhelming at first, but it will be an important tool. Type q to exit and return to coding.

2.3 Numeric Vectors

In the second case, R assumes that since we did not name the input we intended the variable y to be assigned to the first (and in this case only) input x. The result shows that y is described as an object of type numeric; this is a generic class that holds any type of real number.

Everything in R is an object, including functions. Therefore we can even pass the function `class` to itself.

```
> class(x=class)
[1] "function"
```

We see here that "function" is a type of class. Another useful basic function is `ls` (LiSt objects). It does not require any arguments, and prints out the names of all the objects we have created.

```
> ls()
[1] "x" "y"
```

Notice that this list does not include the function class, even though we have determined that it exists and is a type of object. The reason is that by default only user-created objects are returned. If we really wanted to see all of the objects created in the base of R, like class, we need to override one of the default parameters of the function `ls`.[2]

```
> ls(envir=baseenv())
...
  [303] "chol.default"              "chol2inv"
  [305] "choose"                    "class"
  [307] "class<-"                   "clearPushBack"
  [309] "close"                     "close.connection"
...
```

The output is quite long, so we only display the few lines where the function `class` is shown. We show this as an example of the power in R's function syntax; allowing functions to have default values makes it easy to get simple results while not limiting the ability of users to customize functions as necessary.

2.3 Numeric Vectors

In R, a *vector* is a data structure containing a collection of multiple values with the same type. There are several types of vectors, six to be exact, with one of the most common being a numeric vector. A special function c(...) combines multiple values into a single vector object. For example, to create an object with the values 1, 10, and 100 run the following.

---

[2] We suggest trying this on your machine as well (do not worry about fully understanding the function call) in order to get an appreciation of the number of functions which are available by default within the base R language.

```
> vecObj <- c(1,10,100)
> vecObj
[1]   1  10 100
> class(vecObj)
[1] "numeric"
```

The resulting object is referred to as a vector. When we determine the object's class, we see that it is still a "numeric" object just like the single number objects explored in the previous section. The reason for this is that in R a single numeric value is represented as a length one vector rather than a separate type.[3]

We can conduct mathematical manipulations directly on vectors. Consider the following two examples:

```
> vecObj + 10
[1]  11  20 110
> vecObj + vecObj
[1]   2  20 200
```

In the first, we took a vector of length 3 and added a single number to it. The result added the single number to each element in the vector. In the second example, we add together two vectors each of length 3, with a result that adds each element of the vectors. In general, R evaluates expressions involving vectors of different lengths by *recycling* the shorter ones to match the longest one. For instance, if we add a length 6 vector to a length 2 vector, the first element of the shorter vector is added to the 1st, 3rd, and 5th elements of the longer one, whereas the second element of the shorter vector is added to the 2nd, 4th, and 6th elements of the longer one.

```
> c(1,2,3,4,5,6) + c(100,200)
[1] 101 202 103 204 105 206
```

The most common case of manipulating vectors involves expressions that mix vectors of a single given length with length-one vectors, but is important to recognize the more general case.

Constructing vectors by hand can quickly become cumbersome. A shortcut for building a vector of all the integers between two numbers is the colon operator, "`:`".[4] For example `1:84` returns a vector of all integers between 1 and 84.

```
> 1:84
 [1]  1  2  3  4  5  6  7  8  9 10 11 12 13 14 15 16 17 18 19 20 21
[22] 22 23 24 25 26 27 28 29 30 31 32 33 34 35 36 37 38 39 40 41 42
[43] 43 44 45 46 47 48 49 50 51 52 53 54 55 56 57 58 59 60 61 62 63
[64] 64 65 66 67 68 69 70 71 72 73 74 75 76 77 78 79 80 81 82 83 84
```

---

[3] The lack of a *scalar* type in R to represent individual objects is a major departure from many other programming languages such as Python, C, and Java.

[4] In R there is a formal distinction between *integer* ("whole" numbers) and *numeric* objects. However, for the level of this text, the distinction will not be important. R will silently convert between the two as necessary and should never cause unexpected behavior due to the distinction. We will use the term "integer" throughout to describe something which should be a whole number, but may be formally represented by an object of class numeric.

2.4 Logical Vectors

Finally, it is often useful to know the length of a given vector. In order to determine this, the `length` function is used. For example, `length(x=10:42)` would return the number 33.

2.4 Logical Vectors

Another useful and common type of vectors in R are logical vectors, which can be constructed as the output of using the expressions > (greater than), >= (greater than or equal), < (less than), <= (less than or equal), == (equal), and != (not equal).

```
> numericVec <- 1:10
> logicalVec <- (numericVec >= 5)
> logicalVec
 [1] FALSE FALSE FALSE FALSE  TRUE  TRUE  TRUE  TRUE  TRUE  TRUE
> class(logicalVec)
[1] "logical"
> numericVec == 4
 [1] FALSE FALSE FALSE  TRUE FALSE FALSE FALSE FALSE FALSE FALSE
```

In addition to creating logical vectors by manipulating numeric ones, we can also construct vectors by using the symbols TRUE and FALSE.

```
> logicalVec <- c(TRUE,TRUE,FALSE,TRUE)
> class(logicalVec)
[1] "logical"
```

Logical vectors can be manipulated via the ! (not), | (or), and & (and) expressions.

```
> logicalVec1 <- c(FALSE,FALSE,TRUE,TRUE)
> logicalVec2 <- c(FALSE,TRUE,FALSE,TRUE)
> logicalVec1 | logicalVec2
[1] FALSE  TRUE  TRUE  TRUE
> logicalVec1 & logicalVec2
[1] FALSE FALSE FALSE  TRUE
> !logicalVec1
[1]  TRUE  TRUE FALSE FALSE
```

Finally, logical vectors are converted to numeric ones when appropriate by mapping TRUE to the number 1 and FALSE to the number 0. Examples include using logical vectors in mathematical expressions.

```
> logicalVec1 + logicalVec2
[1] 0 1 1 2
> logicalVec1 + 1
[1] 1 1 2 2
> class(logicalVec1 + 1)
[1] "numeric"
```

We shall see that logical vectors are useful tools for filtering and manipulating other R objects.

2.5 Subsetting

There are four basic methods for accessing a subset of an R vector. We will discuss the three most common here. Constructing subsets of vectors in R is straightforward in principle, but it does quickly lead to fairly intricate, and often complex, code.

The syntax for all subsetting commands uses square brackets, [and], immediately following the name of the vector. If an integer i is placed in-between the brackets the element in position i is returned.[5] Here, for example, we pull out the 20th element of the vector vectorObj.

```
> vectorObj <- 101:132
> vectorObj[20]
[1] 120
```

The integer index notation can also use an assignment. Here is an example of setting the 17th element to -2:

```
> vectorObj[17] <- -2
> vectorObj
 [1] 101 102 103 104 105 106 107 108 109 110 111 112 113 114 115 116
[17]  -2 118 119 120 121 122 123 124 125 126 127 128 129 130 131 132
```

The integer input inside of the brackets need not be of length one (remember that "numbers" are just vector of length one). We use the same notation to extract four elements of the vector; notice the usefulness of the colon operator for accessing a consecutive sequence of a vector.

```
> vectorObj[c(6,17,20,30)]
[1] 106  -2 120 130
> vectorObj[5:10]
[1] 105 106 107 108 109 110
```

Again, the same notation can be used to assign multiple values to a vector.

The integer subsetting mechanism provides some powerful operations that may not be immediately obvious. There is no restriction on how often an element can be returned. For example, we can create a length three vector where every element is equal to element 20 from our vector vectorObj.

```
> vectorObj[c(20,20,20)]
[1] 120 120 120
```

Or, by using an index that runs from the length of the vector down to 1, the reverse of the vector will be returned.

```
> vectorObj[length(vectorObj):1]
 [1] 132 131 130 129 128 127 126 125 124 123 122 121 120 119 118  -2
[17] 116 115 114 113 112 111 110 109 108 107 106 105 104 103 102 101
```

---

[5]Note that R starts indexing at 1 instead of 0 unlike many other languages (Python, Java, C, etc.).

2.5 Subsetting

The concept of recycling values from vector arithmetic can also be applied to subset assignment. For example, we can assign the number 1 to the first 10 elements of the vector.

```
> vectorObj[1:10] = 1
> vectorObj
 [1]   1   1   1   1   1   1   1   1   1   1 111 112 113 114 115 116
[17]  -2 118 119 120 121 122 123 124 125 126 127 128 129 130 131 132
```

The single value was recycled to set the first 10 elements to 1.

The second method for subsetting a vector uses a vector of negative integers between the square brackets resulting in a vector with the corresponding elements removed.

```
> vectorObj <- 101:132
> vectorObj[-1]
 [1] 102 103 104 105 106 107 108 109 110 111 112 113 114 115 116 117
[17] 118 119 120 121 122 123 124 125 126 127 128 129 130 131 132
> vectorObj[-c(1,length(vectorObj))]
 [1] 102 103 104 105 106 107 108 109 110 111 112 113 114 115 116 117
[17] 118 119 120 121 122 123 124 125 126 127 128 129 130 131
```

This method is the least likely to be complex as the result is a true subset of the original vector without any duplication or permutation of the results.

The final method for subsetting vectors shown here uses a logical vector in between the square brackets. Only elements corresponding to TRUE are returned.

```
> vectorObj <- 1:8
> vectorObj[c(TRUE,TRUE,FALSE,FALSE,FALSE,TRUE,TRUE,FALSE)]
[1] 1 2 6 7
```

Typically the logical vector will have the same length of the original vector; when this is not the case, elements of the logical index are recycled.

The most common usage of logical subsetting involves constructing the logical vector by inequalities on the original vector. For example, the following code snippet returns the elements of vectorObj that have elements greater than 5.

```
> logicalIndex <- vectorObj > 5
> logicalIndex
[1] FALSE FALSE FALSE FALSE FALSE  TRUE  TRUE  TRUE
> newVectorObj <- vectorObj[logicalIndex]
> newVectorObj
[1] 6 7 8
```

As with the previous two subsetting commands, logical indices can be used for object assignment. Here we take a vector of integers between 1 and 100 and truncate those values that are less than 25 and greater than 75.

```
> vectorObj <- 1:100
> vectorObj[vectorObj <= 25] <- 25
> vectorObj[vectorObj >= 75] <- 75
> vectorObj
  [1] 25 25 25 25 25 25 25 25 25 25 25 25 25 25 25 25 25 25 25 25 25
 [22] 25 25 25 25 26 27 28 29 30 31 32 33 34 35 36 37 38 39 40 41 42
 [43] 43 44 45 46 47 48 49 50 51 52 53 54 55 56 57 58 59 60 61 62 63
 [64] 64 65 66 67 68 69 70 71 72 73 74 75 75 75 75 75 75 75 75 75 75
 [85] 75 75 75 75 75 75 75 75 75 75 75 75 75 75 75 75
```

Notice that we did not explicitly construct and save a logical vector. Instead the expressions `vectorObj <= 25` and `vectorObj >= 75` were directly passed inside the square brackets; the indexing vector was constructed "on the fly" and thrown away at the end. This is a common paradigm in R scripts for taking subsets of numeric vectors.

2.6 Character Vectors

In addition to numeric and logical vectors, R has a class for character vectors.[6]

```
> stringVec <- c("pear","apple","pineapple")
> class(stringVec)
[1] "character"
> stringVec
[1] "pear"      "apple"     "pineapple"
```

Many functions are available specifically for working with character vectors. For example, the `paste` function combines two or more character vectors. Here we paste the word "juice" onto the character vector of fruits. Because of the recycling logic in R, "juice" only needs to be typed once rather than three times. We do need to make sure to indicate the separator by using `sep = " "`. In this case, a space is desired.

```
> paste(stringVec, "juice", sep = " ")
[1] "pear juice"    "apple juice"    "pineapple juice"
```

The `substr` command returns substrings of the inputs by using the character offsets. Here we take the second, third, and fourth characters from every element in the vector:

```
> > substr(stringVec, start=2, stop=4)
[1] "ear" "ppl" "ine"
```

The parameters `start` and `stop` can be passed inputs, which are the same length as the string in order to take different subsets of each element. This can be used together with the `nchar` function which returns the number of characters in each

---

[6] As mentioned earlier, there are formally six primitive types of vectors, but we will not need to use *raw* or *complex* vectors. As well, we do not need to distinguish between *numeric* and *integer* vectors.

2.6 Character Vectors

element of the character vector to return a set of substrings that removes just the first two characters of each string.

```
> nchar(stringVec)
[1] 4 5 9
> substr(stringVec, 3, nchar(stringVec))
[1] "ar"       "ple"      "neapple"
```

The function `grep` takes a pattern and returns the indices that have characters containing the given pattern. These indices can be used with the subsetting commands to return a subset of a character vector corresponding to those elements containing the particular pattern. For example, if we use the pattern "apple" in the `grep` function, the elements "apple" and "pineapple" can be extracted.

```
> index <- grep(pattern="apple", x=stringVec)
> index
[1] 2 3
> stringVec[index]
[1] "apple"     "pineapple"
```

The pattern element to `grep`, which stands for global regular expression print, need not be a fixed string and may contain wildcard characters such as `*`. The input can in fact be any pattern corresponding to a *regular expression*; see the help page `?regexp` for a complete description.

We have already seen that logical vector gets converted to numeric ones when we try to use them in arithmetic. What happens when we try to use a character vector that contains a number in quotes in addition?

```
> "1" + 1
Error in "1" + 1 : non-numeric argument to binary operator
```

An error gets thrown refusing to use character vectors in arithmetic operations. However, if we try to use a numeric vector in a character operation such as paste, the command runs without a problem by silently converting the numeric values to characters.

```
> paste(4:12, "th", sep = "")
[1] "4th"  "5th"  "6th"  "7th"  "8th"  "9th"  "10th" "11th" "12th"
```

The reason for this is that R has the concept of implicit type *coercion*. Accordingly, objects are automatically converted to the appropriate type, but only when this can be done unambiguously and without any possible errors. Generally, this means that logical and numeric vectors are converted between one another and into character vectors whenever needed; however, character vectors must be explicitly cast into numeric objects because this may cause errors when a string does not actually represent a number (such as "pear").

The function `as.numeric` is used to cast any vector into a numeric one; it can be used to fix our previous error:

```
> as.numeric("1") + 1
[1] 2
```

Other casting functions such as as.logical and as.character can be used to explicitly convert vectors into their respective types.

2.7 Matrices and Data Frames

Matrices (plural form of matrix) provide an extension to vectors by providing a dimensionality to the data. A matrix object can be constructed from a given vector by providing the desired number of rows and columns. The resulting object, when printed, displays the data in a grid with the given number of columns and rows.

```
> mat <- matrix(data=1:12, nrow=3, ncol=4, byrow=FALSE)
> mat
     [,1] [,2] [,3] [,4]
[1,]    1    4    7   10
[2,]    2    5    8   11
[3,]    3    6    9   12
> class(mat)
[1] "matrix"
```

The option byrow determines whether the vector fills up the matrix over rows or columns.

```
> mat <- matrix(data=1:12, nrow=3, ncol=4, byrow=TRUE)
> mat
     [,1] [,2] [,3] [,4]
[1,]    1    2    3    4
[2,]    5    6    7    8
[3,]    9   10   11   12
> class(mat)
[1] "matrix"
```

To access a given element, the same bracket notation is used except that now two sets of indices are given and separated by a comma with the first number denoting the desired rows and the second giving the columns. Any of the subsetting vectors (integers, negative integers, and logical vectors) can be used.

```
> mat[2,3]
[1] 7
> class(mat[2,3])
[1] "integer"
> mat[1:2,1:2]
     [1] [,2]
[1,]    1    2
[2,]    5    6
> class(mat[1:2,1:2])
[1] "matrix"
```

In the case of only wanting to subset by one dimension, the other dimension's index can simply be left blank (understood to mean all rows/columns). For example,

2.7 Matrices and Data Frames

grabbing all rows from the 2nd and 3rd columns uses [,2:3] as the subsetting command.

```
> mat[,2:3]
     [,1] [,2]
[1,]    2    3
[2,]    6    7
[3,]   10   11
```

Care should be taken when extracting only a single row or column, as by default R will convert the matrix into a vector. The additional parameter ,drop=FALSE can be passed inside the brackets to stop this behavior.

```
> class(mat[1,])
[1] "integer"
> class(mat[1,,drop=FALSE])
[1] "matrix"
```

The automatic demotion to vectors is a common cause of subtle bugs in R scripts.

It is also possible to use matrices in arithmetic calculations. When used in combination with vectors, the vector values are recycled throughout the length of the matrix.[7] Basic operations between matrices require each to have the same dimensions and the operations are applied element-wise.

```
> matCol <- matrix(data=1:12, nrow=3, ncol=4, byrow=FALSE)
> matCol + 1
     [,1] [,2] [,3] [,4]
[1,]    2    5    8   11
[2,]    3    6    9   12
[3,]    4    7   10   13
> mat + matCol
     [,1] [,2] [,3] [,4]
[1,]    2    6   10   14
[2,]    7   11   15   19
[3,]   12   16   20   24
> mat + matCol[,2:3]
Error in mat + matCol[, 2:3] : non-conformable arrays
```

It is possible to construct matrices from any vector class (such as logical, numeric, or character), though by far the most common is the numeric case.

In many cases, it is advantageous to have a matrix-like object where each column has a different data type. The *data frame* object was created for exactly this purpose; the prevalence of such an object in the base language of R is a result of the language's history as a tool for statistics and data analysis. To construct a data frame, the function *data.frame* is used with each desired column of data passed as a separate argument; these are usually named in order to denote the meaning of each column. Here we construct a data frame with three columns named "a", "b", and "c".

---

[7] A warning is given if the vector's length does not divide the length of the matrix; an error is thrown when the vector is longer than the matrix.

```
> df <- data.frame(a = 1:5, b=21:25, c=1:5 + 0.5)
> df
  a  b   c
1 1 21 1.5
2 2 22 2.5
3 3 23 3.5
4 4 24 4.5
5 5 25 5.5
> class(df)
[1] "data.frame"
```

Three useful properties called *attributes* are attached to every data frame object in R: the dimension of the data frame, the column names, and the rownames. These are accessed as follows:

```
> dim(df)
[1] 5 3
> colnames(df)
[1] "a" "b" "c"
> rownames(df)
[1] "1" "2" "3" "4" "5"
```

The dimension command returns a vector with the number of rows as the first element and number of columns as the second. The vectors resulting from these three commands can also be changed by assigning to them. For example, the following changes the second variable name from "b" to "newName".

```
> colnames(df)[2] <- "newName"
> df
  a newName   c
1 1      21 1.5
2 2      22 2.5
3 3      23 3.5
4 4      24 4.5
5 5      25 5.5
```

These three commands also work for matrices. The output of dim for matrices is in exactly the same format as for data frames; the column names and row names are slightly different because by default matrices have missing names (data frames always have these). However, these can be set and manipulated manually in the same way.

The matrix subsetting commands work the same way on data frames. There is also an additional (and very useful) way to access a single column of a data frame by using the $ operator followed by the variable name.

```
> df$newName
[1] 21 22 23 24 25
> class(df$newName)
[1] "integer"
```

2.8 Data I/O

The dollar sign notation can also be used to construct a new variable attached to a data frame. Any referenced variable will be constructed at the end of the data frame when referenced.

```
> df$newColumn <- 5:1
> df
  a newName    c newColumn
1 1      21  1.5         5
2 2      22  2.5         4
3 3      23  3.5         3
4 4      24  4.5         2
5 5      25  5.5         1
```

The dollar sign notation does not work for matrices, even when column names are manually constructed.

2.8 Data I/O

Beyond typing vectors, matrices, and data frames directly, we can also load external data into R. As a prelude to this, we will need to interact with the computer's file system. At any given point, R has a notion of a current working directory; this is a location in the file system where it will read and write inputs and outputs. The default location will depend on your specific operating system and the method by which you are accessing R (i.e., RStudio, the console, an executable, or the terminal).

The current working directory is displayed with the getwd function and can be changed via the setwd function. For example, the following code snippet changes the working directory from a user's home to their desktop on Mac OSX.

```
> getwd()
[1] "/Users/myUserName"
> setwd("/Users/myUserName/Desktop")
> getwd()
[1] "/Users/myUserName/Desktop"
```

On Windows, here is an example of the same process changing from a users' home directory to their documents directory.

```
> getwd()
[1] "C:/Users/myUserName"
> setwd("C:/Users/myUserName/Documents")
> getwd()
[1] "C:/Users/myUserName/Documents"
```

Notice that we have used the forward slash / rather than the more typical to Windows backslash \; this is because R recognizes the backslash as an escape character and would otherwise throw an error.[8]

---

[8] It is also possible to use double backslashes on Windows machines. We recommend the forward slash as it makes code cross-compatible between operating systems.

The first step to reading in a dataset is to set the working directory to the location containing the data. Once there, the `dir` function displays a character vector of all the files in the current working directory. Here we have navigated to a directory containing two small files regarding properties of fruit.

```
> dir()
[1] "fruitData.csv"        "fruitNutrition.csv"
```

The extensions "csv" indicate that these are *comma separated value* files; data is written in a tabular form in plain text with rows separated by newline characters and columns separated by commas. Files in this format can be exported from various database and spreadsheet programs. To read one of these files use the `read.csv` function and save the result as an R object.[9] Note that we have set the option `as.is=TRUE`. We will do this regularly for loading and manually constructing data frames. It is necessary in order to stop R from constructing factors as in general we will not be using them.[10]

```
> fruitData <- read.csv(file="fruitData.csv", as.is=TRUE)
> fruitData
   Fruit   Color  Shape Juice
1  apple     red  round   1.0
2 banana  yellow oblong   0.0
3   pear   green   pear   0.5
4 orange  orange  round   1.0
5   kiwi   green  round   0.0
> class(fruitData)
[1] "data.frame"
> class(fruitData$Juice)
[1] "numeric"
```

The output is a data frame containing five rows and four columns. Notice that in reading the data, R has detected that the column named "Juice" should be stored as a numeric variable.[11]

An analogous function `write.csv` exists for saving data in R as a csv file. Consider saving only the "Juice" variable as a new plain text file.

```
> write.csv(x=fruitData$Juice,file="fruitDataJuice.csv")
```

The output will be saved in the current working directory. Opening the resulting file in a text editor shows that more than just the five Juice numbers have been saved.

---

[9]The function `read.csv` is a shortcut to the more general function `read.table`, which has over a dozen options for reading in a number of plain text formats.

[10]Factors are mainly used for statistical modeling. Even in those cases, most avoid them until absolutely necessary. As a result, we too will avoid factors as they are more likely to cause complications than help with humanities data.

[11]Juice = 1 indicates fruits commonly sold in juice form in the U.S. and Juice = 0.5 to those sometimes available in juice form.

2.8 Data I/O

```
"","x"
"1",1
"2",0
"3",0.5
"4",1
"5",0
```

The additional data on the first line and the first column are there to represent row and column names. Prior to saving the fruitDataJuice vector, it was coerced to a data frame. In the process, default row and column names were attached (recall that data frames always have these). Reading the data back into R shows that the fruitDataJuice data is now saved as a data frame object.

```
> fruitDataJuice <- read.csv(file="fruitDataJuice.csv")
> class(fruitDataJuice)
[1] "data.frame"
```

We could have avoided the additional row and column names from existing in the plain text csv file by specifying additional parameters in the function call, but there is no way of using `read.csv` to output anything other than a data frame.

An alternative way of saving R data is to save a serialized object as an R data file. The extension ".rds" is commonly used for the output.

```
> saveRDS(object=fruitData$Juice, file="fruitDataJuice.rds")
```

Opening this in a text editor shows an uninterpretable jumble of characters. It will look different in different text editors, all of which will be unreadable. Below is one example.

```
??b'''b'fdb'b2?????
????1??>
```

However, reading it back into R is a simple matter of calling the `readRDS` function.

```
> fruitDataJuice <- readRDS(file="fruitDataJuice.rds")
> class(fruitDataJuice)
[1] "numeric"
> fruitDataJuice
[1] 1.0 0.0 0.5 1.0 0.0
```

In this case, the result was returned exactly as we saved it: a numeric vector.

As a general rule of thumb, plain text files such as csv are best used when sharing data with others or when storing the final results of an analysis. These files are much easier to understand when looking at the output and can be easily imported into other software and programs. On the other hand, R data files are great for storing intermediate results as they can be saved and written without worrying about losing details in the conversion process. When dealing with larger datasets, R data files are beneficial because they take less storage space on the disk and can be loaded back into R significantly faster.

2.9 Advanced Subsetting

There are several functions in R written specifically in order to assist with complex forms of subsetting. Consider the task of taking only those rows in our fruit data frame with color equal to "red" or "green". One method based on our current tools constructs a logical vector using the "or" (|) operator.

```
> index <- (fruitData$Color == "red" | fruitData$Color == "green")
> index
[1]  TRUE FALSE  TRUE FALSE  TRUE
> fruitData[index,]
  Fruit Color Shape Juice
1 apple   red round   1.0
3  pear green  pear   0.5
5  kiwi green round   0.0
```

This can quickly become cumbersome when the number of categories becomes large. The %in% operator provides a convenient shortcut for constructing the logical index vector.

```
> fruitData$Color %in% c("red", "green")
[1]  TRUE FALSE  TRUE FALSE  TRUE
```

Now that we have identified the red and green fruits, we can pull out the corresponding rows. Remember that when we subset a date frame, we need to specify both rows and columns. Because we want all the columns, we will leave a blank after the comma inside of the square brackets.

```
> fruitData[fruitData$Color %in% c("red", "green"),]
  Fruit Color Shape Juice
1 apple   red round   1.0
3  pear green  pear   0.5
5  kiwi green round   0.0
```

Using this, for instance, we can quickly discover that only one fruit in our data has a corresponding color named after it.

```
> fruitData[fruitData$Color %in% fruitData$Fruit,]
   Fruit  Color Shape Juice
4 orange orange round     1
```

Writing without the %in% operator, this would have required a much longer chain of conditional logic.

Another common task is to order a data frame based on a single column. The function order returns the ordering of integer indices that would sort the vector. By default this is done in ascending order, but can be reversed with the decreasing option. The indices can be used to then reorder a vector, matrix, or data frame.

2.9 Advanced Subsetting

```
> index <- order(fruitData$Juice,decreasing=TRUE)
> index
[1] 1 4 3 2 5
> fruitData[index,]
   Fruit  Color  Shape Juice
1  apple    red  round   1.0
4 orange orange  round   1.0
3   pear  green   pear   0.5
2 banana yellow oblong   0.0
5   kiwi  green  round   0.0
```

When presented with ties, as was the case with the Juice variable, the `order` function uses a stable sort so that the relative ordering is preserved. For example, index 1 ("apple") came before index 4 ("orange") because they had the same value and 1 is less than 4.

Often data analysis involves combining independent data sets. Consider a data frame relating fruits to their caloric content.

```
> fruitNutr <- read.csv("fruitNutrition.csv", as.is=TRUE)
> fruitNutr
   Fruit Calories
1 banana      100
2   pear      100
3  mango      200
```

In order to combine this data to our original data, we need to know how to relate the two datasets. The function `match` takes two vectors and, according to the R help documentation, "returns a vector of the positions of (first) matches of its first argument in its second". The result can be used to join the two datasets together. However, in our case, not all of the fruits in our original set have nutritional data, so the match function returns the values NA for the other three fruits.

```
> index <- match(x=fruitData$Fruit, table=fruitNutr$Fruit)
> index
[1] NA  1  2 NA NA
```

These are *missing values*, the abbreviation means "not available". To deal with these, the function `is.na` returns a logical vector of the positions with missing values.[12]

```
> is.na(index)
[1] TRUE FALSE FALSE TRUE TRUE
```

In order to join these datasets, we need a new column to insert the calories data. Therefore, we set the calories variable in the original dataset to missing.

```
> fruitData$Calories <- NA
```

---

[12] You may be tempted to try `index == NA`. It will run without an error but not return the desired result.

Then, use a combination of the `is.na` function and the variable `index`.

```
> fruitData$Calories[!is.na(index)] <-
+                    fruitNutr$Calories[index[!is.na(index)]]
> fruitData
    Fruit  Color  Shape Juice Calories
1   apple    red  round   1.0       NA
2  banana yellow oblong   0.0      100
3    pear  green   pear   0.5      100
4  orange orange  round   1.0       NA
5    kiwi  green  round   0.0       NA
```

The data frame `fruitData` now contains the caloric count for the two matching fruits.

References

[1] Matthew Lee Jockers. *Text Analysis with R for Students of Literature*. Springer, 2014.

[2] William N Venables, David M Smith, R Development Core Team, et al. An introduction to r, 2002.

Chapter 3
EDA I: Continuous and Categorical Data

Abstract In this chapter, basic methods for exploratory data analysis are presented. The focus is on univariate and bivariate graphical techniques such as histograms, bar plots, and tables. Control flow using *for loops* is also introduced.

3.1 Introduction

The R programming language was originally intended as a tool for *exploratory data analysis*. In the previous chapter we covered the basic constructs of the language; here we move into the more data-specific functionality of R. The focus will slowly shift away from the language itself, which is ultimately just a tool, and towards the conceptual methods used for exploring data.

Here, and again in Chap. 4, we use the American Community Survey (ACS) as an example dataset [1]. The ACS is produced annually by the US Census Bureau. Unlike the decennial census, it is a survey of only approximately 1 % of the population, but asks a substantially longer and broader set of questions. This survey is convenient to work with as it is in the public domain and freely downloadable. The variables in the survey, such as age, income, and occupation, are all interpretable without specialized subject domain knowledge. Also, the ACS, and demographic data in general, is likely to be of direct interest and application within a wide range of academic disciplines in both the humanities and social sciences. Due to its size, we have cleaned the data. We will only look at tract-level data from the state of Oregon. Additional states and tables are provided in the supplementary materials for further study.

3.2 Tables

We start by loading the base ACS file into R using the read.csv function.

```
> geodf <- read.csv("data/ch03/geodf.csv", as.is=TRUE)
> dim(geodf)
[1] 826    6
```

Printing the first six rows reveals six variables in this dataset.

```
> geodf <- read.csv("data/ch03/geodf.csv", as.is=TRUE)
> dim(geodf)
[1] 826    6
> geodf[1:6,]
  state    fips county  csa population households
1    or 1950100  Baker None       2725       1225
2    or 1950200  Baker None       3179       1322
3    or 1950300  Baker None       2395       1162
4    or 1950400  Baker None       2975       1397
5    or 1950500  Baker None       2969       1117
6    or 1950600  Baker None       1812        897
```

Each row represents a *census tract*, a county subdivision used for aggregating statistical survey data. They typically correspond to individual towns or small cities, though in larger metropolitan areas tracts more closely represent specific neighborhoods.

Looking closer at the columns, the state variable will not be of much help as all of the data came from Oregon. The fips code is a unique identifier of each row. The county and csa, short for Combined Statistical Area, fields give larger-scale groupings of individual census tracts. The population and household columns are estimated values from the survey sample. Accordingly, all of the data counts we will look at are similarly "scaled-up" from the 1 % sample taken during the survey.

The first few tracts represented by rows of the dataset belong to Baker County. How many counties are there in total in our dataset? Does each county have roughly the same number of tracts? To answer these question, we use the table function, which takes a character vector and provides a count for each of the unique values in the vector.[1]

```
> tab <- table(geodf$county)
> class(tab)
[1] "table"
> tab

     Baker     Benton  Clackamas    Clatsop   Columbia       Coos
         6         18         80         11         10         13
     Crook      Curry  Deschutes    Douglas    Gilliam      Grant
         4          5         24         22          1          2
    Harney Hood River    Jackson  Jefferson  Josephine    Klamath
         2          4         41          6         16         20
```

---

[1] Recall that numeric and logical vectors can be coerced to characters when needed; the table function is able to tabulate numeric variables using this trick.

3.2 Tables

Lake	Lane	Lincoln	Linn	Malheur	Marion
2	86	17	21	7	58
Morrow	Multnomah	Polk	Sherman	Tillamook	Umatilla
2	171	12	1	8	15
Union	Wallowa	Wasco	Washington	Wheeler	Yamhill
8	3	8	104	1	17

The output of the table function is a new object type "table", though it can be manipulated exactly like any named vector for our purposes. From the results, we see a set of 36 counties, with some (Grant, Wheeler, Wasco) having only one tract and others (Multnomah, Washington) having over 100.

By default, a table of a character vector will arrange the results in alphabetical order. To arrange the results based on the frequency counts, we evoke the same `order` function and subsetting commands that were previously used to order numeric vectors. We can also use an additional parameter `decreasing=TRUE` in the function to order the table; the result is the county with the most census tracts.

```
> tab[order(tab, decreasing=TRUE)]
```

Multnomah	Washington	Lane	Clackamas	Marion	Jackson
171	104	86	80	58	41
Deschutes	Douglas	Linn	Klamath	Benton	Lincoln
24	22	21	20	18	17
Yamhill	Josephine	Umatilla	Coos	Polk	Clatsop
17	16	15	13	12	11
Columbia	Tillamook	Union	Wasco	Malheur	Baker
10	8	8	8	7	6
Jefferson	Curry	Crook	Hood River	Wallowa	Grant
6	5	4	4	3	2
Harney	Lake	Morrow	Gilliam	Sherman	Wheeler
2	2	2	1	1	1

The rearranged table makes our observations from the original table more obvious; the advantage becomes more noticeable with larger tables. Notice that the table has reordered both the names and the counts together. To access just the counts we can convert the table to a numeric vector via `as.numeric`. Accessing just a character vector of names requires calling the function `names`, a variation of the `colnames` and `rownames` we used when working with data frames and matrices.[2] In order to get the names of the five counties with the highest number of tracts, we use the following code snippet:

```
> names(tab)[order(tab,decreasing=TRUE)][1:5]
[1] "Multnomah" "Washington" "Lane"        "Clackamas" "Marion"
```

We will see that this is a useful way of extracting values from character vectors with a large number of unique values.

The `table` function is not restricted to creating univariate tables with just one input. It can be used to tabulate an arbitrary number of inputs. For example, the

---

[2] The `names` function should not be used with matrices; for data frames it returns the column names.

number of counties in each combined statistical area (CSA) might be of interest. To understand the relationship between the CSA and counties within Oregon, we build a two-way table of these two variables.[3]

```
> table(geodf$county,geodf$csa)

            Bend Medford None Portland
  Baker        0       0    6        0
  Benton       0       0   18        0
  Clackamas    0       0    0       80
  Clatsop      0       0   11        0
  Columbia     0       0    0       10
  Coos         0       0   13        0
  Crook        4       0    0        0
  Curry        0       0    5        0
  Deschutes   24       0    0        0
  Douglas      0       0   22        0
  Gilliam      0       0    1        0
  Grant        0       0    2        0
  Harney       0       0    2        0
  Hood River   0       0    4        0
  Jackson      0      41    0        0
  Jefferson    0       0    6        0
  Josephine    0      16    0        0
  Klamath      0       0   20        0
  Lake         0       0    2        0
  Lane         0       0   86        0
  Lincoln      0       0   17        0
  Linn         0       0   21        0
  Malheur      0       0    7        0
  Marion       0       0   58        0
  Morrow       0       0    2        0
  Multnomah    0       0    0      171
  Polk         0       0   12        0
  Sherman      0       0    1        0
  Tillamook    0       0    8        0
  Umatilla     0       0   15        0
  Union        0       0    8        0
  Wallowa      0       0    3        0
  Wasco        0       0    8        0
  Washington   0       0    0      104
  Wheeler      0       0    1        0
  Yamhill      0       0    0       17
```

The result shows the relationship between Oregon's three CSA's and 36 counties (counties that are not in a specific CSA have coded as the CSA 'None' in our data). For example, CSA Bend consists of only two counties, whereas the Portland CSA is a collection of five counties. The resulting table object can be manipulated using the same subsetting commands used with matrices; the column and row names, similarly, are accessible via `rownames` and `colnames`.

---

[3] CSAs represent groupings of counties with close social and economic ties; we have coded the typically verbose CSA names with the name of the largest city contained within each area.

3.3 Histogram

Tables provide a quick summary of categorical variables. In some cases a numeric variable may have a small discrete set of potential values, in which case a table can also be useful for summarizing the data. For example, a variable giving the number of bedrooms in a dataset of housing units must be a nonnegative integer, typically between 0 and 5. Many numeric variables are either continuous (where nearly every value is unique) or take far too many unique values to be represented well by a table.

A *histogram* is a visualization used to quickly understand the distribution of a numeric variable. The R function `hist` produces this visualization from a numeric vector; the resulting graphic may be displayed in a new window, tab, frame, or application depending on the installation being used.[4] For example, the following code produces a histogram of the people per household by census tract.

```
> ppPerHH <- geodf$population / geodf$households
> hist(ppPerHH)
```

The result is shown in Fig. 3.1a. The height of each bar shows the number of data points that fall between its ranges. We see that most tracts have between 2 and 3 people per household, with a smaller set in the ranges 1–2 and 3–4. Looking closely at the small bump all the way to the right, there is at least one tract with as many as 9 people per household. A default labeling of the plot and its axes has been given.

Much of the visual space in the default histogram is taken by representing a few outliers on the right half of the window. We can remove these by filtering out any tract with more than five people per household.

```
> hist(ppPerHH[ppPerHH < 5])
```

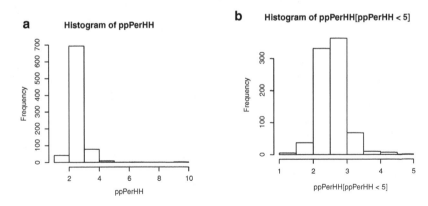

Figure 3.1: (**a**) Default histogram of population by household at a census tract level. (**b**) Histogram of population by household at a census tract level, truncating households of five people or more.

---

[4]We discuss how to save these as external images in Sect. 5.2.

The new histogram is shown in Fig. 3.1b, with the scale now ranging from 1 to 5. The bars have automatically adjusted so that each bucket has length 0.5, compared to the previous plot that had buckets of length 1. The finer grain shows that the tracts with between 2 and 3 people are approximately evenly distribution between 2 and 2.5 and 2.5 and 3, with only slightly more in the latter group.

By default, the histogram command automatically tries to pick "nice" intervals for breaking up the data. We have already seen that the length of a bucket decreases as the range decreases, so that the number of bars remains relatively constant. Also, the function attempts to pick interpretable breaks points; in our first example these are whole integers, and in the second these are half integers. The exact algorithm comes from a classic paper by Herbert Sturges published in 1926 [2].

As dataset sizes have grown considerably over the past 90 years, it is often desirable to increase the number of buckets to better understand the fine grain detail of the data. The buckets can be manipulated by passing an input to the parameter breaks. A single integer input to breaks indicates that the plotting function should construct breaks number of (equally sized) intervals. For example, the following asks for 30 buckets.

```
> hist(ppPerHH[ppPerHH < 5], breaks=30)
```

The output, Fig. 3.2a, shows a finer grain plot than our previous version. We now see that the distribution has an approximately bell-shaped curve, centered somewhere around 2.6 people per household. If we count the buckets, we see that the hist function has taken our request for 30 intervals as a suggestion; it ultimately decided to split at every tenth of a unit resulting in 34 buckets.[5] The histogram command, even when asking for a fixed number of breaks, attempts to find "nice" split points and uses them instead of exactly producing the desired bucket count. Usually this behavior is helpful. We can change the coarseness of the plot as needed while allowing R to construct interpretable break points. Occasionally, it is necessary to manually set the split points of the histogram. To do this, the breaks parameter takes a vector of split locations. These are taken verbatim and will not be manipulated by the plotting function. For example, to recreate the breaks from Fig. 3.2a, we can specify the following:

```
> hist(ppPerHH[ppPerHH < 5], breaks=(13:47) / 10)
```

The code (13:47) / 10 is simply a convenient shortcut for specifying a sequence of between 1.3 (where the x-coordinate starts) and 4.7 (where the y-coordinate ends) in steps of size 0.1. Manually setting histogram breaks can be useful when creating a collection of plots where it can be helpful to keep the scales consistent. When the numeric data are from a discrete set of numbers, such as grades on a 0–100 scale, it may also be helpful to construct a histogram where each bucket has exactly one unique value inside of it.

---

[5] We still count buckets even if they are zero. So, in our case, there are three empty buckets.

3.4 Quantiles

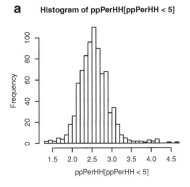
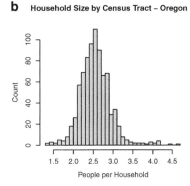

Figure 3.2: (**a**) Histogram of population by household at a census tract level, setting the number of break points to 30 (which is used only as a suggestion). (**b**) Histogram of population by household at a census tract level, with title, axis labels, and shading.

The `hist` function allows for a great deal of aesthetic customization. For example, the parameter `main` can be used to set the title of the plot. Similarly, `xlab` and `ylab` provide means for altering the axes labels. Setting the color parameters shades the inside of the buckets with the desired color. For a list of available color names type `colors()` in the R terminal; most of the standard English color names are available, along with hundreds of additional shades.

```
hist(ppPerHH[ppPerHH < 5], breaks=30,
     col="gray",
     xlab="People per Household",
     ylab="Count",
     main="Household Size by Census Tract - Oregon")
```

The result in Fig. 3.2b shows the same core histogram, but with buckets shaded in grey and the descriptive custom plot labels.

3.4 Quantiles

We now load a separate dataset derived from the ACS describing primary means of transportation to work. The rows correspond exactly to the original dataset `geodf`. As the entire dataset consists of numeric values, we will immediately convert the result of reading into R as a matrix object.[6]

```
> meansOfCommute <- read.csv("data/ch03/meansOfCommute.csv",
+                            as.is=TRUE)
> meansOfCommute <- as.matrix(meansOfCommute)
```

---
[6] Recall that `read.csv` will always return a data frame.

```
> meansOfCommute[1:5,]
     total car public_trans bus subway railroad ferry bike walk taxi
[1,]  1242 984            0   0      0        0     0    8   62   40
[2,]  1199 1036           0   0      0        0     0   34   38   14
[3,]   999 849            0   0      0        0     0   21   16    0
[4,]  1035 954            0   0      0        0     0    4   43    0
[5,]  1123 938            0   0      0        0     0   40   55   21
     work_at_home
[1,]          148
[2,]           77
[3,]          113
[4,]           34
[5,]           69
```

The first column gives a total population count, which may differ slightly from the population in the original dataset for various technical reasons.[7] Other columns count the primary modes of transportation to work. The first few rows indicate that these are highly skewed, with more common modes of transit such as "car" greatly preferred to more specialized forms such as "ferry".

Raw counts of this data are not particularly interesting as the census tracts are not all the same size. Working with percentages makes an easier comparison between rows of data. Let us say we want to know the percentage of the population walking to work. Notice that we can access a column of the matrix by using the column name as an index inside the square braces.[8]

```
> walkPerc <- meansOfCommute[,"walk"] / meansOfCommute[,"total"]
> walkPerc = round(walkPerc * 100)
```

We round the percentage of walkers to a whole number to make it easier to work with the output.

To explore the distribution of this variable, we might start by constructing a histogram as in the previous section. A popular alternative is the *five number summary*, which is returned by default by the quantile function.[9]

```
> quantile(walkPerc)
  0%  25%  50%  75% 100%
   0    1    3    5   50
```

The first and last numbers give the minimum and maximum value of the variable, respectively. Accordingly, there is at least one tract where no one walks to work and one tract where half of the people walk to work. The middle number is the *median* of the dataset, defined as the value such that half of the input values are less than the

---

[7] The Census Bureau will not release counts that might identify an individual. For example, if only one person takes a ferry to work from a given tract, it will not be included in either the total or ferry column. As a result, population numbers can vary slightly across the data set.

[8] This is the fourth and final method for subsetting as referenced in Sect. 2.5.

[9] There is, mostly for historical reasons, also a function fivenum in base R that returns the same numbers.

3.4 Quantiles

median and half of the input values are greater than it.[10] The second number is the 1st (or lower) quartile, often represented by the symbol Q_1; it is defined similarly to the median, such that $1/4$ of the input values are less than it and $3/4$ of the input values are greater than it. The fourth number is the 3rd (or upper) quartile and is defined analogously; in other words, this means that in 75 % of the tracts, 5 % or less of the population walks to work.

The five number summary gives a compact description of a numeric variable. In this case we know that at least one tract has zero walking commuters, whereas at least one has one out of every two people commuting by foot. A typical census tract has roughly 1–5 % of the population commute by walking, with 3 % being the most typical value. The median being closer to the first quartile compared to the third quartile, and much closer to the minimum compared to the maximum, indicates that the data are *positive skewed*. In other words, there are a sizable number of oddly large values compared to the oddly small values. Recomputing the five-number summary for the percentage of people commuting by car gives an example of a dataset that is *negative skewed*.

```
> carPerc <- meansOfCommute[,"car"] / meansOfCommute[,"total"]
> carPerc <- round(carPerc * 100)
> quantile(carPerc)
  0%  25%  50%  75% 100%
  22   78   85   89   98
```

Here there are a sizable number of particularly small values compared to overly large values.

The five number summary is an example of the more general concept of *quantiles*. If a numeric dataset is sorted and divided up into q equally sized buckets, the q-quantiles give the breakpoints for these breaks. The five number summary consists of the 4-quantiles, also known as quartiles (hence the name of the 1st and 3rd). Another common set of quantiles are the 10-quantiles, or deciles. To calculate these with the `quantile` function we pass the set of desired probabilities to the `prob` parameter.

```
> (0:10)/10
 [1] 0.0 0.1 0.2 0.3 0.4 0.5 0.6 0.7 0.8 0.9 1.0
> quantile(walkPerc, prob=(0:10)/10)
  0%  10%  20%  30%  40%  50%  60%  70%  80%  90% 100%
   0    0    1    2    2    3    3    5    6   10   50
```

By setting the `prob` parameter to a range of values between 0 and 1 in steps of size 0.1, the deciles are returned. These give additional information to the distribution of the walking as a means of commuting, particularly with the higher deciles. We see that tracts with more than 10 % of the population walking to work are particularly rare, indicating that the one value of 50 % is particularly anomalous.

By far the most frequently used quantile in nontechnical work is the 100-quantile, also known as a percentile. In order to help calculate these, we use the function `seq` which constructs a sequence of numbers between a start point and

---

[10] Technically, if there are n data points, for odd datasets it is the $\frac{n+1}{2}$ th largest value and for even datasets it is the average of the $\frac{n}{2}$ th and $(\frac{n}{2}+1)$ th largest variables.

end point using a given step size.[11] To simplify the output, we also set the names parameter in the quantile function so that only the values and not their names are returned. Additionally, we will round with the round function to three decimal places.

```
> cent <- quantile(walkPerc,prob=seq(0,1,length.out=100),
+                  names=FALSE)
> round(cent,1)
 [1]  0.0  0.0  0.0  0.0  0.0  0.0  0.0  0.0  0.0  0.0  0.0  0.0  1.0
[14]  1.0  1.0  1.0  1.0  1.0  1.0  1.0  1.0  1.0  1.0  1.0  1.0
[27]  1.0  1.0  2.0  2.0  2.0  2.0  2.0  2.0  2.0  2.0  2.0  2.0
[40]  2.0  2.0  2.0  2.0  2.0  2.0  2.0  3.0  3.0  3.0  3.0  3.0  3.0
[53]  3.0  3.0  3.0  3.0  3.0  3.0  3.0  3.0  3.0  4.0  4.0  4.0  4.0
[66]  4.0  4.0  4.0  4.0  4.0  5.0  5.0  5.0  5.0  5.0  5.0  5.0  6.0
[79]  6.0  6.0  6.0  7.0  7.0  7.0  7.0  8.0  8.0  9.0  9.0 10.0 10.0
[92] 11.0 12.0 13.0 15.0 18.0 20.0 22.3 31.7 50.0
```

The middle values are somewhat hard to parse, but the percentiles do a nice job of characterizing the extreme ends of the distribution. For instance, we see that about 10% of the data have almost no walking commuters, whereas 4% (i.e., the top 4 centiles) have at least one in five people walking to work.

For understanding the entire distribution of a numeric variable, histograms often give an easier to digest representation of the data's distribution. Quantiles can be more useful when looking at the extreme values of skewed data. The five number summary is also very useful in communicating the results of an analysis because a single five column matrix can summarize datasets with dozens of variables.

Another powerful application of quantiles is their ability to be used in subsequent analyses. For example, the quantile at 10% can be used to label tracts with particularly low car usage.[12] The resulting categorical variable can be used in conjunction with the CSA designations, which were loaded in Sect. 3.2, to understand whether there is any regional trend to the presence of low-car usage.

```
> coff <- quantile(carPerc, prob=0.10)
> coff
10%
 66
> lowCarUsageFlag <- (carPerc < coff)
> table(lowCarUsageFlag, geodf$csa)

lowCarUsageFlag Bend Medford None Portland
          FALSE   28       54  336      327
          TRUE     0        3   23       55
```

By looking at those tracts where car usage is among the lowest decile (specifically, 66% or fewer people drive to work), we see that the majority of the low-car using tracts are located in the Portland metro area. This result is not too surprising given the increased housing density and prevalence of public transit within Oregon's largest metropolitan area.

---

[11] It is also possible to specify the desired output length and let the function determine the necessary step size.

[12] The R function can handle any vector of probabilities in the prob parameter, not just formal q-quantiles. We make extensive use of this throughout this text.

3.5 Binning

There is a close conceptual link between histograms and quantiles. Histograms take evenly size intervals and count the amount of data within each interval, whereas quantiles take equal proportions of a numeric dataset and calculate where the splits occur. Histograms are also typically displayed as a graphic and quantiles as a string of numbers, but both can exist in either tabular or graphical form.[13] *Binning* is a conceptual cousin to both of these methods and is a generalization of the previous example where car usage percentages were bifurcated into two categorical variables. Data samples are placed into groups, the "bins", according to where one variable falls in a set of cut-off values. Often these cut-off values come from a set of quantiles, though they may be any set which spans the range of the variable of interest.

Consider the deciles of the proportion of people commuting by car by census tract.

```
> breakPoints <- quantile(carPerc, prob=seq(0,1,length.out=11),
+                         names=FALSE)
> breakPoints
 [1] 22 66 76 80 83 85 87 89 90 92 98
```

An interesting next step is to assign each data point to one of the ten buckets implied by the deciles. This can be done by the `cut` function available in R. It takes a numeric vector and set of break points and assigns each point to one of the implied buckets. Two parameters that should be altered from their defaults are `labels` and `include.lowest`. Setting these to FALSE and TRUE yield the most useful results for our purpose.[14]

```
> bin <- cut(carPerc, breakPoints, labels=FALSE, include.lowest=TRUE)
> bin[1:42]
 [1]  3  6  5  9  5  3  2  4  4  2  6  2  1  1  1  1  7  5  5  4  1
[22]  1  3  3  4  3  3  4  5  6  4  2  7  6  5  4  6  3  6  3  7  5
> table(bin)
bin
  1   2   3   4   5   6   7   8   9  10
 87  93  86  89  68  94 104  45  88  72
```

The values returned by `cut` are integer values assigning each input into one of the deciles. For example, the fourth row of the dataset is in the ninth decile (the second highest) of car commuters. A table of the bins shows that the number of samples in each is similar but not completely uniform. As we used quantiles for the cut offs, it would be reasonable to assume that the sizes would all be the same. The discrepancy comes about because we rounded the percentages. Looking at the raw data, we see 51 tracts with 89 % car commuters, which are all currently placed in bin 7. If these were moved to bin 8 (the smallest), bin 7 would be left with only 53

---

[13] A visualization of two sets of quantiles, a *Q-Q* plot, is a very popular statistical tool. It is used mostly in conjunction with inferential statistics, which is outside the scope of this text.

[14] We encourage readers to try `cut` with other choices to see why these are needed.

tracts. In short, there is no way to evenly split the tracts up given the discreteness of the data; the quantile and cut functions do the best job possible.

We will see many uses for the values from binning data. Typically these consist of using techniques designed for categorical variables with numeric ones by transforming into bin ids. For example, using methods already covered, we can now use the bin ids to look at our ten bins in a two-way table showing the relationship between car ownership and CSA designation.

```
> table(bin, geodf$csa)

bin  Bend Medford None Portland
  1     0       3   24       60
  2     2       5   28       58
  3     4       4   30       48
  4     1       3   41       44
  5     1       3   34       30
  6     1       5   44       44
  7     8      15   43       38
  8     2       5   22       16
  9     6       8   48       26
 10     3       6   45       18
```

We see again that Portland dominates the low end of the distribution; those tracts not in a CSA (likely to be the most rural) dominate the upper quantiles. Given that in rural areas automobiles are often the only method of transit, this result confirms our common assumptions about car usage.

While it is often useful to bin data based on the result of calling the quantile function, the cut function may be used to create buckets with any set of break points.[15] One option is to use equally spaced cuts for the binning. For example, consider cutting the people per household data (truncated from above at 5) using a sequence of breaks based on what we did previously in Sect. 3.3.

```
> bins <- cut(ppPerHH[ppPerHH < 5], breaks=seq(1.3,4.7,by=0.1),
+             labels=FALSE, include.lowest=TRUE)
> table(bins)
bins
  1   2   3   4   5   6   7   8   9  10  11  12  13  14  15  16  17
  2   3   2   5   4   8  18  26  57  69  83  96 110  90  66  68  29
 18  19  20  21  22  23  24  25  26  27  28  29  32  34
 34  18   8   5   3   2   2   2   1   3   2   4   1   1
```

The resulting bins, seen as a table, are the exact heights of the bars shown in the histogram from Fig. 3.2a! Likewise, if we used quantiles as the breaks in a histogram, the resulting histogram will consist of bins with equal area, rather than equal widths. This is shown in Fig. 3.3.[16]

---

[15] If the break points do not span the data set, missing values will be returned for data outside the range of breaks.

[16] We originally described the height of the bins in a histogram as the counts, but this was only because the widths of the buckets were the same. In reality, it is the area of the buckets that matter; these are not the same with unequally spaced cuts.

3.6 Control Flow

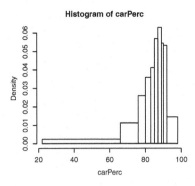

Figure 3.3: Histogram of the percentage of census tract residents who primarily use a personal automobile to commute to work. Uneven breaks are used, with splits occurring at the deciles of the data. Each histogram bar, therefore, has approximately the same area.

```
> hist(carPerc, breaks=breakPoints)
```

Clearly these three techniques are closely related. Successful data exploration of a single continuous variable requires adeptly employing all three to their respective strengths.

3.6 Control Flow

The next set of data from the ACS we will look at gives counts of household-level income. As before, we read the csv file into R and convert the result into a numeric matrix, which has the same number of rows as the data frame dfgeo. We do need one additional parameter to read.csv called check.names to be manually set to FALSE to prevent R from changing the column names.[17]

```
> hhIncome <- read.csv("data/ch03/hhIncome.csv",as.is=TRUE,
+                       check.names=FALSE)
> hhIncome <- as.matrix(hhIncome)
> hhIncome[1:5,]
  total  0k 10k 15k 20k 25k 30k 35k 40k 45k 50k 60k 75k 100k 125k
1  1225 113  60  42  87  50  27  48  90  77  86 183  94  132   86
2  1322 119 162  93  81  91  15  27  72  43 139 113 160   56  106
3  1162 107  69 107 116  60 127  44  88  92 129  86  94    4    8
4  1397 168 188  89  98  84  89  51  58  83 107 146 140   34   24
5  1117  70 131  93  73  66  60  76  89 112 107  90  93   29    3
```

---

[17]The column names we constructed start with a number, which is technically allowed for column names but not allowed for object names. This means that, as a data frame, we would not be able to access the columns of hhIncome using the $ operator. As we are converting into a matrix this is not a concern, so we instruct R not to try to paste an "X" to the front of all the variable names using check.names=FALSE.

```
      150k 200k
1      24   26
2      22   23
3       5   26
4      24   14
5       0   25
```

We have labeled the columns with short names to make them easier to access and print. Column "20k" represents a count of the number of households that earned between 20,000 and 25,000 (the next column name) dollars per year. The final column denotes the number of households that earns 200,000 or more dollars per year. The first column represents the total number of households represented by this analysis.

Consider just one row of data from this set, removing the first column of totals.

```
> oneRow <- hhIncome[1,-1]
> oneRow
   0k   10k   15k   20k   25k   30k   35k   40k   45k   50k   60k   75k  100k  125k
  113    60    42    87    50    27    48    90    77    86   183    94   132    86
 150k  200k
   24    26
```

The raw data are interesting in their own right, but perhaps more insightful would be to convert this into a cumulative count of the number of households that have an income below some threshold. We could calculate each of these cumulative values by hand, but R provides a function called cumsum. The function takes a numeric input and cumulatively adds each element to the one before it. For our row of data the result is as follows:

```
> cumsum(oneRow)
   0k   10k   15k   20k   25k   30k   35k   40k   45k   50k   60k   75k  100k  125k
  113   173   215   302   352   379   427   517   594   680   863   957  1089  1175
 150k  200k
 1199  1225
```

So 863 of the households in this tract make less than 75k dollars per year. Notice that we need to look at the number right before the value labeled 75k (the one for 60k) rather than its value directly.

How might we go about computing this cumulative sum for the entire dataset? Clearly we would not do this manually for each row of data; at worst we would forgo the cumsum function and manually compute each column using vectorized notation (there are only 16 columns but hundreds of rows). Fortunately, we do not have to resort to either method. The R language provides a set of tools for what is referred to as *control-flow constructs*. One example of these is a *for loop*, which iteratively executes a block of code, with one variable taking on each and every value in a given vector. That is a mouthful that can be better explained through an example. Take the set of integers 1:5. The *for loop* in the following code

```
> for (j in 1:5) {
```

3.6 Control Flow

```
+     print(j)
+ }
```

will actually execute the following:

```
> j <- 1
> print(j)
> j <- 2
> print(j)
> j <- 3
> print(j)
> j <- 4
> print(j)
> j <- 5
> print(j)
```

So when we run the *for loop* in R, this is what we see:

```
> for (j in 1:5) {
+     print(j)
+ }
[1] 1
[1] 2
[1] 3
[1] 4
[1] 5
```

The function `print` needs to be called explicitly, as inside a *for loop* printing of unassigned variables is not done automatically as would otherwise be the case. In all other respects, the code executed by the for loop is exactly the same as the expanded version given.

With this new construct, we can now use a *for loop* to cycle over the rows of our dataset. As is often the case with such loops, prior to doing that we need to construct an empty matrix in which we will store the results. Here, we make a matrix filled with zeros that contain the same number of rows and one fewer column (as we do not need one for the total) than the raw data.

```
> cumIncome <- matrix(0, ncol=ncol(hhIncome)-1, nrow=nrow(hhIncome))
```

We now write a for loop where the index j cycles over a sequence of numbers from 1 to the number of columns in hhIncome. In each iteration, the cumulative sum function is applied to a given row and the counts are divided by the total of the row. The calculation is saved in a row of our result matrix cumIncome.

```
> for (j in 1:nrow(hhIncome)) {
+     cumIncome[j,] <- cumsum(hhIncome[j,-1]) / hhIncome[j,1]
+     cumIncome[j,] <- round(cumIncome[j,] * 100)
+ }
> colnames(cumIncome) <- colnames(hhIncome)[-1]
```

At the end, we assign the correct column names to the outcome vector.

We see that the desired values have been filled into our matrix.

```
> cumIncome[1:5,]
     0k 10k 15k 20k 25k 30k 35k 40k 45k 50k 60k 75k 100k 125k 150k
[1,]  9  14  18  25  29  31  35  42  48  56  70  78   89   96   98
[2,]  9  21  28  34  41  42  44  50  53  64  72  84   89   97   98
[3,]  9  15  24  34  40  50  54  62  70  81  88  96   97   97   98
[4,] 12  25  32  39  45  51  55  59  65  73  83  93   96   97   99
[5,]  6  18  26  33  39  44  51  59  69  79  87  95   97   98   98
     200k
[1,]  100
[2,]  100
[3,]  100
[4,]  100
[5,]  100
```

As a nice check, the entire final column is filled with 100s, which is expected as 100 % of the data for each row should be included when cumulatively summing all of the columns. We will use this cumulative data later in Chap. 4.

3.7 Combining Plots

Returning to the original household income data, notice that it has 16 numeric columns. If we were actually fully exploring this data, a first good step would be to pick a single column and to build exploratory histograms and quantile bins to first understand it by itself.[18] As a second step, it would be nice to automate this process so that we do not manually construct 16 sets of exploratory data figures. The *for loop* makes this relatively easy.

R provides a way of adding multiple plots to the same graphics window using the function par, which sets the parameters of our graph. Prior to any plots being drawn, the par function is called with the parameter mfrow equal to a vector of two integers; subsequent graphics will be plotted *by row* in a grid with dimensions equal to the inputs to the mfrow parameter.[19] Drawing all 16 histograms is then possible through the following.[20]

```
> par(mfrow=c(4,4))
> for(j in 1:16) {
+   hist(hhIncome[,j+1] / hhIncome[,1],
+        breaks=seq(0,0.7,by=0.05), ylim=c(0,600))
+ }
```

To begin adjusting the plots aesthetics, we specified the exact break points and limits on the y-axis so that each of these histograms is on exactly the same scale.

---

[18] In the interest of verbosity, we skip that here but encourage readers working along to try this themselves.

[19] A similar parameter mfcol can be used to plot figures by column.

[20] It is possible that you will get the error Error in plot.new() : figure margins too large, which can often be remedied by closing the plot window and running the code from scratch.

3.7 Combining Plots

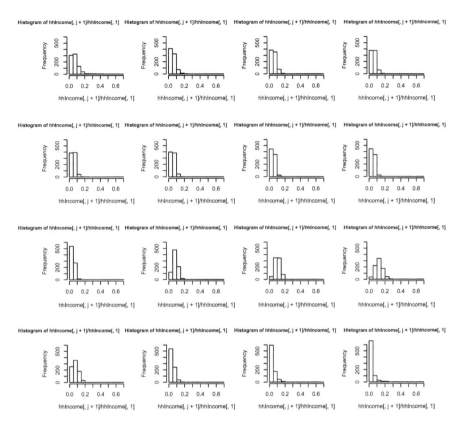

Figure 3.4: Grid of income band distributions at a census tract level using default margins and titles. Axes ranges are held constant.

The output is shown in Fig. 3.4. As we may have expected, the distribution of proportions becomes higher for the middle ranges before shrinking towards zero again for the higher income bands. In other words, there are typically the highest counts of households making 50–100k dollars per year, compared to the counts of households making significantly less or significantly more.

The default histograms plotted in our grid does a reasonable job of conveying the distribution of income throughout the tracts in the state of Oregon. However, it is not possible to read the income bands off of the plot, and a lot of space is wasted on uninteresting default labels. How might we fix this? To start, we need a vector of length 16 giving a nice label for each plot. This can be constructed by pasting together the column names from our data set. After removing the first name "total", the first 15 names are pasted, with a dash in between them, to the last 15 names to show the ranges given in the buckets. The final bucket label is manually added.

```
> bands <- colnames(hhIncome)[-1]
> bandNames <- paste(bands[-length(bands)],"-",bands[-1], sep="")
> bandNames <- c(bandNames, "200k+")
```

```
> bandNames
 [1] "0k-10k"      "10k-15k"     "15k-20k"     "20k-25k"     "25k-30k"
 [6] "30k-35k"     "35k-40k"     "40k-45k"     "45k-50k"     "50k-60k"
[11] "60k-75k"     "75k-100k"    "100k-125k"   "125k-150k"   "150k-200k"
[16] "200k+"
```

These can now be plotted over the histograms using the function text that puts a label at a given set of coordinates.[21] As all of the plots have the same x and y ranges, we can hard code this to be at $x = 0.33$ and $y = 500$.

In order to make the plot fill up more of the image with interesting data rather than repeating titles and axes labels, three steps are needed. Within the hist function call, we set axes to FALSE, and the labels xlab, ylab, and main to empty strings. Secondly, we make another call to the par function, setting the parameter mar (margin) to a vector of four zeros. These values correspond to the bottom, left, top, and right margins of the plot; we are setting them all to zero. Finally, because turning off the axes also turns off the box around the plot, which is visually useful in a grid of histograms, we make an additional call to the function box in each iteration.

```
> par(mfrow=c(4,4))
> par(mar=c(0,0,0,0))
> for(j in 1:16) {
+   hist(cumIncome[,j], breaks=seq(0,1,length.out=20),axes=FALSE,
+        main="",xlab="",ylab="", ylim=c(0,600), col="grey")
+   box()
+   text(x=0.33,y=500,
+        label=paste("Income band:", bandNames[j]))
+ }
```

The output from this code is shown in Fig. 3.5. It is much more visually pleasing and conveys additional meaning from the original plot due to the inclusion of readable band labels.

3.8 Aggregation

Another use of *for loops* is to aggregate a continuous variable over the unique values of a categorical one, for example, summing up the tract populations in geodf by their CSA designation to get a population total for each of the combined statistical areas in Oregon. As before, we first need to create an empty object in which to store the output of the *for loop*. Here we do this with the help of the unique function, which returns the unique values of a vector, in order to construct a named vector of population totals.

```
> csaSet <- unique(geodf$csa)
> popTotal <- rep(0, length(csaSet))
> names(popTotal) <- csaSet
```

---

[21] We will see more advanced uses of this function in Sect. 4.

3.8 Aggregation

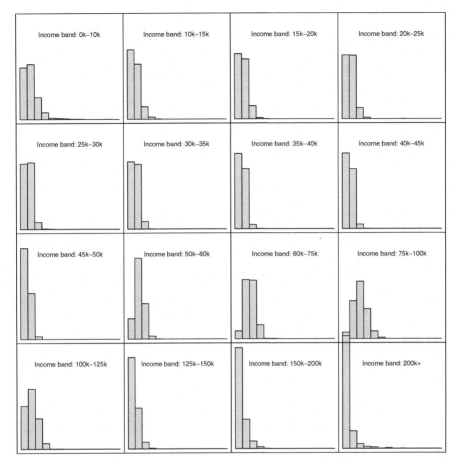

Figure 3.5: Grid of income band distributions at a census tract level with repressed margins and titles. Axes ranges are held constant across the plots. Income ranges are printed in each box.

The data frame is then looped over by row, with each row assigned to a particular element of `csaSet` using the `match` function and its population added to the corresponding running total.[22]

```
> for (j in 1:nrow(geodf)) {
+     index <- match(geodf$csa[j], csaSet)
+     popTotal[index] <- popTotal[index] + geodf$population[j]
+ }
> popTotal
    None Portland     Bend  Medford
 1582446  1816916   181459   287900
```

---

[22] See Sect. 2.9 for a refresh of the match function, a common point of confusion for new R users.

The resulting vector shows that 1.8 million people live in the Portland CSA (at least within Oregon; technically the region spills over the state boundary into Washington State).

Looping over the rows of the data frame is not the only method of using loops to aggregate over the four CSA designations. An alternative is to cycle over the set of CSA values, extracting the matching rows of the data frame and adding them together in each iteration. As an example, here is an example implementing this aggregation to count the number of individuals who work at home in each CSA region.

```
> csaSet <- unique(geodf$csa)
> wahTotal <- rep(0, length(csaSet))
> names(wahTotal) <- csaSet
> for (csa in csaSet) {
+     index <- which(geodf$csa == csa)
+     wahTotal[csa] <- wahTotal[csa] +
+                 sum(meansOfCommute[index,"work_at_home"]) * 100
+ }
```

Dividing this count by the total population shows the percentage of each CSA who works from home.

```
> wahTotal / popTotal
    None   Portland       Bend    Medford
2.488805   3.083247   3.177026   2.755818
```

It is commonly known that R slows down considerably when executing loops; so this second method will scale better when working with large data sets as it requires fewer iterations. At the scale of data we are working with here, though, the difference is practically unnoticeable.

3.9 Applying Functions

We have used loops to apply a function over the rows of a matrix. In addition to this method, R has a special syntax for applying functions over the rows or columns of a matrix using the `apply` function. The following code snippet, for example, applies the function `sum` over the rows of the matrix `meansOfCommute`. The parameter `MARGIN` determines which dimension to apply the function over, with rows having a value of 1 and columns having a value of 2.

```
> apply(meansOfCommute[1:10,-1],MARGIN=1,FUN=sum)
 [1] 1242 1199  999 1035 1123  729 4080 2042 3608 1315
> meansOfCommute[1:10,1]
 [1] 1242 1199  999 1035 1123  719 3932 2042 3559 1275
```

Looking at the `apply` function of the first ten rows, notice that the function has verified that the first column is the total of the other columns. Accordingly, 1242

3.9 Applying Functions

is the aggregate of the means of commute such as car and bike. Applying the sum function over MARGIN=2 shows the total counts of transportation types over the entire dataset.[23]

```
> apply(meansOfCommute,2,sum)
      total          car public_trans          bus       subway
    1700451      1394475        70714        55784         5119
   railroad        ferry         bike         walk         taxi
       2751           32        39789        69285        17085
work_at_home
     109103
```

We see, among other things, that only 32 people claim to take a ferry to work.

The apply function can be used even when the result of applying a function to a row is a vector rather than a single number. The result, assuming each vector is the same length, is a new matrix with the results combined together. As a practical example, consider the process of taking the cumulative sum of each row in the household income dataset. The following one line of code can replace the previous code block that used *for loops*:

```
> cumIncome <- apply(hhIncome[,-1],1,cumsum)
> dim(cumIncome)
[1]  16 826
```

The result is a flipped version of our previous code because apply always combines the results by column. In order to exchange the rows and columns of a matrix, the function t (one letter, standing for transpose) is used.

```
> cumIncome <- t(cumIncome) / hhIncome[,1]
> cumIncome <- round(cumIncome * 100)
> cumIncome[1:5,]
      0k 10k 15k 20k 25k 30k 35k 40k 45k 50k 60k 75k 100k 125k 150k
[1,]   9  14  18  25  29  31  35  42  48  56  70  78   89   96   98
[2,]   9  21  28  34  41  42  44  50  53  64  72  84   89   97   98
[3,]   9  15  24  34  40  50  54  62  70  81  88  96   97   97   98
[4,]  12  25  32  39  45  51  55  59  65  73  83  93   96   97   99
[5,]   6  18  26  33  39  44  51  59  69  79  87  95   97   98   98
     200k
[1,]  100
[2,]  100
[3,]  100
[4,]  100
[5,]  100
```

The result being the exact same as constructed in Sect. 3.6.

Another variant of the apply function is the tapply function, which applies a function over one vector by the unique values of another vector. Among other things, this allows aggregations to be done in a single function call. The following, for example, applies the function sum to counts of people who work from home by the unique values of CSAs.

---
[23] The MARGIN and FUN parameters are typically unnamed and set positionally, as they are here.

```
> wahTotal <- tapply(X=meansOfCommute[,"work_at_home"],
+                    INDEX=geodf$csa,
+                    FUN=sum)
> wahTotal
    Bend Medford     None Portland
    5765    7934    39384    56020
```

The result is exactly the same as derived in Sect. 3.8, but with significantly less code and without the need to pre-calculate the unique values of the CSA variable.

Other variants of apply functions exist in R: lapply, mapply, eapply, vapply, sapply, and parApply. These are all well documented in their respective help pages; we will mostly stick to the two previously mentioned variants throughout this text as they provide the majority of the required functionality.

References

[1] UC Bureau. American community survey. *Washington, DC*, 2009, 2005.

[2] Herbert A Sturges. The choice of a class interval. *Journal of the American Statistical Association*, 21 (153): 65–66, 1926.

Chapter 4
EDA II: Multivariate Analysis

Abstract In this chapter, techniques for exploring the relationship between multiple continuous variables are shown, using scatter plots as basic building blocks.

4.1 Introduction

In Chap. 3 we presented numerous methods for exploring and visualizing datasets. These techniques were either restricted to a single variable, such as histograms and quantiles, or involved categorical variables. Here we investigate methods for exploring the relationship between two (or more) continuous variables. These visualizations allow for a high degree of customization by varying color, shape, sizes, and other graphical parameters. The power of using a programming language for creating graphs, rather than a point and click GUI, is shown.

4.2 Scatter Plots

A scatter plot is a visualization of two numeric variables using a two-dimensional region. For each data point, a mark is placed at the horizontal location value of the first variable and the vertical position of the second variable. Drawing a basic scatter plot in R involves calling the `plot` function with the two vectors of interest. As an example, we plot the number of households and the population of each census tract:

```
> plot(geodf$households, geodf$population)
```

The output in Fig. 4.1a shows the default scatter plot, which roughly resembles similar plots frequently displayed in newspapers, magazines, television shows, and other popular media. An impressive amount of information is succinctly displayed in this plot. We can see the range of the two variables, visually identify outliers (a few tracts with almost no households, and a few with over 4000), and approximately

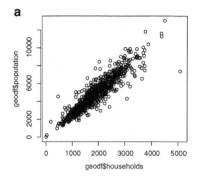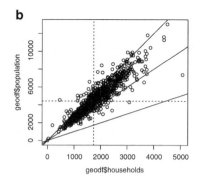

Figure 4.1: (**a**) Scatter plot showing number of households against population for census tracts in Oregon. (**b**) Scatter plot showing number of households against population for census tracts in Oregon. *Solid lines* plot have slopes equal to 1, 2, and 3 and run through the origin. The *dashed lines* denote the median of each component.

identify that most tracts have between 1000 and 2500 households and 2000–6000 people. The roughly linear relationship between the two variables is also seen, with most tracts having two to three people per household. The small set of outliers from this relationship are also quickly identifiable.

The flexibility of scatter plots in R comes mostly from the ability to layer additional information over a pre-existing plot. We have seen one example of this already when adding income band labels to histograms in Sect. 3.7. For the current scatter plot, a useful addition would be to add lines to help understand the ratio between population and the number of households. The function abline takes two numbers and draws a line using the first as the y-intercept (point where the line crosses the y-axis) and the second as the slope of the line. Running the following commands adds lines that run through the origin and have slopes of 1, 2, and 3. A point lying on the second line would, for example, represent a census tract with exactly two people per household.

```
> abline(0,1)
> abline(0,2)
> abline(0,3)
```

It is also possible to add vertical and horizontal lines using abline, by specifying (by name!) the parameter v or h. Here we add lines denoting the median of each coordinate through the parameter prob=0.5. The additional parameter lty indicates that these lines should be dashed rather than solid.

```
> abline(v=quantile(geodf$households,prob=0.5), lty="dashed")
> abline(h=quantile(geodf$population,prob=0.5), lty="dashed")
```

4.2 Scatter Plots

The output from these adding these lines is shown in Fig. 4.1b. While conveying the same underlying points, the new plot helps to strengthen and refine our previous observations. For example, we now see that the majority of tracts have between two and three people per household and none have fewer than one person per household.

We will now turn to another example and explore household income in Oregon looking specifically at income in the Portland metro area in relation to the rest of the state. In particular, we can further customize the outputs through additional parameters in our `plot` function to make our graph easier to read. We will use three of these functions frequently to manipulate the way the points are represented on the plot: `cex`, `pch`, and `col`. The parameter `cex` defines the relative size of the points (with one being the default); `pch` gives a number code to indicate the shape of the points; and `col` determines the color of the points. These can all be provided as single inputs, in which case they effect every point in the scatter plot. Otherwise, vectors of the same length as the input can be given, with each element effecting only the corresponding data value. This provides a mechanism for seeing additional variables in the scatter plot, differentiated by color, shape, or size.

The values for `cex` are defined as multipliers to the default point sizes given the scale of the plot. Generally, we will not want a size smaller than 0.5 or larger than 2. Here we set the size of values corresponding to tracts outside of Portland to be 0.5, with those in the Portland metro area set to 1.

```
> cexVals <- rep(0.5, nrow(geodf))
> cexVals[geodf$csa == "Portland"] = 1
```

Making the points in Portland larger than the dots is helpful as otherwise the plus signs we are about to add will get lost in a sea of solid dots.

The two shape codes we use most are 19 (solid dots) and 3 (plus signs); for a complete list of the codes used in defining the input `pch`, see the help page by typing `?pch` in the R console. Here we will create vector pch values, first setting all of the values to 19 and then switching those corresponding to the Portland metro area to 3.

```
> pchVals <- rep(19, nrow(geodf))
> pchVals[geodf$csa == "Portland"] = 3
```

Using these values, points from tracts in the Portland area will be plus signs and other tracts will be solid dots.

Finally, to illustrate the point, we can define a custom vector of colors. We have already seen how to define color using character vectors as described in the list `colors()`. Another approach is through the function `grey`, which takes a number between 0 and 1 and returns shades of grey with lower numbers being darker and higher number lighter. For example, the following will make the Portland points a light grey and the non-Portland points a darker grey.

```
colVals <- rep(grey(0.2), nrow(geodf))
colVals[geodf$csa == "Portland"] <- grey(0.8)
```

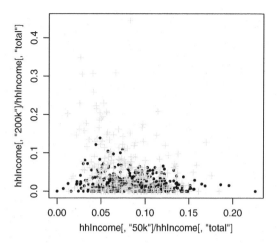

Figure 4.2: Scatter plot of tract level income band data from Oregon, showing the proportion of households earning $45–50k per year against those earning $75–100k. Tracts in the Portland metro area are denoted by *silver plus signs*; other tracts by *dark circles*.

The function `grey`, and its multi-chromatic version `rgb`, is useful when needing a larger set of colors as we can pass it a vector of values in order to get a long vector of shaded colors.

We now use these three graphical parameters in a scatter plot between the two income variables used in Sect. 3.6.

```
> plot(hhIncome[,"50k"]/hhIncome[,"total"],
+      hhIncome[,"200k"]/hhIncome[,"total"],
+      cex=cexVals,
+      pch=pchVals,
+      col=colVals)
```

The output shown in Fig. 4.2 shows the various differentiations between the Portland and non-Portland data points. We see that the set of tracts with a high percentage of households with incomes above $200,000 are almost entirely from the Portland metro area.

4.3 Text

Using the `tapply` function introduced in Sect. 3.9, we can quickly calculate the proportion of households in each county that fall within a given income band.

```
> county30k <- tapply(hhIncome[,"30k"], geodf$county, sum)
> county200k <- tapply(hhIncome[,"200k"], geodf$county, sum)
> countyTotal <- tapply(hhIncome[,"total"], geodf$county, sum)
> county30k <- county30k / countyTotal
> county200k <- county200k / countyTotal
```

4.3 Text

We could construct a scatter plot of the resulting data to understand the relationship between these two income buckets. Given that each data point has a well-defined name (the county) and the relatively small sample size, it would be even better if we could label these points with the county names.

In order to add labels to a plot, the `text` function is used. We already saw one application of this when adding income band labels to a grid of histograms. Here we give the function two vectors of coordinates and vector of labels in order to plot all the counties at once. In order to have the labels appear slightly above the points, rather than awkwardly plotting directly over them, we use an offset of 0.001 to the horizontal components.

```
> plot(county30k, county200k)
> text(county30k, county200k+0.001, labels=names(county30k), cex=0.5)
```

The text command accepts the same `cex` and `col`, which can again be a single number or a vector corresponding to each data point. The `pch` input is not applicable as text labels do not have a shape. Here we reduced the default sizes by half in order to keep the plot from becoming too cluttered.[1] The labeled plot is shown in Fig. 4.3. We see that there is not a clear linear relationship between these variables. Grant County has the second highest percentage of households making between $30,000 and $35,000 per year, and it is also one of the top counties for having top earners.

With the CSA values, we have a method for further grouping the individual counties. These groupings can be denoted on the plot using color. We first need to construct a vector with the same length of `county30k` and `county200k`, describing the corresponding CSA to each county. This is done via the match function:

```
> csaValues <- geodf$csa[match(names(county30k), geodf$county)]
> csaValues
 [1] "None"     "None"     "Portland" "None"     "Portland" "None"
 [7] "Bend"     "None"     "Bend"     "None"     "None"     "None"
[13] "None"     "None"     "Medford"  "None"     "Medford"  "None"
[19] "None"     "None"     "None"     "None"     "None"     "None"
[25] "None"     "Portland" "None"     "None"     "None"     "None"
[31] "None"     "None"     "None"     "Portland" "None"     "None"
```

These strings values now need to be converted into numeric levels; one way of doing this is to construct a set of the unique CSA values and save the raw index output of the `match` function.

```
> csaSet <- unique(geodf$csa)
> index <- match(csaValues, csaSet)
> index
 [1] 1 1 2 1 2 1 3 1 3 1 1 1 1 4 1 4 1 1 1 1 1 1 1 1 2 1 1 1 1 1
[33] 1 2 1 2
```

---
[1] Tweaks like this are generally done by trial and error.

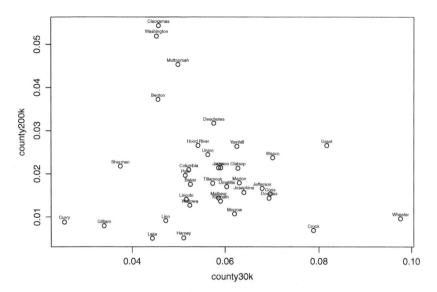

Figure 4.3: Scatter plot of county level income band data from Oregon, showing proportion of households earning $25–30k against those earning $200k or more.

Finally, we take a vector of four colors (one for each CSA) and construct a vector of color values matching the points in the scatter plot.

```
> colVals <- c("orchid1","navy","wheat3","olivedrab")
> colVals[index]
 [1] "orchid1"   "orchid1"   "navy"      "orchid1"   "navy"
 [6] "orchid1"   "wheat3"    "orchid1"   "wheat3"    "orchid1"
[11] "orchid1"   "orchid1"   "orchid1"   "orchid1"   "olivedrab"
[16] "orchid1"   "olivedrab" "orchid1"   "orchid1"   "orchid1"
[21] "orchid1"   "orchid1"   "orchid1"   "orchid1"   "orchid1"
[26] "navy"      "orchid1"   "orchid1"   "orchid1"   "orchid1"
[31] "orchid1"   "orchid1"   "orchid1"   "navy"      "orchid1"
[36] "navy"
```

These colors are then used in both the plot and text functions.

```
> plot(county30k, county200k, col=colVals[index], pch=19)
> text(county30k, county200k+0.001, names(county30k),
+      col=colVals[index],cex=0.5)
```

Notice that the points have been set to solid dots using the pch; we will use this frequently in order to accentuate point colors.

The result of this labeled and colored plot is shown in Fig. 4.4. The mapping between colors and CSA values is given by the following data frame.

```
> data.frame(csaSet,colVals)
    csaSet   colVals
1     None   orchid1
```

4.4 Points

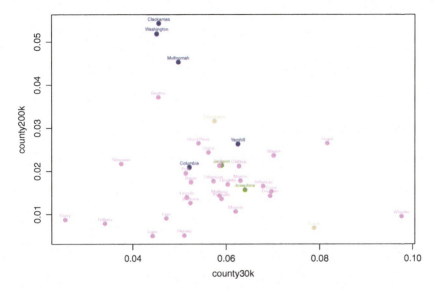

Figure 4.4: Scatter plot of county level income band data from Oregon, showing proportion of households earning $25–30k against those earning $200k or more. *Color* denotes the CSA of the county, with Portland counties in *navy*, Bend counties in *wheat* (*dark yellow*), and Medford counties in *olive*. Counties outside of a Combined Statistical Area are colored in *orchid* (*purple-pink*).

```
2 Portland      navy
3     Bend    wheat3
4  Medford  olivedrab
```

For understanding the data, the plot does a good job of showing the relationship between the two income bands and labeling the points with the various county names and coloring based on the CSA of the county. The plot clearly has some aesthetic issues; some of the text labels run into one another, a legend mapping colors to CSAs should be shown directly on the graph, and the colors may not be ideal. We will address these and other concerns later in Chap. 5.

4.4 Points

Just as we might add text to an already constructed plot, it is also sometimes useful to add additional points to an existing scatter plot. Consider a scatter plot of two income band percentages, here at the basic tract level.

```
> plot(hhIncome[,"30k"] / hhIncome[,"total"],
+      hhIncome[,"200k"] / hhIncome[,"total"],
+      col="black",
+      pch=19,
+      cex=0.5)
```

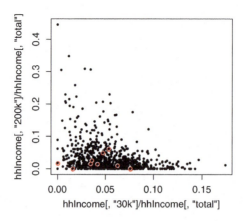

Figure 4.5: Scatter plot of tract level income band data from Oregon, showing the proportion of households earning $25–30k per year against those earning $200k+. *Red circles* highlight tracts where 30 % or more of the population walk to work.

If we are interested in studying places with a higher number of bike commuters, it would be helpful to call out where these points exist on the plot. One method would be to color them differently in the first place; alternatively we can identify them after the fact and plot red circles around the tracts of interest.

Selecting the tracts with a high proportion of bike commuters, the `points` command can then be used similarly to the `plot` command. However, `points` draws on top of the current plot rather than creating a new graphic window; it also does not accept parameters which describe the plot as a whole such as axes limits (`ylim`) and titles (`main`).

```
> index <- which(walkPerc > 0.3)
> points(hhIncome[index,"30k"] / hhIncome[index,"total"],
+        hhIncome[index,"200k"] / hhIncome[index,"total"],
+        col="red")
```

The resulting Fig. 4.5 now clearly calls out the location of these high-bike commuter tracts.

4.5 Line Plots

The next, and final, dataset from the American Community Survey that we investigate calculates the time of day in which people typically leave their house for work. Like the other datasets, we convert this to a matrix; we also immediately convert the raw counts into proportions using the "total" column.

```
> timeOfCommute <- read.csv("data/ch03/timeOfCommute.csv",
+                           as.is=TRUE,check.names=FALSE)
> timeOfCommute <- as.matrix(timeOfCommute)
> timeOfCommute[,-1] <- timeOfCommute[,-1] / timeOfCommute[,1]
```

4.5 Line Plots

The columns represent time ranges, with the labels giving the end of the time range. So, the column labeled "5am" gives the proportion of the population who leave for work between midnight and "5am".

```
> timeOfCommute[1:5,]
     total        5am       5:30am         6am       6:30am         7am
[1,]  1094 0.05850091  0.053016453  0.05210238  0.12888483  0.11060329
[2,]  1122 0.03297683  0.070409982  0.04188948  0.08288770  0.14171123
[3,]   886 0.02708804  0.049661400  0.11060948  0.06546275  0.05530474
[4,]  1001 0.07492507  0.006993007  0.02397602  0.04795205  0.06593407
[5,]  1054 0.03036053  0.004743833  0.01612903  0.09392789  0.03415560
         7:30am         8am      8:30am          9am        10am        11am
[1,] 0.17093236  0.1755027  0.05667276  0.06032907  0.04753199  0.03747715
[2,] 0.11408200  0.2638146  0.06862745  0.02852050  0.03119430  0.03208556
[3,] 0.14785553  0.1591422  0.14672686  0.03611738  0.05079007  0.00000000
[4,] 0.13586414  0.3336663  0.07892108  0.06193806  0.06193806  0.00000000
[5,] 0.09962049  0.1764706  0.16129032  0.06925996  0.01707780  0.10056926
            12pm         4pm         12am
[1,] 0.000000000  0.02010969  0.0283363803
[2,] 0.018716578  0.07219251  0.0008912656
[3,] 0.012415350  0.02821670  0.1106094808
[4,] 0.000000000  0.06993007  0.0379620380
[5,] 0.008538899  0.06831120  0.1195445920
```

In this case, we may want to visualize just a single row of data by creating a scatter plot of time of day against the proportion of the population departing for work at that hour. To start with this requires (manually in this case) determining numeric values which write the column name hours as a numeric variable in hours past midnight.

```
> numericTimes <- c(5,5.5,6,6.5,7,7.5,8,8.5,9,10,11,12,16,24)
> plot(numericTimes, timeOfCommute[1,-1])
```

The points in this plot would actually be better represented as a single line passing through each point. To do this in R, the lines function is used; the syntax is similar to text and points.

```
> lines(numericTimes, timeOfCommute[1,-1])
```

The output of this one tract's data is shown in Fig. 4.6.

One problem with our initial plot is that we are using raw proportions even though the time buckets are not evenly distributed. For instance, the last column represents 8 h of the day (4 p.m.-midnight), and it is unfair to compare this count to a bucket with only half an hour of time. To alleviate this we construct a modified version of the time data where each bucket is divided by the number of hours it contains.

```
timeOfCommuteDens <- timeOfCommute[,-1]
timeOfCommuteDens[,1] <- timeOfCommuteDens[,1] / 5
timeOfCommuteDens[,2:9] <- timeOfCommuteDens[,2:9] / 0.5
timeOfCommuteDens[,13] <- timeOfCommuteDens[,13] / 4
timeOfCommuteDens[,14] <- timeOfCommuteDens[,14] / 8
```

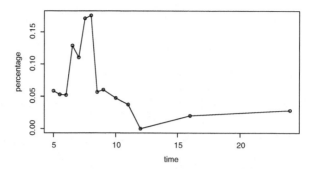

Figure 4.6: Raw values from a particular census tract, showing the proportion of the population who leave at a given hour (shown as hours from midnight).

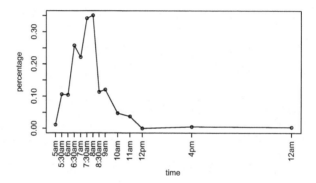

Figure 4.7: Line plot showing the density of people who commute to work at a given hour, from one particular tract.

Using these *densities* rather than raw values will allow for a more accurate description of commute times.

The second issue with the original plot is the difficultly in reading the x-axis labels. This is supposed to represent time, but in converting to a numeric variable for plotting this is not reflected in the axes. To fix these, we must manually construct the axis labels. We have already seen how to turn off the default axes using the `axes` parameter and manually adding back the box around the plot.

```
> plot(numericTimes, timeOfCommuteDens[1,], axes=FALSE)
> lines(numericTimes, timeOfCommuteDens[1,])
> box()
```

To add custom axes to a plot, the `axis` function is used. With a single number, the default axis will be added to the corresponding side.[2] As the y-axis was fine in the

---

[2] 1: bottom, 2: left, 3: top, 4: right.

4.5 Line Plots

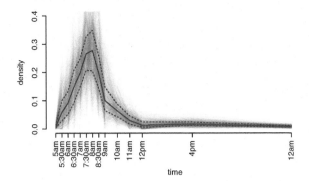

Figure 4.8: Density of time commuters leave for work. The *solid line* shows the hourly median and *dashed lines* indicate the first and third quantiles.

original plot, we use `axis(2)` to add it back in. For the x-axis, we can specify the location of the labels by the `at` parameter and the labels by the `label` parameter.

```
> axis(2)
> axis(1, at=numericTimes, label=colnames(timeOfCommuteDens), las=2)
```

The `las=2` is added to rotate the labels so that they do not run into one another. The improved plot is shown in Fig. 4.7; notice how much easier the plot is to read, and how the densities in the large buckets on the extreme ends have decreased.

Now that we have a nice plot of a single census tract, how might we similarly represent all of the tracts? A separate plot for each would be difficult to use as there are over 800 tracts. A better solution is to use a for loop to plot all of the lines in the same graphics window. If we did this verbatim, the large number of lines would mostly just form a hard-to-read black mass of points. The trick is to use an opaque color for the lines by specifying the `alpha` value in the `grey` function. This fills the lines with a see-through color. Setting the `alpha` to a number close to zero creatively turns the simple line function into a way to visualize all of the tracts on the same plot.

```
> plot(numericTimes, timeOfCommuteDens[1,], type="n", axes=FALSE,
+       xlab="time", ylab="density", ylim=c(0,0.4))
> for(j in 1:nrow(timeOfCommuteDens)) {
+   lines(numericTimes, timeOfCommuteDens[j,],col=grey(0,alpha=0.01))
+ }
```

The output of this is shown in Fig. 4.8, along with the following additional three lines which plot the median, first, and third quartiles over the plot.

```
> medianTimes <- apply(timeOfCommuteDens,2,quantile,probs=0.5)
> lines(numericTimes, medianTimes)
> q1Times <- apply(timeOfCommuteDens,2,quantile,probs=0.25)
> lines(numericTimes, q1Times, col=rgb(0,0,0), lty="dashed")
```

```
> q3Times <- apply(timeOfCommuteDens,2,quantile,probs=0.75)
> lines(numericTimes, q3Times, col=rgb(0,0,0), lty="dashed")
```

From this we see that 8 a.m. is the most popular time to leave, followed very closely by 7:30 a.m. The peak drops off sharply at 9 a.m., at which point most commuters have already left. There is a steadily increasing trickle of early commuters from 5 a.m. to the peak hours.

4.6 Scatter Plot Matrix

We have shown how to construct a scatter plot to visualize the relationship between two continuous variables. By utilizing shapes, colors, sizes, lines, text, and points, we have also been able to incorporate additional variables into a single plot. These are all great techniques, particularly when producing final plots to succinctly present information in a paper, book, or presentation. When dealing with a large set of data, particularly when seeing it for the first time, a less clever solution is often best for understanding the general relationship between the variables. A common tool uses a matrix of scatter plots, showing the relationships between all pairs of continuous variables, as an initial visualization tool. The R function pairs creates such a plot from just a data frame or matrix; in order to illustrate several important concepts, we will show how to instead construct such a graphic manually.

We start by creating a four column dataset of combining selected variables from the means of transportation, time of commute, and income datasets.

```
> tractData <- data.frame(walkPerc, carPerc,
+                         inc30k=timeOfCommuteDens[,"7am"],
+                         inc200k=hhIncome[,"200k"]/hhIncome[,"total"])
```

It turns out that one row of this dataset has a missing value in it. In order to remove this, we combine the is.na function from Sect. 2.9 and apply function from Sect. 3.9, picking out only rows with no missing values.

```
> tractData <- tractData[apply(is.na(tractData),1,sum) == 0, ]
```

We have previously had this missing value floating around in our dataset, but up until now have not needed to remove it because the scatter plot functions handle missing values by simply ignoring them.

In order to construct the scatter plot of matrices, we need to construct *nested* for loops, where one loop is contained inside another. We also need to use a new control flow function if, which evaluates its argument, and only if true execute the remainder of the code. For example, the following code cycles through all combinations of i and j in the set 1 to 5, but prints the result only when i is strictly less than j.

```
> for (i in 1:5) {
+   for (j in 1:5) {
+     if (i < j) print(paste(i,":",j))
```

4.6 Scatter Plot Matrix

```
+   }
+ }
[1] "1 : 2"
[1] "1 : 3"
[1] "1 : 4"
[1] "1 : 5"
[1] "2 : 3"
[1] "2 : 4"
[1] "2 : 5"
[1] "3 : 4"
[1] "3 : 5"
[1] "4 : 5"
```

These nested loops and control statements can become complex, but should be understandable by decomposing them into their respective parts.

The matrix of scatter plot requires setting three graphical parameters. We have already seen how to tell R to put multiple plots on a single image using par and to change the plot margins using mar. For this plot we want to have small margins between the plots, but a larger margin around the entire graphic; this is achieved by manipulating the oma parameter.

```
> par(mfrow=c(4,4))
> par(mar=c(1,1,1,1))
> par(oma=c(2,2,2,2))
```

With these in place, we now cycle through all combinations of the variables i and j to create the matrix of scatter plots. The if statement is used to: (1) add a set of vertical axis labels down the first column, (2) add a set of horizontal axes labels across the bottom row, and (3) add a title using the title function to the top row of the matrix. Opacity has been used to help show overlapping points.

```
> par(mfrow=c(4,4))
> par(mar=c(1,1,1,1))
> par(oma=c(2,2,2,2))
> for (i in 1:ncol(tractData)) {
+   for (j in 1:ncol(tractData)) {
+     plot(tractData[,j],tractData[,i], pch=19,col=grey(0,0.2),
+          axes=FALSE)
+     box()
+     if (i == 1) title(main=colnames(tractData)[j])
+     if (i == ncol(tractData)) axis(1)
+     if (j == 1) axis(2)
+   }
+ }
```

This code constructs the graphic shown in Fig. 4.9. It provides a simple way of visualizing the entire data frame at once. Many useful tweaks can be applied to our basic plot. The diagonal of the plot is not particularly insightful, for example, and could be replaced with a histogram of the associated variable. Also, the top and bottom of the grid are simple mirrors of one another and one copy could be replaced

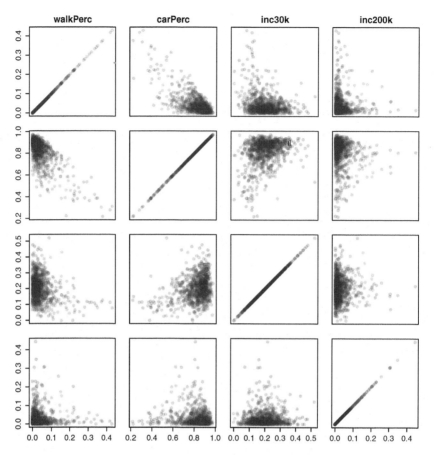

Figure 4.9: Manually constructed pairs plot of four derived variables from the American Community Survey for tracts in the state of Oregon.

with alternative information or graphics. For examples of these alternatives, see the help pages for `pairs`.

4.7 Correlation Matrix

We have focused on simple tables and graphical methods for exploratory data analysis, avoiding model-based approaches such as t-tests and qq-plots. One numerical technique which deserves at least a passing mention are correlation matrices. The correlation between two variables is a number between -1 and 1 describing the strength of the linear relationship between them.[3] A value close to 1 indicates that one variable is approximately a positive multiple of the other. For example, the number of households and the population in a census tract have a correlation of

---

[3]Technically this is known as the Pearson correlation, but when "correlation" is used without a qualifier this is generally what is meant.

4.7 Correlation Matrix

0.92. Negative correlations close to −1 indicate a similar relationship, but where one variable tends to increase as the other decreases. Correlations near zero indicate the lack of linear relationship between the variables in question.

A correlation matrix calculates all pairs of correlations in a dataset, analogous to a scatter plot matrix. Calculating a correlation matrix in R is as easy as calling the function cor on a numeric matrix.

```
> corMat <- cor(tractData)
> round(corMat,2)
         walkPerc carPerc inc30k inc200k
walkPerc     1.00   -0.71  -0.27   -0.04
carPerc     -0.71    1.00   0.30   -0.13
inc30k      -0.27    0.30   1.00    0.02
inc200k     -0.04   -0.13   0.02    1.00
```

Unsurprisingly, the percentage of people who walk to work and the percentage who drive to work are negatively correlated. When one proportion is high, we would naturally expect the other to (generally) be low. The two income band counts are relatively uncorrelated, something we saw at the county level in Fig. 4.3. It does seem that tracts with a higher than typical proportion of car commuters have more households in the $30,000 income bracket but a decreased number of high earners.

Chapter 5
EDA III: Advanced Graphics

Abstract In this chapter, we show several methods for increasing the usability and aesthetic quality of graphics in R. Random number generators and color spaces are also introduced as tools for creating quality graphics.

5.1 Introduction

The graphics we constructed in the previous two chapters have done a nice job of allowing us to quickly explore and understand categorical and numeric variables. We used graphical parameters such as color to represent additional information in scatter plots, while tweaking margins, layouts, and color opacity to fit multiple analyses into a single graphics window. The resulting visualizations already generally look clean and professional. The flexibility of the R programming language provides tools for further increasing the aesthetic value of these plots; this chapter explores several of these methods. As a by-product, the resulting graphics are also often better from the standpoint of basic data exploration.

5.2 Output Formats

In order to use R graphics for presentations and publications, we need a way of saving them as external files. There are often several ways to do this such as right-clicking the plot or selecting from a drop-down menu depending on the method of accessing R. These approaches are fine for quickly saving results during an exploratory analysis. It is also possible to save the graphical output to a file by calling a sequence of R functions. We recommend this approach as it is platform and console independent. If you have a long script that produces dozens of graphics, updating all of the graphics is just a matter of copying and pasting the entire script into R. Finally, parameters such as the width and height of the plot are fixed in the code and will not change from run to run. When using the menu-based options, these parameters are usually determined by the current window size (and is very difficult to replicate).

To save R graphics as a *portable document format* (pdf) file, the function pdf is called *prior* to calling any of the graphics commands. The filename of the output as well as width and height of the output in inches should typically all be specified.[1]

```
> pdf(file="filename.pdf", width=4, height=4)
```

After calling this command, functions such as plot and text, which previously created graphics windows inside of R, will now only plot to the pdf file. If multiple commands are called that would have overwritten a previous plot, these are placed in a new page of the pdf file (another benefit of the command over point and click methods). Once all of the graphics command have been executed, we need to tell R to close its connection to the pdf file by turning the device off. This is done with the command dev.off; it should return a short reference to the device to let us know that it has been successfully closed.[2]

```
> dev.off()
null device
          1
```

After closing the pdf file, graphics commands will work as normal with results displayed directly in R windows. The resulting pdf file can be opened using any external pdf viewer and embedded into e-mails, presentations, websites, and other media. Do not try to open the file prior to closing the graphics device, as it will appear corrupted and will not be viewable.

Other output formats can be saved using a similar method. The functions bmp, jpeg, png, and tiff each save files in formats corresponding to their names. These differ from the pdf function in that the default height and width are in pixels (individual points) rather than inches, and they do not support multiple pages. If you plot more than one graphics window with these, only the last graphic appears in the final output. The following code illustrates how to save a scatter plot to a png file:

```
> png(filename="myScatterPlot.png", height=800, width=800)
> plot(1:10,1:10)
> dev.off()
null device
          1
```

While the pdf command saves vector images, the four functions—bmp, jpeg, png, and tiff—save raster images (hence the reason behind the slightly different default values). The distinction between these two file formats, and relative pros and

---

[1] Otherwise a plot named "Rplots.pdf" will be created in the current working directory with a width and height of 7 inches.

[2] The device should also close if you exit the R session entirely, but it is a better practice to manually close it so as to not risk corrupting the file.

5.3 Color

cons of each, is explored at length throughout Chap. 7 in the context of geospatial datasets and again in Chap. 8 when exploring image analysis.

When constructing complex plots, such as the large networks in Chap. 6, plotting can become a painfully slow operation. Writing the output to a file rather than directly to an R windows is often significantly faster; in these cases, it can be advantageous to use these graphics commands even during the initial stages of data exploration.

5.3 Color

Good use of color is an essential part of creating most statistical graphics. We have seen how to use colors by name and through the command grey. Here we show how to easily construct a *color palette*, a small vector of the colors used in a plot, for various tasks. To illustrate these palettes, we load a data set of election results from the 2012 presidential election in France.

```
> election <- read.csv("../raw_data/france_election_2012.csv",
+                     as.is=TRUE)
> election[1:5,]
      department HOLLANDE SARKOZY LE.PEN MELENCHON BAYROU JOLY
1          Paris    34.83   32.19   6.20     11.09   9.34 4.18
2 Seine-et-Marne    27.65   27.27  19.65     11.01   8.55 1.96
3       Yvelines    27.32   34.24  12.44      9.11  11.24 2.50
4        Essonne    30.39   25.46  15.20     12.26   9.33 2.35
5 Hauts-de-Seine    30.16   34.97   8.51     10.35  10.69 2.74
  DUPONT.AIGNAN POUTOU ARTHAUD CHEMINADE HOLLANDE_2 SARKOZY_2
1          1.00   0.67    0.27      0.23      55.60     44.40
2          2.18   1.02    0.46      0.26      49.25     50.75
3          1.73   0.80    0.35      0.28      45.70     54.30
4          3.41   0.94    0.41      0.24      53.43     46.57
5          1.34   0.69    0.30      0.26      49.48     50.52
```

Each row corresponds to the results from a particular department, an administrative division. Columns 2–11 give the percentage of votes won in the first round of voting, with columns 12 and 13 giving the percentage of votes in the second round of voting (when only two candidates were on the ballot).

One variable of interest from the first round of voting is the total percentage of votes from each department that went to candidates other than the two finalists, François Hollande and Nicolas Sarkozy. Using the apply function this is calculated as follows:

```
> otherVotes <- apply(election[,4:11],1,sum)
```

From the binning method developed in Sect. 3.5, these votes can be grouped into ten buckets.

```
> cuts <- quantile(otherVotes,probs=seq(0,1,length.out=11))
> bins <- cut(otherVotes, cuts, include.lowest=TRUE, labels=FALSE)
```

The vector `bins` has numbers 1 to 10, matching the `otherVotes` variable to a discrete categorization of buckets.

We want to map each of these ten buckets to a set of colors. Specifically, we need a *sequential palette* to show a gradual change between two extremes. We use the R package **colorspace** to provide this set of colors. For details on installing R packages, see Chap. 11. The function `heat_hcl`, provided by the package, returns a set of colors ranging from a dark red to a light yellow. The number of colors used to span this set is given as an input parameter, here we use ten to match the number of buckets.

```
> library(colorspace)
> heat_hcl(n=10)
 [1] "#D33F6A" "#DA565E" "#E06B50" "#E57E41" "#E89132" "#EAA428"
 [7] "#E9B62D" "#E8C842" "#E5D961" "#E2E6BD"
```

The colors are represented as hexadecimal codes, which is also the output given by `grey`, and can be used directly by the R plotting functions.[3] As it is more common to have red by the highest value, and yellow the lowest, we reverse this set before saving it as our color palette. These colors are then used to construct a vector `col` from the bins.

```
> heatPalette = heat_hcl(10)[10:1]
> cols = heatPalette[bins]
```

Now the vector `cols` can be used to encode the percentage of the vote taken by the remaining parties in a scatter plot showing the percentages given to the top two candidates.

```
> plot(election$HOLLANDE, election$SARKOZY, col=cols, pch=19,
+      cex=1.5, xlab="HOLLANDE %", ylab="SARKOZY %")
```

The result is shown in Fig. 5.1a. As expected, the reddest points occur in the lower left of the plot (where Hollande and Sarkozy did relatively poorly) and the yellowest points occur in the upper right half of the plot.[4]

Given the two stage election method in France, one interesting metric is to look at how voters for other candidates split their votes in the second round.[5] For example, we can compute the percentage of the remaining votes assigned to François Hollande as follows:

---

[3] Several websites, such as http://www.color-hex.com/, provide a quick way of decoding these into a thumbnail of the color.

[4] The coloring is determined entirely by the other two axes, so this works great as an example of what a sequential palette of heat colors looks like. It does not, however, provide much useful new information to the scatter plot.

[5] We are implicitly assuming that voters for the front-runners are not changing their votes and that the exact same group of people vote in each round.

5.3 Color

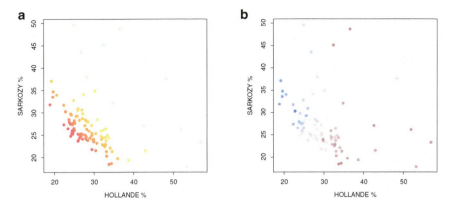

Figure 5.1: (**a**) Scatter plot of first round 2012 French Presidential Elections data, illustrating a sequential color palette. (**b**) Scatter plot of first round 2012 French Presidential Elections data, illustrating a divergent color palette.

```
> percRemain <- (election$HOLLANDE_2 - election$HOLLANDE) /
+                (100 - election$HOLLANDE - election$SARKOZY )
> quantile(percRemain)
       0%       25%       50%       75%      100%
0.3613821 0.4817990 0.5251723 0.5768840 0.8498641
```

By symmetry the remainder of the votes were allotted to Sarkozy. Consider assigning these percentages to colors in the same way we did with the percentages of voters casting votes for candidates not proceeding to the second round. The basic idea would still be conveyed, but the color scheme from dark red to light yellow is not particularly accurate because this data has a natural mid-point at 50 %. Interesting values are not those at one end of the spectrum, but rather values at either extreme. A better choice would be a palette ranging from a dark color, through white, and back to an alternative color. White should correspond to an even 50–50 split of the remaining votes.

To construct the bins to be used with such a color palette, we have to calculate the data cuts separately for values less than and greater than 50. Otherwise there is no guarantee that both of these sets will have the same number of buckets; we need this property so that the "white" value in the middle corresponds to an even split. To calculate these cuts, we use the `quantile` function on only a subset of the data to construct upper and lower break points.

```
> index <- percRemain < 0.5
> cutsLower <-
+     quantile(percRemain[index],probs=seq(0,1,length.out=11))
> index <- percRemain >= 0.5
> cutsUpper <-
+     quantile(percRemain[index],probs=seq(0,1,length.out=11))
```

These breakpoints are combined together into a single vector and used, as before, to bin the output data into chunks.

```
> cuts = c(cutsLower,cutsUpper)
> cuts
        0%        10%        20%        30%        40%        50%        60%
0.3613821  0.4161632  0.4340408  0.4527129  0.4627394  0.4721817  0.4772551
       70%        80%        90%       100%         0%        10%        20%
0.4818796  0.4859240  0.4926577  0.4978733  0.5001059  0.5125271  0.5231833
       30%        40%        50%        60%        70%        80%        90%
0.5351469  0.5482774  0.5606758  0.5760597  0.5874583  0.6174553  0.6376925
      100%
0.8498641
> bins = cut(percRemain, cuts, include.lowest=TRUE, labels=FALSE)
```

The **colorspace** package provides a function diverge_hcl that gives a *divergent palette* of colors. It uses a white value as its mid-point, diverging toward two separate colors on either end point. Here we add an additional parameter alpha to make the colors opaque, and assign colors to each data point using the palette and data bins.

```
> divPalette <- diverge_hcl(20,alpha=0.5)
> cols <- divPalette[bins]
```

The scatter plot of first round results for the two leading candidates using this new color scale is shown in Fig. 5.1b. Here the colors do in fact add new information to the original plot. We see in general that Hollande did a better job of picking up votes in the second round, largely the reason he ultimately won the election. For the most part each candidate did better swaying voters in area where they were already the stronger of the two, though there were two, shown in the upper center, where Sarkozy won the first round but Hollande gained significant ground in the second round.

One interesting way of categorizing the various departments is to see which of the losing first-round candidates had the highest showing. We calculate this by again using the apply function together with a new function which.max, which returns the index of the position with the highest value.

```
> whichOtherParty <- apply(election[,4:11],1,which.max)
> table(whichMaxThirdParty)
whichMaxThirdParty
 1  2  3
94  7  6
```

We see that Front National candidate Marine Le Pen, identified with index 1 by looking at the candidate names in the original data, dominated over all the other candidates by taking 94 of the 107 departments. Parti de Gauche candidate Jean-Luc Mélenchon and the centrist François Bayrou managed to split the remaining 13.

In order to color points by these categories, we need a categorical color palette where each value is highly distinguishable. This final category is a *categorical*

5.3 Color

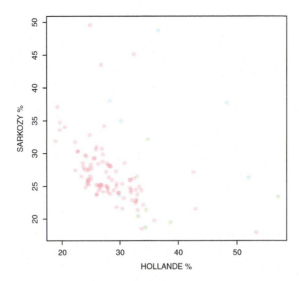

Figure 5.2: Scatter plot of first round 2012 French Presidential Elections data, illustrating a categorical color palette based on the runner-up with the best results by department.

palette and can be calculated by the rainbow_hcl function. It is possible to construct this type of palette by hand, but this function will typically do a better job of finding aesthetically pleasing colors which are maximally differentiated.[6] When dealing with categorical variables which have many levels, hand selecting colors also becomes increasingly difficult.

```
> categoricalPalette <- rainbow_hcl(3, alpha=0.5)
> cols <- categoricalPalette[whichMaxThirdParty]
```

The plot from this is shown in Fig. 5.2. Pink, being the most dominant, is obviously Le Pen, with Mélenchonis the greenish one and Bayrou the blue. We see that the centrist Bayrou performed well when Hollande and Sarkozy captured a high amount of the initial vote. Mélenchonis on the other hand did well where Hollande was also strong; this is reasonable given that Parti de Gauche was a recent off-shoot of Hollande's Parti Socialiste.

All of these palette creation routines have additional parameters for controlling the output (e.g., the divergent palette can be made to instead range between red and green). See the excellent vignette which comes along with the package for additional details.

---

[6] In this particular case hand constructing colors may be a better alternative as we could pick those associated with each party. We use the colorspace function to illustrate the more general approach.

5.4 Legends

The **colorspace** package has given us great color palettes for various types of binned and categorical data. A missing element has been a legend for indicating the meaning behind the values. These can be added to R plots via the `legend` command, which takes the x and y coordinates where it should be plotted and a vector of labels corresponding to the elements in the legend. Additional graphical parameters affect the shape, color, and size of the points plotted in the legend. Here is an example of the legend that would be used in the plot of the runner-ups in the first round of the 2012 French Presidential election:

```
> legend("topright",legend=colnames(election)[4:6],
+        col=categoricalPalette,pch=19,cex=1,
+        bg=grey(0.9))
```

Figure 5.3 shows the much improved plot with the new legend. We used the `bg` parameter to place a light grey background on the image.

A more involved legend can be used to display the levels in a sequential palette. Recomputing the colors for the maximum number of other votes,

```
> otherVotes <- apply(election[,4:11],1,sum)
> cuts <- quantile(otherVotes,probs=seq(0,1,length.out=11))
> bins <- cut(otherVotes, cuts, include.lowest=TRUE, labels=FALSE)
> cols <- heatPalette[bins]
```

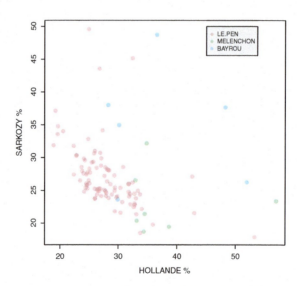

Figure 5.3: Scatter plot of first round 2012 French Presidential Elections data, showing the use of a categorical legend.

5.5 Randomness

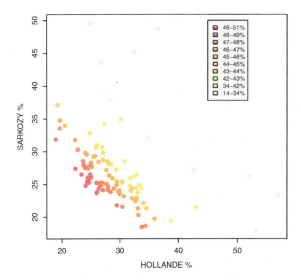

Figure 5.4: Scatter plot of first round 2012 French Presidential Elections data, showing the use of a legend with a continuous response.

We take a rounded version of the break points and paste them together for the legend labels.

```
> cuts <- round(cuts[11:1])
> legendLabels <- paste(cuts[-1],"-",cuts[-length(cuts)], "%",sep="")
```

The legend of the plot is now just as before with the new labels and colors.

```
> legend(45,50,legend=legendLabels, fill=heatPalette, bg=grey(0.9))
```

The output in Fig. 5.4 displays the plot with a legend, which now allows us to give scale to the colors.

5.5 Randomness

When looking at the department by which of the remaining parties did the best, we noticed several interesting patterns but were not able to easily identify the identity of the interesting data points. Using the text command could alleviate this by displaying names next to data points. Here we set the points color to "white", so that only the text values are displayed.

```
> cols <- categoricalPalette[whichOtherParty]
> plot(election$HOLLANDE, election$SARKOZY, col="white",
+       pch=19, cex=2, xlim=c(10,60), ylim=c(10,60))
> text(election$HOLLANDE, election$SARKOZY, election$department,
+       col=cols)
```

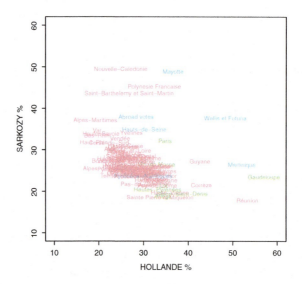

Figure 5.5: Scatter plot of first round 2012 French Presidential Elections data, giving department names.

Unfortunately, the resulting Fig. 5.5 has many overlapping text boxes making the majority of them unreadable. For our own personal use, a simple solution is to make the text size significantly smaller and they just zoom in on each region. This solution is neither elegant nor practical when using the image in print media or as a presentation tool.

As a tool for statistical analysis, the R language has an extensive number of functions for generating and working with randomly generated values.[7] We will not need most of these, but will make use of the function `sample`, which takes a vector and returns a randomly chosen subset of the vector of a given length.

```
> sample(1:10,3)
[1] 8 6 9
```

Running this command many times will yield new results. By default, the sample only picks a value from the set once; the ordering of the output is also randomly generated.

We can use this command to pick out only a random subset of the data to plot. Due to the importance in our visualization of the 13 departments where Le Pen was not the best runner-up, we take a subset consisting of those 13 data points and 15 randomly selected others.

---

[7] Technically R only has the ability to construct *pseudorandom* numbers, but conceptually for most purposes the distinction is unimportant.

5.5 Randomness

```
> index <- which(whichOtherParty %in% c(2,3))
> index <- c(index, sample(which(whichOtherParty == 1), 15))
```

We now create the plot again, but only for the subset of points in `index`.

```
> plot(election$HOLLANDE, election$SARKOZY, col="white",
+      pch=19, cex=2, xlim=c(10,60), ylim=c(10,60),
+      xlab="HOLLANDE %", ylab="SARKOZY %")
> text(election$HOLLANDE[index], election$SARKOZY[index],
+      election$department[index], col=cols[index], cex=0.6)
```

As we see in Fig. 5.6, this is only a modest improvement. We have lost many of the data points which were previously not a problem, but still have over-plotting in the dense middle of the plot because the randomly selected set is likely to still pick several data points from that region.

A clever solution to this problem is to assign every data point to a number giving its approximate location in the plot. Consider the following scheme:

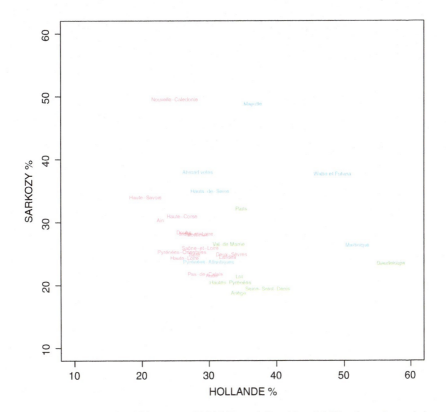

Figure 5.6: Scatter plot of first round 2012 French Presidential Elections data, giving department names. Random sampling used to limit overplotting.

```
> location <- round(election$SARKOZY/2) +
+             round(election$HOLLANDE/10)*100
> location
 [1] 316 314 317 313 317 410 313 313 312 215 215 214 312 213 312 214
[17] 313 312 315 312 314 314 315 314 314 215 314 311 313 214 312 311
[33] 312 213 213 213 217 216 314 213 313 312 313 315 315 313 216 312
[49] 312 313 314 312 314 313 312 311 312 312 313 312 309 313 311 312
[65] 311 310 312 313 411 311 410 215 312 313 312 313 315 214 217 312
[81] 314 312 311 311 212 313 314 313 213 213 219 214 217 214 216 316
[97] 612 513 414 509 309 322 424 519 323 225 319
```

The first two digits give the approximate number of votes assigned to Sarkozy, to a precision of 2, and the hundreds digit gives the votes assigned to Hollande to a precision of 10. Two points now have the same location value only if they gave similar votes to each candidate. If we allow only one text label to appear for any given location value, the plot should not have any intersecting labels; we used a longer box for the horizontal axis because text takes more horizontal than vertical space.[8]

Also, this time we plot a very opaque version of all the data as a base layer; this means that no data points are completely missing, even though some will be lacking a textual label.

```
> colsAlpha <- rainbow_hcl(3, alpha=0.2)[whichMaxOtherParty]
> plot(election$HOLLANDE, election$SARKOZY, pch=19, cex=2,
+      xlim=c(10,60), ylim=c(10,60),
+      xlab="HOLLANDE %", ylab="SARKOZY %")
```

We now use a *for loop* to cycle through the data, plotting a text label only if we have not seen a point with that given location value. Because this would unfairly prioritize the rows of data near the top of our data frame, we use the sample command to randomly permute the indices.[9]

```
> index <- c()
> for (i in sample(1:nrow(election))) {
+   if (!(location[i] %in% index)) {
+     text(election$HOLLANDE[i], election$SARKOZY[i]+1,
+          election$department[i], col=cols[i], cex=0.7)
+     index = c(index, location[i])
+   }
+ }
```

Figure 5.7 shows a very professional looking plot with many of the points labeled and others only have lightly shaded dots. In particular, notice that all of the points outside the densely populated center are completely labeled as they share a location value with no other points.

---

[8] If this scheme seems confusing, try running the code yourself and tweaking the 2 and 10 values. It is significantly easy to describe this in code and examples than via a textual description.

[9] If sample is used without a sample size, it returns a random permutation of the entire input. This is the same as would occur when the sample size is manually set to the length of the input.

5.5 Randomness

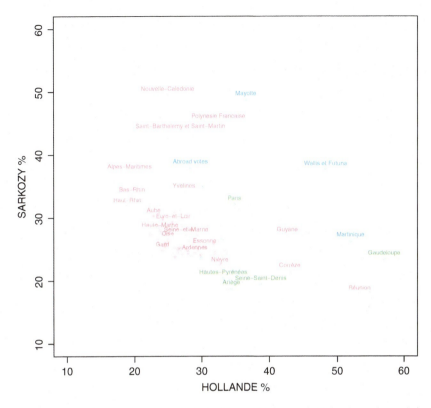

Figure 5.7: Scatter plot of first round 2012 French Presidential Elections data, giving department names. A grid-base version of sampling is used to limit overplotting of the text boxes.

When using the `sample` command, we expect the results to change with each call. If this were not the case, the whole purpose of the function would be lost. Sometimes, however, we want to make sure that a block of R code using a random sample will pick the same sample each time it is run. For example, in this text we wanted to make sure that each plot looks the same when we update the code so that our description of the output does not also need to be updated. In order to fix the result of subsequent calls, the function `set.seed` is used and given an arbitrary integer at which to set itself. The following code should produce the same subsets every time it is run.

```
> set.seed(42)
> sample(1:10,3)
[1] 10  9  3
> sample(1:10,3)
[1] 9 6 5
```

5.6 Additional Parameters

Typing `par()` in an R session prints out 72 parameters that effect the output of an R plot. Dozens of other parameters are set directly within the plot function and the calls to the graphics devices such as `pdf` and `jpeg`. We will not take the time to explain the massive amount of customization that is ultimately possible from within R.[10] We have covered some of the most important and difficult ones already in this and the proceeding two chapters. Many data type specific plotting parameters are mentioned throughout the remainder of this text. We touch briefly on two additional commands which accomplish tasks which are often asked by new users of R graphics.

The plain white background of R plot windows are nice for print media, but can be a bit boring for digital uses. Adding a grey background requires only one line of code, though it is not a particularly intuitive piece of code:

```
> rect(par("usr")[1],par("usr")[3],par("usr")[2],par("usr")[4],
+      col = gray(0.9))
```

To understand what this is doing look at the examples in the help pages for `rect` and `usr`. It can otherwise be copied and pasted as is to add colorful background to existing plots. With white freed from being a background color, it can now be used to provide grid lines for the final plot using the `grid` command.

```
> grid(lty="solid", col="white")
```

The result of adding a background and grid to our French election data is shown in Fig. 5.8. Note that we had to make a separate call to the `points` after adding the background and grid as these had over-writing the initial plot.

In busy plots, it is often useful to put the legend outside of the main graphics window. In order to make this work, the margin command must first be used to create additional margin space outside the plot window.

```
> par(mar=c(5.1, 4.1, 4.1, 10))
> plot(election$HOLLANDE, election$SARKOZY, col=cols, pch=19,
+      cex=1.5, xlab="HOLLANDE %", ylab="SARKOZY %")
```

The legend command is then used with the additional parameter `xpd=TRUE` (which tells R that it is okay to let it plot outside the main window). The x and y coordinates are specified assuming they continue outside of the plot window. Here we use $x = 60$ because it falls just to the right of the plot.

---

[10] For a good description to many of these additional parameter, see Paul Murrell's text *R graphics* [1].

5.7 Alternative Methods

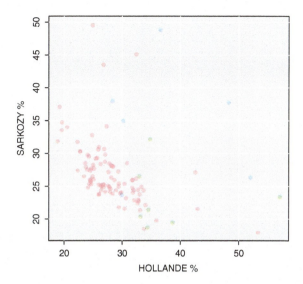

Figure 5.8: Scatter plot of a grey background with white grid lines. Closely mimics the default style of **ggplot2**.

```
> legend(60,50,legend=colnames(election)[4:6],
+        col=rainbow_hcl(3),pch=19,cex=1,
+        xpd=TRUE,
+        bty = "n")
```

This legend outside the plot is shown in Fig. 5.9. When plots have a large number of levels, or span the entire region, this trick can be particularly helpful.

5.7 Alternative Methods

The style of visualization we have been using, and will continue to use, are called *base* R graphics. We find them to be the easiest to work with for new users, while allowing for a wide range of customization for more advanced work. Several alternatives with completely different plotting commands and constructs do exist and are also quite popular. The packages **lattice** and **grid** are shipped with the standard installation of R and each have their own constructs for plotting. The third-party package **ggplot2** has an even further modified set of functions for plotting, built around Leland Wilkinson's text *Grammar of Graphics* [2, 3]. We mention these as they are frequently mentioned in various help forums and mailing lists.

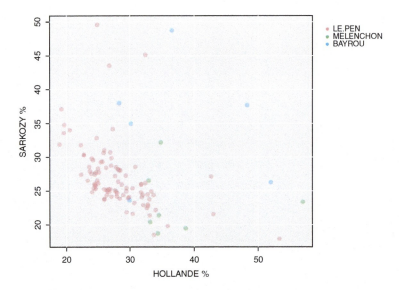

Figure 5.9: Example showing a legend outside the main plotting region.

References

[1] Paul Murrell. *R graphics*. CRC Press, 2011.

[2] Hadley Wickham. *ggplot2: elegant graphics for data analysis*. Springer Science & Business Media, 2009.

[3] Leland Wilkinson, D Wills, D Rope, A Norton, and R Dubbs. *The grammar of graphics*. Springer Science & Business Media, 2006.

Part II
Humanities Data Types

Chapter 6
Networks

Abstract In this chapter, we introduce the concept of a network (also known as a graph). Working with a citation network build from United States Supreme Court opinions, the topics of graph drawing, centrality measures, and community detection are all explored.

6.1 Introduction

Networks form a very generic data model with extensive applications to the humanities. A network consists of a set of objects and a collection of links identifying some relationship between these pairs of objects. The assumption is that a connection exists between these objects that will help us better understand what we are studying. In mathematics, networks are called *graphs*, the set of objects are known as *vertices*, and the links between them are referred to as *edges*. The study of these objects constitute a sub-field of mathematics known as graph theory, which is a large and active area of current research. We will stick to the mathematic terminology, as it is the most commonly found in software directed at data analysis.

Graphs can be a great way to understand connections and relationships between a wide range of objects or types of data. For example, one might want to explore the friendship relationships between people, citations between books, or network connection between computers. Whenever there exists a set of relationships that connects the objects to each other, a graph can be a useful tool for visualization and data exploration.

6.2 A Basic Graph

A simple and well-known example of a graph is a family tree. In a family tree, the vertices are people and an edge between two people represents a direct familial relationship. As an example of a family tree that many people are familiar with, we will construct a tree for four generations of the British royal family. It will be small enough to construct this by hand; in the next section we will explore methods for creating much larger graphs from external datasets.

In order to work with graphs, we make use of custom data structures, domain-specific algorithms, and customized plotting routines. Several R packages provide these functionalities; we will use the **igraph** as it is relatively simple to use and rich with features [2]. There are also versions of the **igraph** package for Python, Ruby, and C++, making it ideal when collaborating with others who may be using a different set of tools.

Graphs come in two basic varieties: *directed* and *undirected*. In the directed case, edges have a distinction between the "to" vertex and the "from" vertex. Edges of directed graphs are often visualized by arrows. In undirected graphs, edges are simply line segments with no such distinction. In the case of a family tree, if we were to have edges represent that two people are married, it would be natural to make this relationship undirected. Conversely, if edges were used to represent parent–child relationships, this would be best represented by a directed graph with an arrow going from a parent toward their children.

In our family tree example, we want to represent parent–child relationships. We therefore start by loading the **igraph** library and constructing an empty directed graph.

```
> library(igraph)
> g <- graph.empty(directed=TRUE)
```

Next, we need to manually add our data. First, each person in the family tree is added to the set of vertices by literally adding (with the + operator) each vertex (singular of vertices) to the graph object g. Notice that we must reassign the new graph back into the variable g.

```
> g <- g + vertex("Elizabeth II")
> g <- g + vertex("Philip")
> g <- g + vertex("Charles")
> g <- g + vertex("Diana")
> g <- g + vertex("William")
> g <- g + vertex("Harry")
> g <- g + vertex("Catherine")
> g <- g + vertex("George")
```

Here just first names are used, as dealing with full formal titles becomes quite cumbersome when dealing with royalty!

We will also manually add edges to the graph for every parent–child relationship. As the graph g is directed, it is important that each edge is created with the parent first and their child second. For example, William (Prince William) and Catherine (Princess Catherine, née Middleton) are the parents of Prince George.

```
> g <- g + edges("Elizabeth II", "Charles")
> g <- g + edges("Philip", "Charles")
> g <- g + edges("Charles", "William")
```

6.2 A Basic Graph

```
> g <- g + edges("Diana", "William")
> g <- g + edges("Charles", "Harry")
> g <- g + edges("Diana", "Harry")
> g <- g + edges("William", "George")
> g <- g + edges("Catherine", "George")
```

We now have the complete structure of our family tree inside the R object g. The process outlined here is fairly verbose to explicitly illustrate the steps in constructing a basic graph. We could have, for example, skipped the step of manually adding each vertex, as the R library would silently construct the nodes when adding edges.

What does this graph object actually do for us? Printing it in an R console is fairly unexciting. It compactly shows that we have a directed (D), named (N), graph with eight vertices and eight edges, but offers little further insight into the graph we have constructed.

```
> g
IGRAPH DN-- 8 8 --
+ attr: name (v/c)
```

If we plot the graph using plot.igraph(g), we get something a bit more interesting, as shown in Fig. 6.1a. The vertices and edges are plotted and laid out in an aesthetically pleasing way; none of the edges overlap, the edges are roughly the same length, and the vertices are spread out over the entire plot. While not bad for a first pass, this plot still does not look like a traditional family tree. In order to do this, we need to tell R exactly where we want each point plotted.

In order to create a custom plot of a graph in R, a two-column matrix with a row for each vertex needs to be passed to the plotting function. The first column gives the x-coordinate of the vertex and the second column provides the y-coordinate of the vertex. The vertices in an igraph object have an internal ordering, which can be seen by using the V() function. The rows in the matrix correspond to the internal ordering of vertices.

```
> V(g)
Vertex sequence:
[1] "Elizabeth II" "Philip"      "Charles"   "Diana"   "William"
[6] "Harry"        "Catherine"   "George"
> lout <- matrix(c(1,3,3,3,2,2,3,2,1,1,3,1,2,1,1,0),8,2,TRUE)
> lout
     [,1] [,2]
[1,]    1    3
[2,]    3    3
[3,]    2    2
[4,]    3    2
[5,]    1    1
[6,]    3    1
[7,]    2    1
[8,]    1    0
```

In this example, Harry's vertex will be positioned as coordinates $(3, 1)$. We have defined a layout where the y-coordinate is a proxy for generation. The reigning

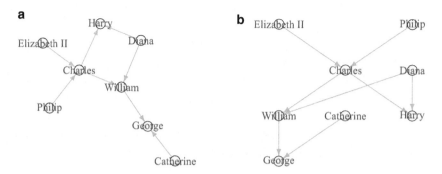

Figure 6.1: A simple graphical depiction of Queen Elizabeth II's family tree. (**a**) Generic layout. (**b**) Family tree format.

monarch is at the top of the plot, her children are slightly lower, her grandchildren even lower, and the baby Prince George is on the bottom. To turn this layout into a plot, we simply pass the matrix as an argument to the `layout` parameter. The edges will be automatically constructed to connect the relevant nodes.

```
> plot.igraph(g, layout=lout)
```

The output shown in Fig. 6.1b shows the same graph structure as the previous plot, but in a more natural layout expected in a family tree.

6.3 Citation Networks

Consider looking through a repository of articles published in *African Studies Review*, the journal of the African Studies Association. How might one use this information to determine which articles and authors have been particularly influential in the field of African Studies? A common metric used in academia is the number of citations made to a given article within the first 5 years of publication. Using citations as a measure of influence is reasonable, but simple counts only tell part of the story. Peter Uvin's article "Prejudice, crisis, and genocide in Rwanda" has 97 citations on Google Scholar, compared to Gregory H Maddox's 18 citations for "Gender and Famine in Central Tanzania: 1916–1961" [7, 12]. Clearly Uvin's article had, in some sense, a wider reach, but there is potentially a more complex story to tell. It may be that both articles are equally central within their own sub-fields, but more scholars are interested in Rwanda or genocide compared to the number who are interested in famine or Tanzania. Or, perhaps, the 18 citations to Maddox's article are of a higher average quality compared to the 97 to Uvin's. A *citation network* is a graph where the vertices are publications and edges represent the relationship that one publication was cited by the other [8]. Using this more complex graphical representation helps to discern these, and many more, nuances which may be obfuscated when using simple counts.

6.3 Citation Networks

Citation networks may be constructed from many datasets that may not at first appear to be a set of citations. For example, one can take a set of course syllabi and pick out which readings are assigned to each course. In this case, the vertices are a set consisting of all the course syllabi and all of the unique readings cited within them. The edges associate each reading to one or more syllabi in which it has been assigned. A graph where vertices can be split into two groups such that edges only occur between vertices in different groups is called a *bipartite graph*. Such graphs have a myriad of applications and mathematical properties (most of which are outside the scope of this book). The **igraph** library even has several functions and algorithms for efficiently working with bipartite graphs.

For the remainder of this chapter, we will be working with a citation network built from United States Supreme Court case opinions. It is a convenient dataset to work with because Supreme Court records are in the public domain and are often of broad interest. We will start by showing how to build a graph object of court citations without resorting to adding each citation as in Sect. 6.2.

The citation data we will use comes from Supreme Court Citation Network Data, developed and provided by James H. Fowler and Sangick Jeon [4, 3]. Their data have been parsed (and is available in the Supplementary Materials) into a two column dataset containing about 216,000 citations between majority opinions written by the US Supreme Court. The first column gives the id of the case which cited the case in the second column; this structure is called an *edge list*, as each row represents an edge in the graph. For instance if we read into R the entire dataset and look at just the first six rows,

```
> allCounts <- as.matrix(read.csv("data/ch06/ac.csv", as.is=TRUE))
> head(ac)
     to         from
[1,] "4US6"     "3US320"
[2,] "4US6"     "4US1"
[3,] "6US280"   "1US393"
[4,] "6US280"   "1US53"
[5,] "6US280"   "3US133"
[6,] "14US179"  "5US321"
```

We see that the majority opinion in 4 U.S. 6 (*New York v Connecticut*, 1799) cited only two cases: 3 U.S. 320 (*Grayson v. Virginia*, 1786) and 4 U.S. 1 (*New York v Connecticut*). The full text of the case conveniently shows exactly the same two citations.[1]

Constructing a graph object in R from an edge list involves a simple call to a single igraph function. Rather than having to specify explicitly, the set of vertices are inferred as the set of all vertices in the edge list. While it certainly is reasonable to model citation networks as directed graphs (with arrows pointing into the citing document), in our case it will be simpler and just as interesting to have an undirected graph.

---

[1] https://supreme.justia.com/cases/federal/us/4/6/

```
> G <- graph.edgelist(allCounts, directed=FALSE)
> G
IGRAPH UN-- 25417 216738 --
+ attr: name (v/c)
```

The entire citation graph has over 25,000 nodes. It is possible to work with a graph of this size R, but it will be far easier for us to take a subset of the graph to work with instead. If 100 nodes were randomly sampled from this graph, we would likely be left with a sparse (very few edges) and uninteresting graph. A better approach is to pick out a subset of cases that deal with similar legal topics. To do this, we will use the Supreme Court Database from the University of Washington—St. Louis to assign thematic categorization to all of the cases in our dataset [11]. The data we need consists of a two-column table mapping each court case to one or more "issue" codes, which can be subsequently looked up in an accompanying code book.

```
> themes <- read.csv("data/ch06/themes.csv", as.is=TRUE)
> head(themes)
      usid issue
1   329US1 80180
2  329US14 10500
3  329US29 80250
4  329US40 20150
5  329US64 80060
6  329US69 80100
```

In the first row, for example, 329 U.S. 1 *Halliburton Oil Well Cementing Co. v. Walker* (1946) is labeled as issue 80180, "patents and copyrights, patents". In the second row case 329 U.S. 14 is labeled as 10500, "statutory construction of criminal laws: Mann Act and related statutes".

With this metadata, it is now possible to restrict the graph G to only cases dealing with a few closely related issues. We will choose to use the topics 20040 and 20050, which deal with "desegregation (other than as pertains to school desegregation, employment discrimination, and affirmation action)" and "desegregation, schools", respectively. The **igraph** library makes this easy with the induced.subgraph function, which takes a set of vertex names and returns a graph (the *vertex induced subgraph*) which extracts only the edges with endpoints in the specified set.

```
> rowNumberOfMatchingCases <- which(themes$issue %in% c(20040,
    20050))
> usidsOfMatchingCases <- themes$usid[rowNumberOfMatchingCases]
> H <- induced.subgraph(G, usidsOfMatchingCases)
> H
IGRAPH UN-- 132 729 --
+ attr: name (v/c)
```

Our graph now has only 132 vertices and is certainly small enough to easily plot. It would still be difficult, however, to hand select where each point should be plotted as we did in Sect. 6.2. Thankfully an entire area of mathematics and computer science known as *Graph Drawing* is dedicated to algorithms for visually arranging graphs

6.4 Graph Centrality

in a two-dimensional plot. A particularly popular and general purpose example is the Fruchterman–Reingold algorithm [5, 10]. It consists of running a simulated physics experiment where edges are modeled as springs and vertices are modeled as positively charged particles. The algorithm can be run in the **igraph** library, where it returns a two-dimensional matrix of coordinates; it is in the same format we created by hand for the British Royal Family's family tree.

```
> set.seed(1)
> lout <- layout.fruchterman.reingold(H)
> head(lout)
           [,1]        [,2]
[1,]  -8.276299   91.980889
[2,] -35.387460   68.329024
[3,] -88.142586    7.486661
[4,] -32.217773  -28.709860
[5,] -18.855028   -9.418584
[6,] -30.091857   34.827377
```

Notice that we have called the function set.seed just prior to running the layout algorithm. We do this because the algorithm is nondeterministic (the result depends on the random starting points of the vertices) and we want to make sure each call returns exactly the same graph. Because we set the random seed, if you run this code on your own machine it should give exactly the same layout displayed here.

We can now use the layout matrix to plot the citation network of our subgraph H. The exact same code from our previous family tree example would produce a decent visualization; here we have added two small tweaks to make the vertex sizes (the default is 10) and labels slightly smaller.

```
> plot.igraph(H, layout=lout, vertex.size=5, vertex.label.cex=0.5)
```

The resulting plot is shown in Fig. 6.2. We see that some cases are not connected to any others, whereas many form two fairly tight clusters in the center of the plot. In the next two sections we will explore tools for studying and visualizing these structures. Unfortunately many of the individual labels are hard to see given the size limitation of a textbook. A digital version of the plot, which uses a smaller font size and can be zoomed in and out on, provides a better solution to the over-plotting seen here.

6.4 Graph Centrality

Centrality is a measurement of how important a vertex is within the context of the entire graph. It is a broad conceptual idea and does not have a single formal definition. Instead, there are several different forms of centrality that capture different notions of importance.

Applications of centrality are numerous and depend on both the nature of the graph being studied and the type of centrality used. Centrality can identify the most influential people in social networks or the most vulnerable targets in a computer

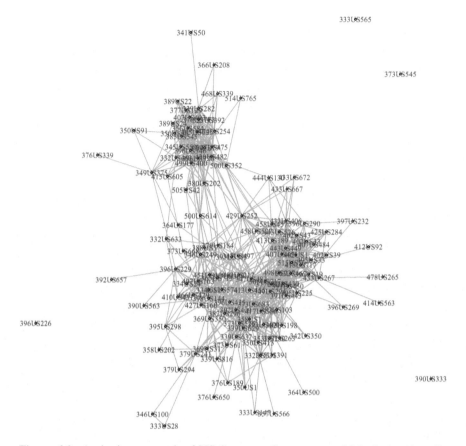

Figure 6.2: A citation network of US Supreme Court cases which dealt primarily with the topic of segregation.

network. The PageRank algorithm used by Google to order search results is a particular example of a centrality measure over the graph of websites [9]. In our example of a citation network, centrality can help identify the most influential opinions to a particular area of case law.

The simplest centrality measure is *degree centrality*. Vertices are ranked only on the number of edges to which it is connected. In citation networks, degree centrality is analogous to just counting the number of citations a document has. We have already argued that this is a reasonable first solution, but may miss the larger picture. A refinement known as *eigenvector centrality* assigns a higher weight to a vertex for being connected to vertices which are themselves important. Formally, it assigns a weight to every vertex such that the weight of a particular vertex is proportional to the sum of the weights of its neighbors. It may seem that this is very hard to calculate given that we need to simultaneously calculate all of the weights at the same time.

6.4 Graph Centrality

It turns out that there is a very efficient way of calculating these weights using the language of matrices (there is a whole subfield of mathematics called *spectral graph theory* that studies the matrix properties of graphs).

Calculating eigenvector centrality for our subgraph H in R is very simple using the evcent function. A list with many components is returned, though only the element named "vector" will be useful for us. This element is a named vector relating each node a numerical score between 0 and 1.

```
> eigenCent <- evcent(H)$vector
> sort(eigenCent,decreasing=TRUE)[1:10]
  347US483   391US430   349US294     402US1   443US449   413US189   418US717
 1.0000000  0.8933058  0.8011224  0.7770846  0.7493045  0.7275929  0.7023205
  503US467   407US451    515US70
 0.6538141  0.6298709  0.6009171
```

Sorting the output shows the top ten cases by their eigenvector centrality values. The top score goes to 347 U.S. 483, *Brown v. Board of Education*, largely considered the most pivotal case in school desegregation, in which the court unanimously argued that racially segregated public schools were unconstitutional [1]. Knowing that the opinion widely regarded as the most influential can be successfully identified in this way lends a great deal of credibility to both the general approach of citation methods and the specific use of eigenvector centrality. This is particularly true after looking back at the graph in Fig. 6.2. Would you have been able to visually identify the most important case from the plot?

Centrality measures are useful for identifying a list of the most influential vertices. They can also be useful in adding context to a visualization of the entire graph by coloring vertices based on their centrality scores. Eigenvalue centrality scores are known to typically decay very rapidly; in our example over 90 % of the vertices have a score of less than 0.5 and the median score is only 0.11. It will therefore be advantageous to convert our centrality scores into quantized buckets.

```
> bins <- unique(quantile(eigenCent, seq(0,1,length.out=30)))
> vals <- cut(eigenCent, bins, labels=FALSE, include.lowest=TRUE)
> colorVals <- rev(heat.colors(length(bins)))[vals]
```

To assign these colors to a plot, the easiest way is to attach a new element named color to the vertex set V(H). From this, the plotting function will automatically pick up these colors and use them to shade the vertices; to reduce clutter we also turn off the vertex labels, which were already hard to read.

```
> V(H)$color <- colorVals
> plot.igraph(H, vertex.label=NA, vertex.size=5)
```

The output of these commands is given in Fig. 6.3a. As we would expect, more centrally located points are shaded darker (or more red, in color) with the isolated points the lightest. The eigenvector centrality assigned higher scores to those cases in the bigger of the two clusters, a known artifact of the method.

The concept behind eigenvector centrality is that the most important vertices should be connected to many other well-connected vertices. A slightly different notion of importance comes from identifying those vertices which connect disjoint parts of the graph. The *betweenness centrality* measures this property of a graph by (approximately) determining the shortest path between every pair of nodes and calculating how many of these run through each vertex; it can also be easily calculated in the **igraph** library using a single call to the betweenness function.

```
> betweenCent <- betweenness(H)
> sort(betweenCent,decreasing=TRUE)[1:10]
 347US483    430US482    429US252    403US217    392US409    413US189    391US430
1964.8653    637.3044    591.0348    589.3720    519.2219    476.9320    388.6452
 380US202    347US475    396US229
 343.9670    333.3813    328.9941
> cor(betweenCent,eigenCent)
[1] 0.5003805
```

The highest betweenness score comes again from *Brown v. Board of Education*, but the next three cases are not in the top ten list from the eigenvector centrality scores. The correlation between the two measurements is only 0.5; clearly the betweenness score is significantly distinct from the eigenvector scores. These new values can be plotted on the graph using the same code as before; the output is shown in Fig. 6.3b. This new score does seem to favor vertices which connect disjoint parts of the graph, but many points in the interior of the graph (such as *Brown v. Board of Education*) also have high betweenness values. To identify those points which function purely as links, rather than central hubs, we need to identify points that have *both* high betweenness and low eigenvector centrality. With a bit of trial and error, taking points with eigenvector centrality less than 0.36 and betweenness greater than 200 results in a set of 9 interesting points.

```
> betweenCent <- betweenness(H)
> eigenCent <- evcent(H)$vector
> colorVals <- rep("white", length(betweenCent))
> colorVals[which(eigenCent < 0.36 & betweenCent > 200)] <- "red"
> V(H)$color <- colorVals
```

Plotting this, as shown in Fig. 6.4a, reveals a more natural categorization of vertices which serve primarily as bridges between disparate sections of the graph.

6.5 Graph Communities

We have referenced several times that the basic plot of our citation network appears to roughly have two distinct clusters of points; unsurprisingly, this is a result of the fact that we have chosen two issues to pull out of the Supreme Court dataset (school desegregation and "other" desegregation cases). Taking a closer look, it appears that there may be more precise ways of splitting the graph into even smaller clusters. Many methods for calculating these smaller clusters, known as *communities* given their importance to social networks, exist, several of which are available within the **igraph** package.

6.5 Graph Communities

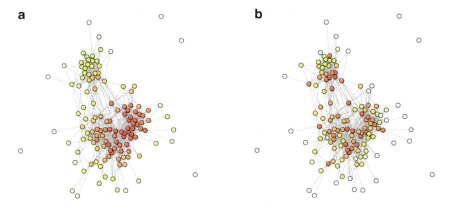

Figure 6.3: Graph centrality scores. Darker (*more red*) nodes have a higher centrality score. (**a**) Eigenvector. (**b**) Betweenness.

In the previous section we calculated the number of minimal paths running through each vertex and assigned this as a score for centrality. The same process can be applied to the edges in a graph to give a score indicating the degree to which the edge connects various sections of the graph. Repeatably removing edges with the highest levels of betweenness will eventually result in a disconnected graph; the disconnected parts, which managed to stay together despite the removal of many edges, are then identified as the graph's *communities*.

Once again, calculating community structures requires only a simple function call. However, creating a visualization with the result does take a little bit of data manipulation. Take a look at the membership ids returned from running the betweenness community detection algorithm.

```
> w <- edge.betweenness.community(H)
> sort(table(w$membership))

 2  4  7  8  9 11 12 13 14 15 16 17 18 20 21 22 23 24 25 27 28 29 30
 1  1  1  1  1  1  1  1  1  1  1  1  1  1  1  1  1  1  1  1  1  1  1
31 32 33 34 35 19 26  3  5  6  1 10
 1  1  1  1  1  2  2  4  6 22 29 39
```

There are three large communities with 22, 29, and 39 members and four smaller communities with no more than six members. The other vertices are contained in 29 isolated singletons. We want to color the nontrivial communities (greater than three) with different colors, while making the orphaned groups uncolored.

```
> V(H)$color <- rep("white", length(w$membership))
> keepTheseCommunities <- names(sizes(w))[sizes(w) > 3]
> matchIndex <- match(w$membership, keepTheseCommunities)
> colorVals <- rainbow(5)[matchIndex[!is.na(matchIndex)]]
> V(H)$color[!is.na(matchIndex)] <- colorVals
```

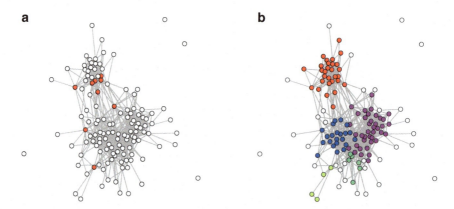

Figure 6.4: Vertices with high betweenness but low centrality (*left*) and communities (*right*) as determined by edge betweenness. (**a**) Gate-keeper vertices. (**b**) Communities.

A plot of the final community structure is given in Fig. 6.4b. The cluster of vertices corresponding to noneducational segregation are all within one cluster, whereas the educational segregation cases have been split into two large communities and two small communities.

6.6 Further Extensions

In this chapter, we have explored some of the major areas of graph theory and network analysis: graph drawing, measures of centrality, spectral graph theory, and community detection. We have tried to give a general overview; however all of these areas are far richer than what can be fit into a few pages. For further study, the **igraph** documentation is a good place to start; it contains dozens of additional graph drawing, centrality, and community detection algorithms. Beyond this, Stanley Wasserman's text on social network analysis gives a lot of depth (in an applicable way) while remaining fairly accessible [13]. For a more technical treatment, Eric Kolaczyk's *Statistical analysis of network data* provides even more detail, while still being written from the perspective of conducting applied data analysis [6].

Practice

1. Rerun the graph layout algorithm a few times for the subgraph H, but without resetting the seed. Plot the graph with these new layouts. In what way does the randomness of the algorithm seem to affect the outcome?

2. Calculate the closeness centrality of the Supreme Court citation network using the function `closeness`. Using plots and correlations, how does it relate to the two previously mentioned centrality scores?

3. Include cases under the topic 20070, "affirmative action", into the analysis. Does the list of the most central (eigenvector) cases change? Does the community detection algorithm detect the set of affirmative action cases as a unique community?

4. Using the communities detected in Sect. 6.5, and metadata contained in the supplementary materials, can you determine what caused the education desegregation cases to be split into two main groups?

References

[1] Erwin Chemerinsky. *Constitutional law, principles and policies (introduction to law series)*. New York,(NY): Aspen Publishers, 2006.

[2] Gabor Csardi and Tamas Nepusz. The igraph software package for complex network research. *InterJournal*, Complex Systems:1695, 2006.

[3] James H Fowler and Sangick Jeon. The authority of supreme court precedent. *Social networks*, 30(1):16–30, 2008.

[4] James H Fowler, Timothy R Johnson, James F Spriggs, Sangick Jeon, and Paul J Wahlbeck. Network analysis and the law: Measuring the legal importance of precedents at the us supreme court. *Political Analysis*, 15(3):324–346, 2007.

[5] Thomas MJ Fruchterman and Edward M Reingold. Graph drawing by force-directed placement. *Software: Practice and experience*, 21(11): 1129–1164, 1991.

[6] Eric D Kolaczyk. *Statistical analysis of network data: methods and models*. Springer Science & Business Media, 2009.

[7] Gregory H Maddox. Gender and famine in central tanzania: 1916–1961. *African studies review*, 39(01):83–101, 1996.

[8] Sridhar Nerur, Riyaz Sikora, George Mangalaraj, and VenuGopal Balijepally. Assessing the relative influence of journals in a citation network. *Communications of the ACM*, 48(11):71–74, 2005.

[9] Lawrence Page, Sergey Brin, Rajeev Motwani, and Terry Winograd. The pagerank citation ranking: Bringing order to the web. 1999.

[10] Bruce Russett and Taylor Arnold. Who talks, and who's listening? networks of international security studies. *Security Dialogue*, 41(6):589–598, 2010.

[11] Harold J Spaeth. *The Supreme Court Database*. Center for Empirical Research in the Law at Washington University, 2009.

[12] Peter Uvin. Prejudice, crisis, and genocide in rwanda. *African Studies Review*, 40(02):91–115, 1997.

[13] Stanley Wasserman. *Social network analysis: Methods and applications*, volume 8. Cambridge university press, 1994.

Chapter 7
Geospatial Data

Abstract In this chapter, we will look at how to work with raster and vector spatial data in R. Particular attention is placed on the process of merging various data types to create enriched datasets for further analysis.

7.1 Introduction

There is a popular phrase thrown around by those working with spatial data claiming that "80 % of data contains a spatial component", likely dating to a weaker statement made by Franklin and Hane specifically regarding data contained in government databases [6]. While actually quantifying the "amount of data" with a spatial component is likely impossible (and meaningless), the premise that a majority of datasets contain some spatial information is a valid one. Consider a dataset containing a record for every item held in a particular public library. It may contain explicit geospatial data such as the address of the branch where each item is housed, but there is a substantial amount of implicit spatial data which could also be added and explored such as the location of first publication or the birthplaces of the authors. Given the preponderance of geospatial data in general, and its particular importance to work in the humanities, this chapter introduces methods for exploring and visualizing a number of spatial data types within the R language.

Another popular set of tools for working with geospatial data are geographic information systems (GIS) such as the open source QGIS [12] and the proprietary ArcGIS [1]. Almost all of the same analytic functionality offered by these systems is also available within R, though ArcGIS does benefit from coming with a massive amount of ready to use data. We mention these here because GIS is sometimes mis-attributed as a type of *analysis*, rather than a type of *tool*.

7.2 From Scatter Plots to Maps

Basic geospatial plots can be thought of as simple scatter plots with an x-coordinate equal to longitude and a y-coordinate equal to latitude. Consider the following dataset of major border crossings into West Berlin between 1961 and 1989.[1]

```
> berlin <- read.csv(file="data/ch07/berlinBorderCrossing.csv",
+                    as.is=TRUE)
> berlin
                              Crossing Latitude Longitude
1                    Bornholmer Straße 52.55474  13.39766
2                       Chausseestraße 52.54048  13.36966
3                      Invalidenstraße 52.52790  13.37406
4                      Friedrichstraße 52.50762  13.39042
5                Heinrich-Heine-Straße 52.50472  13.41161
6                        Oberbaumbrücke 52.50197  13.44587
7                           Sonnenallee 52.46167  13.47844
8              Friedrichstraße station 52.52028  13.38704
9     Grenzübergangsstelle Drewitz-Dreilinden 52.41547  13.19716
10                     Glienicker Brücke 52.41349  13.09014
11                             Heerstraße 52.52906  13.11922
12                    Berlin-Heiligensee 52.62806  13.24160
```

We will start by just identifying the crossings clustered in the city center, specifically crossing 1–6 and 8. These could have been determined by an initial plot, though here we will just take them as known. A simple labeled plot suffices to visually display these locations, as seen in Fig. 7.1a.

```
> cityCenterId <- c(1:6,8)
> plot(x=berlin$Longitude[cityCenterId],
+      y=berlin$Latitude[cityCenterId],
+      pch=19,
+      axes=FALSE,
+      xlim=range(berlin$Longitude[cityCenterId]))
> text(x=berlin$Longitude[cityCenterId],
+      y=berlin$Latitude[cityCenterId],
+      labels=berlin$Crossing[cityCenterId],
+      pos=4,
+      col="blue")
```

Unless someone has a very good sense of Berlin's geography, however, this plot is not particularly interesting. No additional information such as streets, political borders, parks, and other landmarks is present.

It would be great if we could display a map of the city underneath the points, similar to the way a web-based platform such as Google or Apple displays a street map underneath search results. Fortunately, this is easy to do in R using the **snippets** package [14].[2] The function osmap pulls map images from an application known as a *tile map service*, a web-based application which stores a set of small map images

---

[1] Rough locations are from http://www.berlin.de/mauer/grenzuebergaenge/index/index.de.php; exact coordinates were determined by hand.

[2] See Chap. 11 for special installation instructions for this package.

7.2 From Scatter Plots to Maps

in a hierarchical fashion [11]. When trying to load a map on a website with a large amount of tiles or with a slow connection, often square patches of the map sporadically appear. Each of these patches is a single image served by a tile map service. By default, the osmap function determines the coordinates of the current plot, pulls approximately 25 tiles to cover the plot region from OpenStreetMaps (the namesake of the function) [10], and overlays these map images onto the current plot.

```
> library(snippets)
> plot(x=berlin$Longitude[cityCenterId],
+      y=berlin$Latitude[cityCenterId],
+      pch=19,
+      axes=FALSE,
+      xlim=range(berlin$Longitude[cityCenterId]))
> osmap()
> points(x=berlin$Longitude[cityCenterId],
+        y=berlin$Latitude[cityCenterId],
+        pch=19)
```

Notice the need to make a call to the points function due to the original points being covered up by the map tiles. The output is shown in Fig. 7.1b. We have succeeded in adding a significant amount of additional detail but unfortunately the resulting maps have come out rather distorted. From a pragmatic standpoint, most of the features are legible, but on aesthetic grounds it would be better if we could adjust this distortion. When running the code in an interactive R session, it is easy to simply resize the window as appropriate. If plotting to a graphics device, a bit of trial and error will all quickly suffice in producing a reasonable plot.

What if you need the map to fit into a pre-determined image size, or simply do not want to be bothered with trial and error? There is an additional input parameter to the default plot function in R that comes to the rescue. When set, the asp parameter sets the *aspect ratio*, the ratio of the scale on the y-axis to the scale of the x-axis, of a plot. If this is set to the ratio of the length of a degree of latitude to the length of a degree of longitude, the resulting map will be undistorted. Such an effect is achieved by extending the range of one of the axes. The correct ratio changes depending on the latitude, with a value of 1 at the equator and 2 at 60°N and 60°S; the exact value is given by the inverse of absolute value of the cosine of the degree of latitude (in radians). The parameter is not overly sensitive for small plots; here it is sufficient to take the exact ratio implied by the first data point (approximately 1.64):

```
> plot(x=berlin$Longitude[cityCenterId],
+      y=berlin$Latitude[cityCenterId],
+      pch=19,
+      axes=FALSE,
+      asp=1/abs(cos(berlin$Latitude[1]*pi/180)),
+      xlim=range(berlin$Longitude) + c(0,0.2))
```

Following this command with a call to osmap and re-plotting the points as before yields Fig. 7.1c. Notice that the new plot extends slightly farther in the horizontal directions in order to maintain our desired aspect ratio.

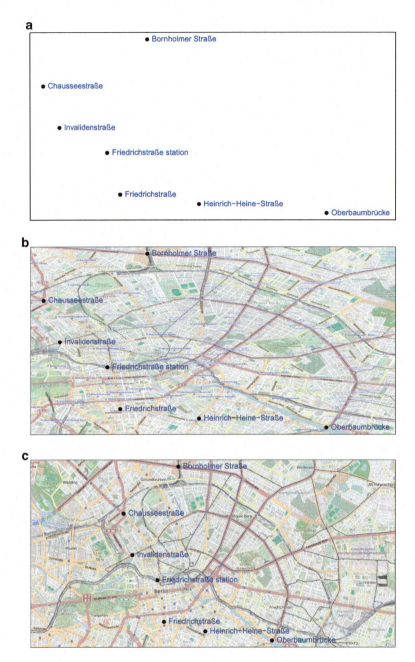

Figure 7.1: Location of the primary civilian ground border crossings between West Berlin and East Germany between 1961 and 1989. (**a**) Geospatial data as a scatter plot. (**b**) Open street map data of the city center. (**c**) View of crossings with adjust aspect ratio.

7.2 From Scatter Plots to Maps

We have now constructed a map which is both aesthetically pleasing and useful in adding a geographical perspective to the West Berlin border crossing dataset. It highlights, for example, how arbitrarily the city was split in half, adding perspective to the challenges faced by those living on either side of wall in post-war Berlin. The tiles we used to construct map are based on modern-day roads and landmarks, not all of which existed in 1961. Could we use historic data for the maps?

There are no technical limitations to setting up a tile map service based on historic data. Configuring and maintaining a tile map service, however, is quite involved and outside the scope of this text. Doing so would also require access to a substantial amount of historic data in order to be able to construct the map tiles; such data does not typically exist in an easily digestible format (if at all). A solution to this problem, which should suffice for most uses, is to pull tiles from a server that is built from modern data but does so in a minimalistic fashion. For example, Stamen Design provides high contrast black and white minimalistic tiles for free under a fairly permissive Creative Commons licence. Using these tiles requires only one additional parameter to the osmap function.

```
> osmap(tiles.url="http://c.tile.stamen.com/toner/")
```

The result of this map, Fig. 7.2a, still labels a few major streets and parks, which existed well before the 1960s, and removes many of the potentially anachronistic features. We also think it looks better when printed in black and white, but, of course, customize to your taste. The map certainly is not perfect, but it does a reasonable job of representing post-war Berlin without the hundreds, if not thousands, of hours spent curating historical street data and building a tile service. Another solution for historic locations and areas that have recently undergone rapid development is plain terrain maps.[3] Fortunately, many more open tile map services exist with varying features and aesthetics.[4]

Finally, let us briefly consider building a larger plot of the entire border crossing dataset to include those locations that are not within the city center. Programmatically altering the map region is very easy; the same exact code without the subsetting command, [cityCenterId], produces the larger map without any changes required to the osmap function. The output shown in Fig. 7.2b demonstrates that the new tiles have been pulled and the aspect ratio handled correctly. Notice that the larger map has not just pulled *more* tiles but has instead pulled a *different* set of tiles. The same number of images were requested from Stamen Design's servers in both versions of the map. Each tile in the larger region plot simply shows a less detailed version of a larger area (notice the omitted streets). The labeling has also changed to be appropriate for the lower resolution plot: the Großer Tiergarten is still shaded in but now lacks a label, whereas a label has been added to indicate the position of the city of Berlin (which is over-plotted by our text for Friedrichstraße).

---

[3] Stamen Design also produces a nice terrain tile map service under the same permissive license at: http://maps.stamen.com/terrain-background.

[4] See the links at http://wiki.openstreetmap.org/wiki/Tile_servers for a good starting point.

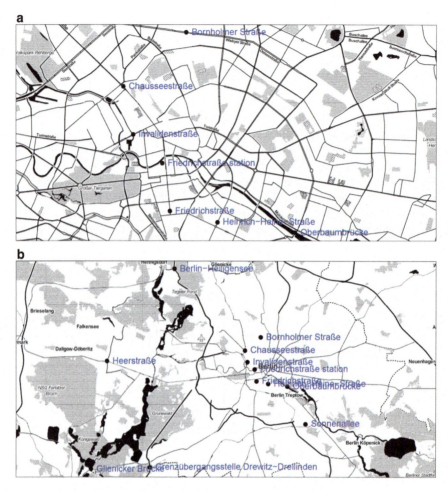

Figure 7.2: Location of the primary civilian ground border crossings between West Berlin and East Germany between 1961 and 1989. (**a**) Geospatial data as a scatter plot. (**b**) Open street map data of the city center.

7.3 Map Projections and Input Formats

A tile map service is a great way to quickly turn a basic geospatial scatter plot into a publication ready visualization with a single extra line of code. If we want to add anything more involved a different approach is required. A map tile has no information *per se* about roads, cities, or geographic features. It is simply a collection of pixels, an example of a *raster graphics format*, and nothing more than an image. This is the reason that our previous example of mapping two plots with slightly different zoom levels required an entirely new set of tiles. In contrast to raster data, *vector graphics* are instead content aware, with information regarding

7.3 Map Projections and Input Formats

the shape of every element embedded into the data. Metadata, such as an element name or classification, is often also attached to each object, such as a road or body of water, in a vector graphic. Vector graphics often require significantly larger file sizes, which is why they are not used to send data through web-based mapping services. However, the additional information they contain allow a wide range of geospatial visualizations and analyses, which we will explore for the remainder of this chapter.

Shapefiles are a very popular format for storing vectorized geospatial data. Developed by ESRI, the company responsible for the proprietary ArcGIS software system, the standards for the format were published as an open data specification in a 1998 white paper [13]. Data are distributed in this format by organizations such as the United Nations, the European Union, and the United States Census Bureau. The term shapefile is a misnomer, as the format actually requires a collection of three or more files with various file extensions to be co-located in the same directory (often distributed as a zip archive). At a minimum the .shp, .shx, and .dbf files are required; a .prj is almost always also included.

Two R packages will provide us with the majority of the functionality needed to work with vectorized geospatial data: **sp** and **maptools** [4, 2]. Loading a shapefile into R can be done with a single function call; the input string should point to the filenames for the data without specifying the extension (e.g., .shp). To start, we load a file provided by the US Census Bureau providing basic census data from 2010 at a state level attached to geospatial vector data defining the shape of all 50 states.

```
> library(sp)
> library(maptools)
> state <- readShapeSpatial(fn="data/ch07/State_2010Census_DP1")
> class(state)
[1] "SpatialPolygonsDataFrame"
attr(,"package")
[1] "sp"
> dim(state)
[1]  52 195
> dim(as.data.frame(state))
[1]  52 195
```

The resulting object is a `SpatialPolygonsDataFrame`, a special class constructed by the **sp** package. In addition to purely geospatial information, it also has an internal data frame with metadata for each shape in the shapefile. We were able to access this internal data frame with the `as.data.frame` function. In this case, the data frame has 195 columns, primarily containing raw counts of un-sampled, self-reported data from the 2010 Census. The 52 rows correspond to the 50 states, Washington D.C., and Puerto Rico. Unlike many other R packages we have used that define customized objects, the **sp** package did not define a way of nicely printing spatial polygon data frames; printing the object simply prints a long unstructured list of (usually) unintelligible output.

It will be easier to display a map of the United States in the limited space of this text by first removing Alaska and Hawaii. Taking a subset of the objects in a spatial polygon data frame conveniently uses the same notation used for taking a subset of rows in a standard data frame.

```
> index <- (as.data.frame(state)$STUSPS10 %in% c("AK", "HI"))
> state <- state[!index,]
> dim(state)
[1] 50 195
```

A basic plot of a spatial polygon object can be generated by calling the plot function of the object.

```
> plot(state)
```

Figure 7.3a shows the output of this command. As a basic plot of spatial data, it works quite well. As vector data, we can output this plot to a device of any size without the output becoming grainy, a powerful benefit of this type of data.

The spatial plot we already produced plotted shapes the same way we treated scatter plots in Sect. 7.2 by treating raw longitude and latitude as the x and y coordinates of the plot. Such a simplification was fine when dealing with data at the scale of a city. However, when looking at large scales, it is often advantageous to plot spatial data in a projection format that accounts for the spherical nature of the world. Converting between projection formats can be done within R; the first step involves identifying which projection our current data was originally loaded in with (here, just longitude and latitude) and assigning it to the proj4string of the spatial polygon data frame. The notation used to define projections is known as PROJ.4 [5]. It is very extensive, and rather than explaining it in detail, we will simply lay out how to use it to describe two of the most useful variants.

```
> projectionObj <- CRS(projargs="+proj=longlat")
> proj4string(state) <- projectionObj
```

The process of converting from one projection to another is handled by the R package **rgdal** [3]. It takes an existing spatial object and a new projection format and returns a copy of its input in the new projection format. Here, we will convert to the Universal Transverse Mercator projection [8, 9]. This projection requires specifying the desired reference "zone" (a number between 1 and 60), which roughly specifies where the "middle" of the map should be. For the continental United States, zone 14 works particularly well.

```
> library(rgdal)
> stateTrans <- spTransform(x=state,
+     CRSobj=CRS("+proj=utm +zone=14"))
```

7.3 Map Projections and Input Formats

Calling the plot function directly on the projected object `stateTrans` produces the outline of the states shown in Fig. 7.3b. More information will help make the map legible, so let us add the state names to this plot. A direct call to the `text` function using latitude and longitude would not be sufficient because the shapes are now plotted in a new coordinate system. To determine the location of the new shapes the `gCentroid` function is used; it returns the *centroid* (the geometric center) of each state in the projected coordinate system. Finally, using the coordinates from these centroids, a call to the `text` function produces the final figure.

```
> centroid <- gCentroid(spgeom=stateTrans, byid=TRUE)
> head(centroid)
SpatialPoints:
          x         y
0 -198256.2  4796062
1 2289521.4  4749735
2 1885001.1  4602892
3 -155119.1  3830282
4 2444657.6  4555463
5 2797519.2  4985976
Coordinate Reference System (CRS) arguments: +proj=utm
+zone=14 +ellps=WGS84
> text(x=centroid$x,
+      y=centroid$y,
+      label=as.data.frame(stateTrans)$NAME10,
+      cex=0.7)
```

The resulting map produces a distinctly less distorted representation of the United States.

Now that we have shown the basics of loading, plotting, and projecting vector data in R, we finish this section by showing how to visualize the census data on our map. We will look at housing data from the 2010 US Census.

A researcher might be interested in how housing is used in the United States, focused on the locations of recreational housing. They are confident that Florida will be a popular state for snowbirds seeking respite from the snow in the northeast. To confirm this assumption and to see what other states have a high density of recreational homes, they turn to the census. First, the proportion of housing units (DP0180001) declared as being "seasonal, recreational, or occasional" (DP0180008) for each state is calculated and converted to quantized bin IDs.

```
> stateTransData <- as.data.frame(state)
> perHouseRec <- stateTransData$DP0180008 / stateTransData$DP0180001
> bins <- quantile(perHouseRec, seq(0,1,length.out=8))
> binId <- findInterval(perHouseRec, bins)
```

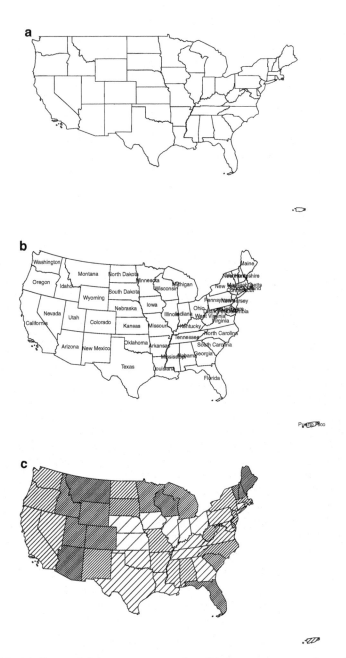

Figure 7.3: (**a**) Geospatial data as a scatter plot. (**b**) Open street map data of the city center. (**c**) View of additional crossings farther outside the city center.

7.4 Enriching Tabular Data with Geospatial Data

These bins are scaled to a factor of 5 (trial and error to achieve a visually pleasing plot) and simply given as an additional parameter to the plot function.

```
> densityVals <- seq_len(length(bins)) * 5
> plot(stateTrans, density=densityVals[binId])
```

The output is shown in Fig. 7.3c, with a higher proportion of seasonal or recreational houses corresponding to darker shaded states. The relatively high values in Florida, Arizona, South Carolina, and Maine correlate with the commonly held assumption that these are popular spots for Winter/Summer homes.

7.4 Enriching Tabular Data with Geospatial Data

The power of vectorized geospatial data can be best appreciated by seeing how it is used to add context to other datasets. In this section, we study a dataset of metadata corresponding to documentary photographs taken between 1935 and 1945 for the US Federal Government. For each of the 90,000 geo-locatable records (each record corresponds to a single photographic negative) information is available regarding the date, name of the photographer, and the approximate latitude and longitude where the photograph is believed to have been taken. Given that the photographers were often given a great deal of leeway regarding where they traveled, and collectively covered a vast proportion of the country, an interesting academic question arises around comparing and contrasting the subject matter each photographer chose to capture. Here, we address this question by merging the photographic metadata with county-level US Census data to help characterize differences in the locales that were visited.

We begin by loading into R the tabular metadata and removing data rows with missing geospatial data. We further limit the data set to the top 20 photographers (by count) in the collection because the remaining photographers took a very small number of photographs, often just one or two.

```
> z <- read.csv(file="data/ch07/photoDatasetAllRaw.csv", as.is=TRUE)
> z <- z[!is.na(z$latitude) & !is.na(z$longitude) & !is.na(z$pname),]
> pnameSet <- names(sort(table(z$pname),TRUE))[1:20]
> z <- z[z$pname %in% pnameSet,]
> head(z)
            cnumber         pname year longitude latitude
1 LC-DIG-fsac-1a33849 Jack Delano 1941 -71.31617 42.63342
2 LC-DIG-fsac-1a33850 Jack Delano 1940 -71.31617 42.63342
3 LC-DIG-fsac-1a33851 Jack Delano 1940 -71.01838 42.08343
4 LC-DIG-fsac-1a33852 Jack Delano 1940 -71.01838 42.08343
5 LC-DIG-fsac-1a33853 Jack Delano 1940 -71.01838 42.08343
6 LC-DIG-fsac-1a33857 Jack Delano 1941 -71.31617 42.63342
```

We need to convert this data frame into a spatial object in order to manipulate it with the **sp** package. Previously we had loaded the state shapes files as a spatial polygon data frame. Each record in the photographic metadata is a point rather than a polygon; a method exists for constructing a very similar object called a spatial points data frame. It requires a matrix of coordinates and a data frame, with both having the same number of rows.

```
> pts <- SpatialPointsDataFrame(coords=cbind(z$longitude,
+                                            z$latitude),
+ data=z)
```

Shapefiles at the county level are loaded as before using the `readShapeSpatial` function, in order to merge with these spatial points. In this example, we have used the 2010 census data. It would be more accurate to use information from the 1940 census, which is available; however, it is much more difficult to point users wishing to follow along to the 1940s version.[5]

```
> cnty <- readShapeSpatial("data/ch07/County_2010Census_DP1")
```

We now have R objects that represent spatial polygons and spatial points, and need a method for joining the polygons (census) to the points (photographic metadata). The **sp** package provides the function `over` for this purpose. The `over` function is fairly complex, taking at least two arguments, x and y, where its behavior depends on the class of the two objects. We have previously seen many functions such as `head`, `summary`, `print`, and `plot` that change depending on the class of their first input parameter. The `over` method simply takes this one step further by depending on two input classes; this language feature is known as *multiple dispatch* and has the potential to become quite complex. For our purpose, we will provide the over function with a spatial points data frame as the first input and a spatial polygons data frame in the second. This returns a regular data frame with one row for each element in the first input containing data from the second input over the matching polygon (NAs are produced when no match is found).

```
> joinedDataF <- over(x=pts,y=cnty)
> dim(pts)
[1] 81720     21
> dim(cnty)
[1] 3221  195
> dim(joinedDataF)
[1] 81720   195
```

Finally, we construct the population density for the joined counties using the data provided by the `over` function and plot this as a boxplot by photographer.[6] The variable **DP0010001** denotes the total population and **ALAND10** the total area of the county.

---

[5] It requires logging into a system, downloading each state individually, and running code to join the shapefiles to the actual census data.

[6] A *boxplot* is a graphical representation of the quantiles of a distribution. In particular the thick black line indicates the median of the distribution. See the help pages, ?boxplot, for more detailed information.

7.5 Enriching Geospatial Data with Tabular Data

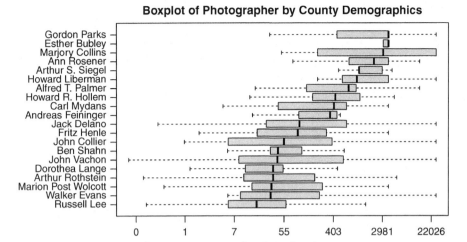

Figure 7.4: Boxplot showing the population density of counties where FSA-OWI staff photographers took photographs.

```
> joinedDataF$popDen <- joinedDataF$DP0010001 / joinedDataF$ALAND10
> joinedDataF$popDen <- joinedDataF$popDen * 1000^2
> medianPerc <- tapply(joinedDataF$popDen, z$pname, median,
+     na.rm=TRUE)
> index <- order(medianPerc)
> joinedDataF$pnameFactor <- factor(z$pname,
+     levels=names(medianPerc)[index])
> boxplot(pnameFactor, log(popDen),
+         data=joinedDataF, axes=FALSE,
+         horizontal=TRUE, las=1,
+         outline=FALSE,
+         col="grey")
```

These results largely fall in line with scholarship on the photographic collection. Walker Evans, known for his photographs of the rural south, has the second least dense median population density. Gordon Parks in the other hand, who largely photographed in the metro Washington, D.C., area, has the highest median population density of photograph locations (Fig. 7.4).

7.5 Enriching Geospatial Data with Tabular Data

In the previous section we joined county census data to the locations where historic photographs had been taken. In more general terms, spatial polygons were used to enhance a tabular dataset. It is possible to also go in the other direction whereby spatial points enhance spatial polygons. In this final section we illustrate how to add a new variable to each county in our dataset: the number of photographs that were taken inside of it.

The raw data we need is the exact same as was used in the previous section. To simplify the resulting plots, and illustrate the process for subsetting spatial data, we will restrict ourselves to only include counties within states found within a bounding box extending roughly from Virginia to Vermont. We have already seen that spatial polygon data frames can be subset using the same syntax as a normal data frame.

```
> centroidS <- gCentroid(state, byid=TRUE)
> state <- state[centroidS$x > -79.3 & centroidS$y > 37 &
+                centroidS$x < -71.0 & centroidS$y < 44,]
> cnty$GEOID10 <- as.character(cnty$GEOID10)
```

The `state` object is now properly subset, but we still need to reduce the set of county polygons to include only those contained in the reduced set of states. To do this, we need to match each county to a given state; this process requires using another variant of the `over` function. When given two spatial polygon objects, the `over` function returns a vector of indices indicating which element in the second input corresponds to the each element in the first input. Here, the function serves as a spatial analogue to calling `match` on two vectors.

```
> matchIndex <- over(cnty, state)
> table(matchIndex,useNA="always")
matchIndex
    1    2    3    4    5    7    8    9   11 <NA>
  104   35   11   67    8    3   13   13  157 2810
> cnty = cnty[!is.na(matchIndex),]
```

Removing counties that do not match (i.e., are not contained inside) the reduced set of states has the desired effect.

In order to count the number of photographs inside of each county, a third method of `over` is evoked. If the first argument to `over` is a spatial polygons object and the second argument is of class spatial points data frame, the result will be a data frame where each county is associated with the (first) point contained inside of it. That is not the behavior we would like, as we want to count all the photographs in a county not just learn about the first, so a third argument called `fn` is given the value `length` so that a count of the number of elements in each county is returned instead.

```
> cnty$photoCount <- as.numeric(over(cnty,pts,fn=length)[,1])
> head(cnty$photoCount)
[1]  89  61  NA   2  51 448
```

With these values in hand, we construct a spatial plot of the desired counties shaded by the number of photographs taken inside of it. Just as we did for specifying the density in Fig. 7.3c, color can be set by simply specifying the `col` argument to `plot` just as it would be when working with a standard scatter plot.

7.5 Enriching Geospatial Data with Tabular Data

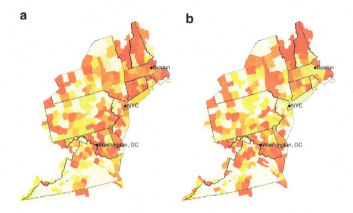

Figure 7.5: Choropleth map showing the density of photographs in the FSA-OWI collection. (a) Raw counts. (b) Normalized by total population.

```
> var01 <- cnty$photoCount
> bins <- unique(quantile(var01, seq(0,1,length.out=30)))
> cnty$binId01 <- findInterval(var01, bins)
> colSet01 <- rev(heat.colors(length(bins)))
> plot(cntyTrans, col=colSet01[cntyTrans$binId01], border=NA)
> plot(stateTrans, add=TRUE)
```

The resulting visualization, an example of a *choropleth map*, is shown in Fig. 7.5a.[7] Notice that many counties bordering against the states of interest are also included; this an artifact of the fact that the state and county datasets were not provided at exactly the same resolution, so our code accidentally assigned some counties to neighboring states. We see that a large number of photographs were taken just outside of Washington, D.C., and in the vicinity of Boston, New York City, and Pittsburgh. There are also localized spikes in the middle of New York State and throughout Vermont.

Raw counts can be a very useful metric to use for visualization, but also have a tendency to be deceiving when comparing regions of different sizes and populations. Calculating the percentage of photographs per person,

```
> var02 <- cnty$photoCount / cnty$DP0010001
```

We can recalculate the original figure in terms of counts per person, as in Fig. 7.5b. Notice that some of the densities have changed drastically. New York City, in particular, went from very dense in the un-normalized plot to very sparse in the normalized one. While a large number of photographs were taken here, on a photo per person basis the count is lower compared to other regions.

---

[7]Three city names have also been added to guide the discussion for anyone unfamiliar with the geography of the Eastern United States. Code for this is contained in the supplementary materials.

7.6 Further Extensions

A natural next step from this chapter is the text *Applied Spatial Data Analysis with R* [4]. It first extends the methods mentioned here to a wider range input formats, projections, and applications. In the second half of the text more analytic techniques for modeling spatial data are explored. The level of presentation is very similar to this text and, similarly, emphasizes applied data analysis and the "how-to" of programming in R. The text *Spatial statistics and modeling* by Carlo Gaetan and Xavier Guyon provides a far more extensive introduction to spatial statistics but requires a background in mathematical analysis and theoretical statistics [7].

Practice

1. Construct a small dataset of important places in your life, possibly including things such as your home location, work location, and favorite coffee shop. Manually add latitude and longitude to the data (can be extracted from many online tools such as Google Maps) and create plots using the `snippets` function. Try increasing and decreasing the extent of the plot by adding/removing locations. What features appear and disappear as the map area becomes smaller?

2. Replicate the plot shown in Fig. 7.3a and save the output in these formats: tiff, pdf, jpeg, png, bmp. Use the default height and width for the plots. What differences do you see between the file sizes of the output? Now construct plots with twice the height and width of the originals. Compare the new and old file sizes. Do they all scale up the same way? Why or why not? When might you prefer a jpeg over a pdf (and vice versa)?

3. We have already worked with point and polygons in this chapter, but there is one other data type we did not use: SpatialLines. The US Census Bureau maintains a shape files (by state) for all primary and secondary streets in the United States, downloadable here: `ftp://ftp2.census.gov/geo/tiger/TIGER2014/ROADS/`. Read in these shapefiles with the command `readShapeLines`. What type of object is returned? It can be manipulated almost exactly like its point and polygon variants; try plotting for instance. Produce a plot with only the primary roads (indicated in the attached data frame). Now produce a plot where all of the roads are present, but the primary roads are colored in red.

References

[1] Hawthorn L Beyer. Hawth's analysis tools for arcgis, 2004.

[2] Roger Bivand and Nicholas Lewin-Koh. *maptools: Tools for reading and handling spatial objects*, 2014. URL `http://CRAN.R-project.org/package=maptools`. R package version 0.8-30.

References

[3] Roger Bivand, Tim Keitt, and Barry Rowlingson. *rgdal: Bindings for the Geospatial Data Abstraction Library*, 2014. URL http://CRAN.R-project.org/package=rgdal. R package version 0.9-1.

[4] Roger S Bivand, Edzer J Pebesma, Virgilio Gómez-Rubio, and Edzer Jan Pebesma. *Applied spatial data analysis with R*, volume 747248717. Springer, 2008.

[5] Gerald Evenden. Proj. 4–cartographic projections library. *Source code and documentation available from trac. osgeo. org/proj*, 1990.

[6] Carl Franklin and Paula Hane. An introduction to geographic information systems: Linking maps to databases [and] maps for the rest of us: Affordable and fun. *Database*, 15(2):12–15, 1992.

[7] Carlo Gaetan, Xavier Guyon, and Kevin Bleakley. *Spatial statistics and modeling*, volume 271. Springer, 2010.

[8] E Grafarend. The optimal universal transverse mercator projection. In *Geodetic Theory Today*, pages 51–51. Springer, 1995.

[9] John W Hager, James F Behensky, and Brad W Drew. The universal grids: Universal transverse mercator (utm) and universal polar stereographic (ups). edition 1. Technical report, DTIC Document, 1989.

[10] Mordechai Haklay and Patrick Weber. Openstreetmap: User-generated street maps. *Pervasive Computing, IEEE*, 7(4):12–18, 2008.

[11] Yun Feng Nie, Hu Xu, and Hai Ling Liu. The design and implementation of tile map service. *Advanced Materials Research*, 159:714–719, 2011.

[12] DT QGis. Quantum gis geographic information system. *Open Source Geospatial Foundation Project*, 2011.

[13] ESRI Software. *ESRI Shapefile Technical Description*, 1998. URL https://www.esri.com/library/whitepapers/pdfs/shapefile.pdf.

[14] Simon Urbanek. *snippets: Code snippets, mostly visualization-related*. URL http://www.rforge.net/snippets/. R package version 0.1-0.

Chapter 8
Image Data

Abstract In this chapter, methods for loading, manipulating, and saving image files in R are presented. Dimension reduction and clustering analysis are developed in order to visually represent a corpus of images in standard scatter plots.

8.1 Introduction

A large amount of humanities data consists of digitized image data, and there is an active push to digitize even more. Examples of large corpora include Google Books, Google Art Project, HathiTrust, the Getty Museum Europeana, Wikimedia, and the Rijksmuseum. In some cases, these image collections represent scans of mostly textual data. In others the images represent digitized art works or photographic prints; in these cases the images serve as direct historical evidence, objects of study in their own right, or both. Converting images of text into raw text data is an interesting problem in computer vision. The process of converting, however, is currently best left to custom proprietary software (and is often run once at the moment of digitization). We will concentrate in this chapter only on the cases where images directly represent artwork or other historical documents.

While many digital humanities projects work with image data, few analyze the actual images themselves. In this chapter we present methods for visualizing an entire corpus of images in a single scatter plot. As an example, we show how these methods can be applied to a collection of outdoor photographs and the degree to which they successfully separate those taken during the day from those taken at night.

8.2 Basic Image I/O

There are many competing formats for storing image data. Three R packages handle the three most commonly used digital repositories: the **tiff** package [10], the **jpeg** package [11], and the **png** package [9]. Each handles exactly one file format

114   8 Image Data

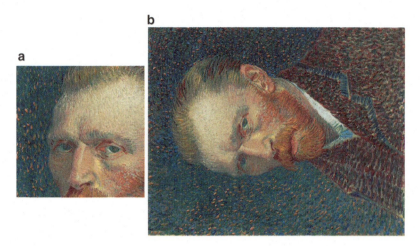

Figure 8.1: Simple examples of manipulating JPEG images within R. (**a**) Cropped image. (**b**) Rotated image.

and provides just two simple functions to read and write their respective formats. They also return and accept the same types of objects. We concentrate on the **jpeg** package here, but keep in mind that png and tiff files can be used in the exact same fashion.

Loading a jpeg image into R is similar to the process of loading a dataset, by using the function `readJPEG`.

```
> library(jpeg)
> vanGogh <- readJPEG("vanGogh_selfPortrait.jpg")
```

The resulting object is of class `array`. This object is not specific to the **jpeg** package and exists as a base object in the R language. Unlike a matrix or data frame, arrays may have more than two dimensions.

```
> class(vanGogh)
[1] "array"
> dim(vanGogh)
[1] 768 608   3
> range(vanGogh)
[1] 0 1
```

An array object is an extension of the concept of a matrix to an arbitrary number of dimensions. We can think of the array `vanGogh` as a collection of three distinct 768-by-608 matrices. The matrices represent pixels in the image, with the first matrix giving the intensity of the red component, the second matrix the green component, and the third the blue component. The values are numbers between 0 and 1, with 0 being no intensity in a given color channel and 1 being full intensity. Note that if all the components are 0 then the pixel will be black (the absence of light), and when all are 1 then the pixel will be white.

8.2 Basic Image I/O

An array object in R is manipulated in the same way that regular matrices are, except that when subsetting the expressions inside the square brackets requires (in this case) three inputs rather than two. As an example, look at the result of taking the red and green intensities of pixels from the upper left corner of the image.

```
> vanGogh[1:4,1:3,1:2]
, , 1

        [,1]      [,2]      [,3]
[1,] 0.6431373 0.5960784 0.5764706
[2,] 0.6117647 0.6509804 0.5176471
[3,] 0.5607843 0.7333333 0.5176471
[4,] 0.7529412 0.8549020 0.6196078

, , 2

        [,1]      [,2]      [,3]
[1,] 0.5882353 0.5529412 0.5607843
[2,] 0.5725490 0.6352941 0.5254902
[3,] 0.5333333 0.7254902 0.5411765
[4,] 0.7098039 0.8274510 0.6274510
```

The subsetting command can be used to produce a cropped version of an image. In order to view the cropped image, we create a new jpeg file using the function `writeJPEG`.

```
> vanGoghCrop <- vanGogh[100:400,100:400,]
> writeJPEG(vanGoghCrop,"vanGoghCrop.jpg")
```

The resulting image is shown in Fig. 8.1a.

In order to rotate the image, we might consider using the transpose function, which we have used to flip the dimensions of a matrix. The array analogue to the transpose function is called `aperm`; it is available by default in the base language of R and does not require any special packages. The function exchanges, or permutes, the order of an array's dimensions. We will use the permutation `c(2,1,3)` to indicate that we want to flip the first two dimensions while keeping the third in place.

```
> vanGoghRotate <- aperm(a=vanGogh,perm=c(2,1,3))
> vanGoghRotate <- vanGoghRotate[dim(vanGoghRotate)[1]:1,,]
> writeJPEG(vanGoghRotate,paste0(OUTDIR,"vanGoghRotate.jpg"))
```

The permutation alone would result in mirror image of the original, so after taking the permutation the first dimension was then reversed. The result in Fig. 8.1b demonstrates that this has resulted in the correct rotation.

It is also possible to manipulate the third dimension of the image array. For example, creating a copy of the `vanGogh` object and setting the green and blue channels to zero result in a representation of the image that is only displayed in red.

Figure 8.2: Isolated rgb color channels for a single image. From *left to right*: red only, green only, blue only, average of three color channels (which results in a black and white image).

```
> vanGoghRed <- vanGogh
> vanGoghRed[,,2:3] <- 0
```

Figure 8.2 shows the red-only image as well as the analogues for green and blue. Notice that these are not simply tinted versions of one another; different features are absent in each version. Most notable are the eyes in the portrait, for which the irises are completely missing in the red channel. It is also possible to construct a black and white image of the portrait by setting each color channel to the average pixel intensity across all three channels. Whenever all three channels are equal, the resulting image will be some shade of gray.

```
> vanGoghBW <- vanGogh
> vanGoghBW[,,1] <- (vanGogh[,,1] + vanGogh[,,2] + vanGogh[,,3]) / 3
> vanGoghBW[,,2] <- (vanGogh[,,1] + vanGogh[,,2] + vanGogh[,,3]) / 3
> vanGoghBW[,,3] <- (vanGogh[,,1] + vanGogh[,,2] + vanGogh[,,3]) / 3
```

The black and white image is shown as the right most panel in Fig. 8.2.

How did we create the single image shown in Fig. 8.2? We bound together the four image arrays along their vertical dimensions, similar to the way that matrices can be combined using cbind and rbind. It requires the use of the package **abind**, which operates almost exact like the matrix equivalents but requires the parameter along to indicate which dimension the combining will occur along.

```
> library(abind)
> vanGoghAll <- abind(vanGoghRed,vanGoghGreen,vanGoghBlue,vanGoghBW,
+                     along=2)
> dim(vanGoghAll)
[1]  768 2432    3
> writeJPEG(vanGoghAll,paste0(OUTDIR,"vanGoghAll.jpg"))
```

As an easy to remember rule, the element specified in the parameter along refers to the element of the output dimension that we expect to grow during the binding. All of the other dimensions must be consistent among the inputs and will be the same in the output.

8.3 Day/Night Photographic Corpus

It will be advantageous to study a small collection of curated images developed for image analysis. This has the advantage of having pre-determined metadata defining the underlying image types. It also will help to have images that are all of roughly the same pixel dimensions. We will use a collection that has outdoor photographs taken during the day and during the night from the Digital Video Multimedia Lab at Columbia.[1]

```
> files <- dir("../data/ch08/columbiaImages", full.names=TRUE)
> meta <- read.csv("../data/ch08/photoMetaData.csv", as.is=TRUE)
```

We filter out only those images taken outdoors and construct a vector of symbols to indicate which category each image falls under.

```
> files <- files[meta$category %in% c("outdoor-night","outdoor-day")]
> meta <- meta[meta$category %in% c("outdoor-night","outdoor-day"),]
> pchSymb <- rep(19,length(files))
> pchSymb[meta$category == "outdoor-day"] = 3
> table(pchSymb)
pchSymb
  3  19
277  34
```

There are 34 night images and 277 day images in the collection. As a first step to understanding these data, let us calculate the median of each color channel over the corpus of images.

```
> outputRGB <- matrix(0,nrow=length(files),ncol=3)
> for (j in 1:length(files)) {
+    z = readJPEG(files[j])
+    outputRGB[j,1] = median(z[,,1])
+    outputRGB[j,2] = median(z[,,2])
+    outputRGB[j,3] = median(z[,,3])
+ }
```

A pair of scatter plots of these values is shown in Fig. 8.3. We already see a decent separation between the night and day images. As a basic heuristic, night images have proportionally more red compared to green and blue. The color intensity values for each channel appear to be positively related; a correlation matrix reveals that the intensities have correlations ranging from 0.77 to 0.95.

```
> round(cor(outputRGB),3)
      [,1]  [,2]  [,3]
[1,] 1.000 0.883 0.766
[2,] 0.883 1.000 0.947
[3,] 0.766 0.947 1.000
```

---

[1] http://www.ee.columbia.edu/~dvmmweb/dvmm/downloads/
PIM_PRCG_dataset/techreport_personal_columbia.html.

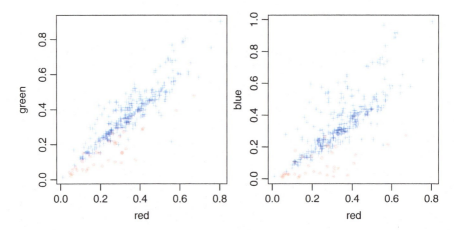

Figure 8.3: Scatter plot of red, green, and blue pixel intensity of photographs from the Digital Video Multimedia Lab at Columbia. *Dots* (*red*) are outdoor images taken at night, and *plus signs* (*blue*) are outdoor images taken during the day.

We are representing each image by the median pixel intensity by channel; however, these values are very highly correlated. If we are going to represent an image with three numbers, it would be advantageous if these numbers offered richer information.

One solution is to use an alternative color representation to the typical red, green, and blue pixel intensities. A common example is the hue-saturation-value (hsv) cylindrical coordinate system. It is often considered a more intuitive model for describing colors as it was devised in the 1970s based on human perception [8]. Here a particular color is represented by a different triplet of numbers between 0 and 1. The *hue* mimics a traditional color wheel, with 0 corresponding to red, $\frac{1}{3}$ to green, and $\frac{2}{3}$ to blue. The *value* corresponds to the highest pixel intensity and *saturation* corresponds to the range of the intensities divided by their maximum. Conceptually, saturation measures how "grey" the output is (with all true greys having a saturation of zero) and value describes how bright it is. For an example of these coordinates, see the decomposition of the Van Gogh portrait in Fig. 8.4. Notice that the various color channels already seem less correlated than the rgb model.

The function `rgb2hsv`, available by default within R, makes converting into the hsv coordinate system straightforward (keeping in mind that `maxColorValue` should be set to 1 as the default is 256). The only additional consideration is that the hue value is circular, so therefore it does not make sense to directly take the median or mean of the raw values. A hue of 0.1 is a slightly orange variant of red and 0.9 a slightly purple version of red. The mean of these two values is 0.5, which is the hue of the color cyan. A more reasonable "average" of the two is the color red. In order to arrive at this more appropriate value, we will use a circular variant to calculate values corresponding to hue; these are provided by the package **circular** [2].[2]

---

[2]The formula for circular median is not too complex; if you want to avoid loading another library, the following:
`atan2(mean(sin(mat[1,]*2*pi)), mean(cos(mat[1,]*2*pi))) / (2*pi)` can be used in place of the `median.circular(...)` call (it is actually much faster).

8.3 Day/Night Photographic Corpus

Figure 8.4: Hue-saturation-value coordinate decomposition of the Van Gogh portrait. *Left* image has saturation and value both set to 1, leaving only hue to distinguish the pixels. The *center* and *left* image are displayed in grey scale. The *center* represented saturation with black a saturation of 0 and white a saturation of 1; the *right* represents value, with a value of 0 displayed as black and a value of 1 displayed as white.

We can now calculate the medians of the hsv model coordinates over the corpus of photographs with a variant of the same code we used for the rgb coordinates.

```
> library(circular)
> outputHSV <- matrix(0,nrow=length(files),ncol=3)
> for (j in 1:length(files)) {
+     z <- readJPEG(files[j])
+     mat <- rgb2hsv(as.numeric(z[,,1]),as.numeric(z[,,2]),
+                    as.numeric(z[,,3]),maxColorValue=1)
+
+     outputHSV[j,1] <-
+     median.circular(circular(mat[1,]*360,units="deg"))
+     outputHSV[j,2] <- median(mat[2,])
+     outputHSV[j,3] <- median(mat[3,])
+ }
```

A correlation matrix indicates again, as we saw in the Van Gogh example, that the median of these coordinates offer more independent information relative to one another than raw pixel channel intensities in the rgb system.

```
> round(cor(outputHSV),3)
        [,1]   [,2]   [,3]
[1,]   1.000 -0.108  0.365
[2,]  -0.108  1.000 -0.223
[3,]   0.365 -0.223  1.000
```

A full scatter plot of the image corpus is given in Fig. 8.5. Notice that the scatter plot is much more evenly distributed across the three dimensions, though blue hues do seem to have suppressed saturation and value. Almost all of the night images

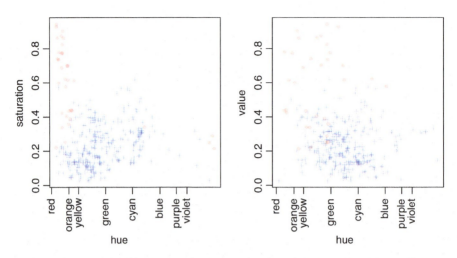

Figure 8.5: Scatter plot of photographs from the Digital Video Multimedia Lab at Columbia in hue-saturation-value coordinates. *Dots* (*red*) are outdoor images taken at night, and *plus signs* (*blue*) are outdoor images taken during the day.

have a median hue between red and yellow and median saturation greater than 0.3, whereas almost none of the daytime images have these two properties. This effect is likely due to composition of artificial light sources, compared with that of the sun. Standard tungsten lamps, for example, are known to be biased toward red wavelengths of light.

8.4 Principal Component Analysis

There are many benefits to being able to represent a dataset in an alternative coordinate system where the correlations between components are smaller. In other words, we are looking at variation in order to understand the differences between the photos. Mapping a set of rgb intensities to hsv coordinates is particularly nice because it was designed with the intention of decomposing color to better capturing human perception. What if such a transformation did not already exist?

A method known as *principal component analysis* (PCA) can be used in these cases. Given a numerical dataset, PCA returns a new set of coordinates such that each component is completely uncorrelated with the others; these new coordinates are referred to as principal components. Furthermore, the first component is chosen such that it explains the maximum amount of variance in the data. Each subsequent component does the same, with the condition that they are uncorrelated with the previously defined components. The prcomp function provided by default within R can be used to compute the principal components of a given matrix. As an illustrative example we also turn off centering and scaling; these should almost always be set to TRUE in practice.

8.4 Principal Component Analysis

```
> pc <- prcomp(outputRGB,center=FALSE,scale.=FALSE)
> pc
Standard deviations:
[1] 0.65734056 0.08510617 0.02810292

Rotation:
            PC1         PC2         PC3
[1,] -0.5552056  0.72964807 -0.3991997
[2,] -0.5983264 -0.01700333  0.8010720
[3,] -0.5777130 -0.68361142 -0.4460080
```

By definition, each PCA component is computed as a linear combination of the original data components. From the output, we see that the first principal component is approximately equal to an equal weighting, with a factor of about -0.58, of the three color channels. Specifically, we can calculate PC1 with the following formula:

$$PC1 = -0.56 * RED - 0.60 * GREEN - 0.58 * BLUE$$
$$\approx -0.58 \cdot (RED + GREEN + BLUE)$$

As the first component is attempting to capture the highest amount of variance, and we have already observed that the majority of variation in our data comes from the overall intensity of the three color channels, we should have expected this component to largely be an equal weighting of the three channels. The second principal component consists, again roughly, of the difference between the red and blue pixel intensities:

$$PC2 = 0.73 * RED - 0.02 * GREEN - 0.68 * BLUE$$
$$\approx 0.7 \cdot (RED - BLUE)$$

Whereas the third and final is approximately the difference between the green intensity and the average of the red and blue intensities:

$$PC3 = -0.40 * RED + 0.80 * GREEN - 0.45 * BLUE$$
$$\approx 0.8 \cdot \left(GREEN - \frac{BLUE + RED}{2} \right)$$

It is often not possible to directly interpret principal components, particularly when using a larger number of variables. Here, we were lucky to find a nice and understandable decomposition of the three components.

In order to compute the principal components of our dataset, we do not need to calculate each component by hand. The function `predict` conveniently handles the computation for us; this is particularly useful when scaling and centering are turned on.

```
> outputPC <- predict(pc)
```

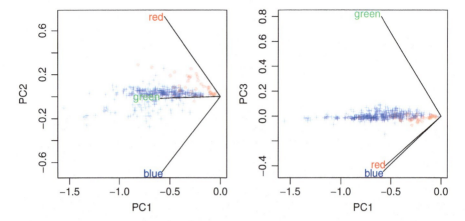

Figure 8.6: Scatter plot of photographs from the Digital Video Multimedia Lab at Columbia using principal components from rgb pixel intensities. The projected *red*, *green*, and *blue* "axes" show the theoretical projected locations of pixels with nonzero intensities in only one channel.

A scatter plot of the principal components is shown in Fig. 8.6. Axes labeled as the three primary colors indicate the locations where pixels having only one nonzero color intensity would be found; these are helpful in understanding the nature of the components. For example, all three rgb lines are equally long when viewed on the PC1 axis; the PC2 axis has almost no variation in the green line and equal but opposite intensities for the other two colors. Notice that as promised, each successive dimension contains more variance of the data than the previous one. The PC3 dimension has almost no variation compared to PC1.

Due to the fact that the first two principal components contain the majority of the variation in the dataset, for many applications it would be possible to use only the first two components. In many cases, even when the input data has a large number of variables, the most interesting effects are contained in the first few principal components. Collapsing the interesting variation in a set of data is called dimension reduction and is an important task for both visualization and predictive modeling. Principal components are popular because they are a fast way to perform aggressive dimension reduction while minimizing the effect of overfitting to a given dataset. In other words, PCA should produce similar rotations when used on a similar but independently constructed dataset (in this case, that might be another set of day/night photographs).

To illustrate the use of PCA in a higher-dimensional setting, consider saving the first and third quartile of the hsv coordinates in addition to the median; this constructs a nine-dimensional representation of the corpus.

```
> output9 <- matrix(0,nrow=length(files),ncol=9)
> for (j in 1:length(files)) {
+     z <- readJPEG(files[j])
```

8.5 K-Means

```
+         mat <- rgb2hsv(as.numeric(z[,,1]),as.numeric(z[,,2]),
+                    as.numeric(z[,,3]),maxColorValue=1)
+
+         output9[j,1:3] <- quantile(mat[1,],probs=c(0.25,0.5,0.75))
+         output9[j,4:6] <- quantile(mat[2,],probs=c(0.25,0.5,0.75))
+         output9[j,7:9] <- quantile(mat[3,],probs=c(0.25,0.5,0.75))
+ }
```

The principal component rotation for this dataset is now a 9-by-9 matrix. Notice that in the higher dimensional case it is harder to directly interpret the actions of each component.

```
> pc9 <- prcomp(output9,center=TRUE,scale.=TRUE)
> outputPC9 <- predict(pc9)
> round(pc9$rotation,3)
        PC1    PC2    PC3    PC4    PC5    PC6    PC7    PC8    PC9
[1,]  0.242  0.396 -0.310 -0.633 -0.251  0.006  0.457 -0.125  0.019
[2,]  0.293  0.325 -0.479  0.032  0.012  0.286 -0.701  0.061  0.042
[3,]  0.314  0.061 -0.485  0.541  0.326 -0.352  0.370 -0.058 -0.024
[4,] -0.306  0.484  0.107 -0.025 -0.039 -0.688 -0.233  0.049  0.357
[5,] -0.360  0.459  0.025  0.126  0.051  0.056  0.019 -0.092 -0.793
[6,] -0.386  0.358 -0.028  0.302  0.059  0.554  0.292 -0.030  0.483
[7,]  0.335  0.220  0.446 -0.128  0.580  0.070 -0.071 -0.522  0.070
[8,]  0.373  0.292  0.368  0.046  0.112  0.070  0.137  0.774 -0.056
[9,]  0.366  0.161  0.304  0.423 -0.688 -0.002 -0.001 -0.307 -0.005
```

A scatter plot of all nine dimensions is shown in Fig. 8.7, where each component is shown on the same scale. Notice that the higher components have almost no variation; conversely, the first component alone provides a very clear separation between the night and day images. For most applications, the first three components would be sufficient for capturing the majority of the variation in the data.

8.5 K-Means

When looking at scatter plots of points, an inclination is to try to identify clusters of points. More precisely, we look for a grouping of the data where the distances between points within a group are consistently smaller than the distance between groups. We saw an example of this in the community detection algorithms over a graph in Sect. 6.5. Algorithmically calculating clusters within a dataset provides a powerful tool for visualizing high-dimensional data. It can be used either in place of or in addition to PCA to understand patterns in such datasets.

There are many clustering algorithms available within R. One popular example available by default is k-means, provided by the function kmeans. We will not give a detailed description of the algorithm here beyond mentioning that it requires pre-specifying the number of clusters in the output and is nondeterministic.[3] When run within R, a vector of cluster ids is returned; due to the nondeterministic nature of the algorithm, we will set the random seed prior to continuing in order to make

---

[3] For a detailed description and visualization of the underlying algorithm see [1].

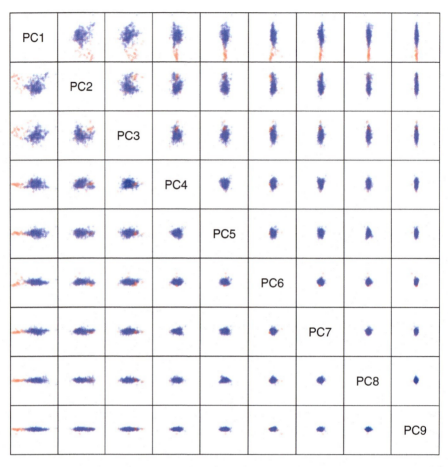

Figure 8.7: Scatter plot of photographs from the Digital Video Multimedia Lab at Columbia using principal components from the Q_1, Q_2, and Q_3 summary of the hue-saturation-value coordinates. All components are plotted on the same scale to illustrate their relative variance.

sure the results are replicable. Here we take the nine-dimensional output from the previous section and apply k-means with six clusters.

```
> set.seed(1)
kmeans <- kmeans(outputPC9, centers=6)
> cluster$cluster
  [1] 1 1 1 1 1 6 1 1 1 2 6 6 2 1 6 1 1 6 6 6 6 1 1 1 6 6 6 1 6 6 1 6
 [33] 1 2 1 1 2 6 6 6 2 1 1 1 2 2 2 5 4 5 5 5 5 5 2 2 2 2 4 2 5 2 2 2
 [65] 2 2 2 5 5 5 2 2 6 6 6 2 1 2 2 2 2 2 1 2 1 6 6 4 2 2 2 3 5 5 5
 [97] 4 2 2 6 6 6 2 4 2 2 6 6 6 2 1 6 4 6 4 1 2 2 5 5 5 5 5 5 5 2 2
[129] 1 6 6 1 6 4 3 4 4 4 4 3 3 3 3 2 5 4 3 6 4 2 2 2 6 2 2 4 4 4 6 4
[161] 2 1 6 2 2 6 6 6 4 6 6 1 2 4 6 6 2 6 4 4 3 3 3 3 3 3 3 3 3 3 3 3
[193] 3 3 3 6 6 3 4 2 2 1 6 6 6 6 4 4 4 4 4 6 2 6 4 2 4 6 2 4 4 2 2 6
```

8.5 K-Means

```
[225] 2 2 4 4 2 4 4 4 4 2 3 2 4 4 4 2 2 4 4 4 2 3 3 3 3 4 2 6 4 4 6 2 2
[257] 2 4 2 4 3 3 4 3 4 4 4 4 4 4 4 4 4 2 6 4 4 2 4 4 2 4 2 2 2 3 3 6
[289] 3 6 6 4 6 2 2 2 4 6 2 4 2 2 6 6 6 6 6 6 4 6 4
```

The values returned assign each input to a particular cluster bucket. Unlike the order of components in PCA, the actual cluster numbers do not mean anything particular: they are just dumb labels.

We can construct a table to show the degree to which these clusters separate the day and night outdoor photographs

```
> table(cluster$cluster,meta$category)

  outdoor-day outdoor-night
1          32             0
2          74            12
3          34             0
4          66             2
5           1            20
6          70             0
```

Clusters 1, 3, 4, and 6 hold the outdoor photographs (with 4 containing two outliers). Cluster 5 contains almost all night images but cluster 2 holds a mixture of both categories. Figure 8.8 shows a plot of the centers of the clusters over the first two principal components.

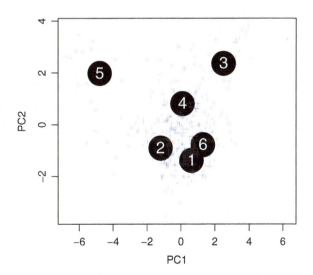

Figure 8.8: Location of k-means clusters over the first two principal components from Fig. 8.7.

8.6 Scatter Plot of Raster Graphics

We have so far developed a series of methods for displaying a corpus of images as points in scatter plots. As a final step we show how to replace the dots with small thumbnail versions of the images in question. This provides a visualization which can capture the features of the images in a way that no scatter plot could do on its own.

As a first step, we convert the principal components into standardized x and y coordinates between 0 and 1 in order to simplify the process of scaling the output correctly.

```
> x <- outputPC9[,1]
> x <- (x - min(x)) / (max(x) - min(x))
> y <- outputPC9[,2]
> y <- (y - min(y)) / (max(y) - min(y))
```

In order to plot a jpeg image onto an R plot, rather than saving it as an individual jpeg image with writeJPEG, we will use the function rasterImage, which is available within the default installation of R. The function takes an image object, which can be the direct output of readJPEG, and the locations of the top, bottom, left, and right corners of the box. By providing these four numbers, the function allows for maximum customization by end users but does force us to manually calculate the size of a box needed to maintain the aspect ratio of the original jpeg.

In order to plot a scatter plot of jpegs, the first step is to create an empty canvas to plot over. Here we also define the parameter rho, which we will use as the length of the maximum size of the plotted image; the x and y variables previously defined will be used as the lower left corner of the box and therefore we need to extend the plot region to contain the range of x and y plus an additional offset of rho.

```
par(mar=c(0,0,0,0))
rho <- 0.1
plot(0,0,type="n", xlim=c(0,1+rho), ylim=c(0,1+rho))
```

From here, we now use a for loop to cycle over the corpus of images. For each image the aspect ratio is calculated and the size of the scaled image is determined based on whether the image has a longer horizontal or vertical dimension. Finally, the rasterImage function is used to plot the image on the plot.[4]

```
> set.seed(1)
> for (j in sample(1:length(files))) {
+     z <- readJPEG(files[j])
+
+     rat <- dim(z)[1] / dim(z)[2]
+     delta_x <- ifelse(rat > 1, 1, rat) * rho
+     delta_y <- ifelse(rat > 1, rat, 1) * rho
+     rasterImage(z, xleft=x[j], ybottom=y[j],
```

---

[4]To improve the final image, we also permute the set 1:length(files) using the sample function. The order matters in this case because the later images are overplotted on the first images. The default order of the files is not as visually pleasing as a random permutation as the original ordering was sorted by size and category.

8.7 Extensions

Figure 8.9: Scatter plot of photographs from the Digital Video Multimedia Lab at Columbia using principal components from the Q_1, Q_2, and Q_3 summary of the hue-saturation-value coordinates.

```
+                    xright=x[j]+delta_x, ytop=y[j]+delta_y)
+   rect(x[j],y[j],x[j]+delta_x,y[j]+delta_y,lwd=2)
+ }
```

The output from this is shown in Fig. 8.9. Notice that the images fall into the same pattern as the scatter plot of points in Fig. 8.8. Many patterns which were not obvious in the original plot are now apparent. For example, the upper right corner is dominated by blue sky and water images. The lower center contains outdoor images taken in heavy shadows and featuring darker streets and buildings, whereas the upper left contains images with reddish incandescent bulbs.

When saving the scatter plot of jpeg images, it is best to save the output as a raster format such as a jpeg. If trying to use a vector graphic format such as pdf, the file size will be massive as a full complete copy of every image will be saved in the output. This is very similar to the issue we saw when plotting shape files in Chap. 7.

8.7 Extensions

We have made considerable progress in visualizing a corpus of images using nothing more than pixel intensities. There are many more features which can be extracted from images which consider more nuanced aspects of images. Low-level examples include image texture via co-occurrence matrices [4] and scale-invariant feature transform (SIFT) [6]. Higher-level algorithms can extract global features such as image segmentation [7] and facial recognition algorithms [3]. Not all of these higher level feature sets are currently supported by R packages; the **glcm** package, however, provides a good starting point for incorporating grey-scale textural features to data [12].

The generic statistical dimension procedures introduced, PCA and k-means clustering, are two of the most popular methods for dimension reduction and clustering. There are many important alternatives and extensions for dealing with high-dimensional data. A very popular, and reasonably accessible, reference for these is given in the text *The Elements of Statistical Learning* [5]. We will also explore further applications of these to textual corpora in Chap. 10.

Practice

1. Take a personal photograph, preferably one with bright colors and many features, convert it into a jpeg/tiff/png if necessary, and read it into R. Construct a histogram of the three color channels with ten buckets each. Then, separately for each color channel truncate the intensities at some reasonable value (the 10th and 90th percentile work well) and save the three resulting jpeg images. How different do the three (red truncated, green truncated, and blue truncated) look? Does truncation in different color channels effect perception differently from the original?

2. One technique for finding the distinctions between day and night images is looking at only the top pixels in the image, as this will often contain a bright blue sky or brightly lit buildings. Rerun the basic analysis on the corpus of images by capturing four numbers from each image: the saturation and value for the top 50 rows of pixels, and the saturation and value for the bottom 50 rows of pixels. Try plotting these new dimensions. Use a PCA and plot the images using the code developed in Sect. 8.6. What differences do you see compared with the original analysis?

3. The image corpus we have has several other categories. Pick two of them and reconstruct Figs. 8.6 and 8.7. Do these methods separate the classes as well, better, or worse than the outdoor day and night classes?

4. Write a loop to calculate the k-means clusters for the day/night photographic corpus with $k = 6$ over the principal components 25 times (use par(mfrow= c(5,5) to display them together), without re-setting the random seed. What do you notice about the clusters? How stable is the output? Try this again with both $k = 3$ and $k = 10$ clusters. How stable are these outputs? How might you use this information to help choose the number of clusters?

References

[1] Elke Achtert, Hans-Peter Kriegel, and Arthur Zimek. Elki: a software system for evaluation of subspace clustering algorithms. In *Scientific and Statistical Database Management*, pages 580–585. Springer, 2008.

[2] C. Agostinelli and U. Lund. *R package* `circular`: *Circular Statistics (version 0.4-7)*. CA: Department of Environmental Sciences, Informatics and Statistics, Ca' Foscari University, Venice, Italy. UL: Department of Statistics, California Polytechnic State University, San Luis Obispo, California, USA, 2013. URL https://r-forge.r-project.org/projects/circular/.

[3] Gary Bradski and Adrian Kaehler. *Learning OpenCV: Computer vision with the OpenCV library.* " O'Reilly Media, Inc.", 2008.

[4] Robert M Haralick, Karthikeyan Shanmugam, and Its' Hak Dinstein. Textural features for image classification. *Systems, Man and Cybernetics, IEEE Transactions on*, (6): 610–621, 1973.

[5] Trevor Hastie, Robert Tibshirani, Jerome Friedman, T Hastie, J Friedman, and R Tibshirani. *The elements of statistical learning*, volume 2. Springer, 2009.

[6] Tony Lindeberg. Scale invariant feature transform. *Scholarpedia*, 7(5):10491, 2012.

[7] Nikhil R Pal and Sankar K Pal. A review on image segmentation techniques. *Pattern recognition*, 26(9):1277–1294, 1993.

[8] Alvy Ray Smith. Color gamut transform pairs. In *ACM Siggraph Computer Graphics*, volume 12, pages 12–19. ACM, 1978.

[9] Simon Urbanek. *png: Read and write PNG images*, 2013. URL http://CRAN.R-project.org/package=png. R package version 0.1-7.

[10] Simon Urbanek. *tiff: Read and write TIFF images*, 2013. URL http://CRAN.R-project.org/package=tiff. R package version 0.1-5.

[11] Simon Urbanek. *jpeg: Read and write JPEG images*, 2014. URL http://CRAN.R-project.org/package=jpeg. R package version 0.1-8.

[12] Alex Zvoleff. *glcm: Calculate textures from grey-level co-occurrence matrices (GLCMs) in R*, 2015. URL http://CRAN.R-project.org/package=glcm. R package version 1.2.

Chapter 9
Natural Language Processing

Abstract An introduction applying low-level natural language processing is given in this chapter. Techniques such as tokenization, lemmatization, part of speech tagging, and coreference detection are described in relationship to text analysis. The methods are applied to a corpus of short stories by Sir Arthur Conan Doyle featuring his famous detective, Sherlock Holmes.

9.1 Introduction

The application of computational tools to textual data is a growing area of inquiry in the humanities. From the culling of "Culturomics" via the 30 million document Google books collections [15], to the painstakingly detailed process of analyzing the text of Shakespeare's plays to ascertain their "true" creator [12, 25], a wide range of techniques and methods have been employed and developed. Text analysis in the humanities has also garnered an impressive level of interest in the mainstream media. For example, a study analyzing the relationship of a professor's gender to their teaching reviews [16] and an overview of Franco Moretti's *distant reading* [21] both recently appeared in the *New York Times*. *The Atlantic* featured a historical critique of the language used in the period drama "Mad Men", where textual analysis of the script revealed departures from the standard American English spoken in the 1960s [20].

Textual data is also highly unstructured. When working with images we saw that we could represent a collection by arranging the pixel intensities in a very wide table. While large and slightly awkward, at least this provided a convenient starting point. Textual data does not offer such a simple representation (at least without losing a substantial amount of information). To address this limitation, textual sources must undergo a large amount of pre-processing.

The form of pre-processing we will focus on will be natural language processing (NLP), which mimics the complex process by which humans parse and interpret language. The areas we will cover include tokenization and sentence

© Springer International Publishing Switzerland 2015
T. Arnold, L. Tilton, *Humanities Data in R*, Quantitative Methods
in the Humanities and Social Sciences, DOI 10.1007/978-3-319-20702-5_9

splitting (Sect. 9.2), lemmatization and part of speech tagging (Sect. 9.3), dependencies (Sect. 9.4), named entity recognition (Sect. 9.5), and coreference detection (Sect. 9.6). It is worth noting that these methods are complex and remain a very active and unsettled area of research.

Given the complexity and importance of textual data, we have decided to split our treatment into two chapters. Here we cover the low-level data cleaning steps known as the *natural language processing pipeline*. We will do this by way of examples. Our primary focus will be on Arthur Conan Doyle's 56 short stories about Sherlock Holmes. We will look at "A Scandal in Bohemia" through the NLP pipeline and then scale up to analyzing all 56 of Doyle's stories. We provide interesting direct applications of these methods; the true power of textual analysis will become even clearer in the next chapter when we show how to apply various high-level analyses to the cleaned data.

9.2 Tokenization and Sentence Splitting

Consider (an English translation of) the opening lines to Albert Camus's *l'Étranger* [1].[1] Let us represent this as a length one character vector in R.

```
> sIn <- "Mother died today. Or, maybe, yesterday; I can't be sure."
```

A practical, and seemingly simple, first step in processing this string is to split it into a longer character vector where each element contains a single word. But what exactly is meant by a word? Are punctuation marks separate words? What about contractions, hyphens, or compound nouns such as "New York City"? If we split this string apart using just the presence of spaces the result seems approximately reasonable, but less than perfect.

```
> strsplit(sIn, split=" ")
[[1]]
 [1] "Mother"      "died"     "today."    "Or,"    "maybe,"
 [6] "yesterday;"  "I"        "can't"     "be"     "sure."
```

The process of splitting text into meaningful elements is called *tokenization*. For English text the difficult task is catching the myriad of rules and exceptions. Rather than re-creating and re-implementing these conditions, it is better to use a well-tested library to tokenize our string. The library we will use throughout this chapter is the Stanford CoreNLP [14]. It is an open source java software with a large user base and has support for a range of languages. We have developed an R package **coreNLP** for calling the library as well as manipulating and visualizing the output. In order to use the R package, call the function `initCoreNLP`.[2]

---

[1] Later, in Sect. 9.8 we explore how to tokenize these lines in the original French.
[2] More detailed instructions on how to set up this package can be found in Chap. 11 and on CRAN.

9.2 Tokenization and Sentence Splitting

```
> library(coreNLP)
> initCoreNLP()
```

The initialization of the library can take a minute or two as a large amount of linguistic data is loaded and processed into memory; a running list of the models should be displayed in the R console window.

In order to process a string of text using **coreNLP**, an annotation object first needs to be constructed. When the text is passed through annotateString, the entire suite of CoreNLP functions such as lemmatization and stemming is applied. We will explore each of these techniques throughout this chapter.

```
> annotation <- annotateString(sIn)
> annotation

A CoreNLP Annotation:
  num. sentences: 2
  num. tokens: 16
```

As the default output shows, this annotation has already (correctly) determined that the text has two sentences and sixteen *tokens*, a generalization of the concept of a word, which includes elements such as punctuation. To see the generated tokenization, the function getToken extracts information regarding each lemma detected in the input. For now we pull out just the word element of the output.

```
> getToken(annotation)$token
 [1] "Mother"      "died"        "today"      "."      "Or"      ","
 [7] "maybe"       ","           "yesterday"  ";"      "I"       "ca"
[13] "n't"         "be"          "sure"       "."
```

Notice that the punctuation symbols have been assigned to their own elements and the contraction "can't" has been split into two words. (Note: In the next step, "ca" and "n't" will be addressed.) However, the input text has not been modified with the exception of removing spaces. In addition to the process of tokenizing the input, the annotation also calculated how to split the input into sentences. As the documentation states:

> Sentence splitting is a deterministic consequence of tokenization: a sentence ends when a sentence-ending character (., !, or ?) is found which is not grouped with other characters into a token (such as for an abbreviation or number), though it may still include a few tokens that can follow a sentence ending character as part of the same sentence (such as quotes and brackets).[3]

To see the assignment of sentences, pull the sentence element out of the tokenization.

```
> getToken(annotation)$sentence
 [1] 1 1 1 1 2 2 2 2 2 2 2 2 2 2 2 2
```

---

[3] http://nlp.stanford.edu/software/tokenizer.shtml.

The algorithm has assigned the first four tokens to the first sentence, and the remainder to the second sentence.

Can we learn anything useful directly from the output of this process of tokenization? In our short 16 lemma example probably not, but consider applying the algorithm to a longer sample of text. The **coreNLP** provides a function for annotating an entire file in one step. It is straightforward to apply but can take a nontrivial amount of time to process a file of text. Reading in the short story "A Scandal in Bohemia", the first of Sir Arthur Conan Doyle's short stories featuring Sherlock Holmes, for example, takes about 4 min on a moderately powerful machine.[4]

```
> anno <- annotateFile(
+             "data/ch09/01_a_scandal_in_bohemia.txt")
> anno

A CoreNLP Annotation:
  num. sentences: 668
  num. tokens: 10448
```

The output object is of exactly the same structure as our short example. In this case 668 sentences and 10,448 tokens have been processed. We can use the tokenization and sentence splitting to determine the length of every sentence in the text.

```
> sentLen <- table(getToken(anno)$sentence)
> hist(sentLen, breaks=30)
```

A histogram of these lengths is shown in Fig. 9.1.[5] The distribution shows a sharp peak of sentences less than ten tokens longer; this is fairly short, particularly when considering that punctuation is included in this count. It is likely a product of the heavy use of dialogue in the text. A very small set of sentences top 60 or more tokens. A close analysis of the original text reveals most of these to be part of a long deductive speech given by Sherlock Holmes towards the end of the story.

9.3 Lemmatization and Part of Speech Tagging

While tokenizing simply splits the raw character input into groups, *lemmatization* goes further by converting each token into a representative *lemma*. For example, "go" is the English lemma for words such as "gone", "going", and "went".[6] Nouns have their own process of lemmatization, such as converting all words into their singular form; for example, "dogs" becomes "dog" and "mice" becomes "mouse".

Notice that lemmatization changes depending on the part of speech. Therefore, much like tokenization and sentence splitting, the task of tagging tokens with parts of speech and lemmatization is often accomplished in tandem. To demonstrate how both work in the **coreNLP** package, we again turn to our annotation of "A Scandal

---

[4] All texts of the short Sherlock Holmes stories were downloaded from Project Gutenberg [9].

[5] A detailed statistical analysis of sentence length distributions is given by Sichel [23].

[6] In the technical terminology of linguistics, a *lexeme* denotes a word meaning along with its orthographic or phonological form; a lemma is then a collection of the lexemes with the same meaning.

9.3 Lemmatization and Part of Speech Tagging

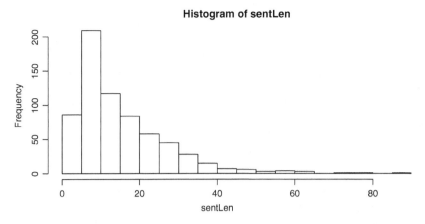

Figure 9.1: Distribution of sentence length in "A Scandal in Bohemia".

in Bohemia" and the `getToken` function [24]. Pulling out the second sentence (and obscuring some of the columns so as not to overwhelm ourselves with the rest of the output) reveals the following data frame.

```
> token <- getToken(anno)
> token[token$sentence==2,c(1:4,7)]
   sentence id   token   lemma  POS
10        2  1       I       I  PRP
11        2  2    have    have  VBP
12        2  3  seldom  seldom   RB
13        2  4   heard    hear  VBN
14        2  5     him      he  PRP
15        2  6 mention mention   VB
16        2  7     her     she PRP$
17        2  8   under   under   IN
18        2  9     any     any   DT
19        2 10   other   other   JJ
20        2 11    name    name   NN
21        2 12       .       .    .
```

The lemmatization process should seem straightforward. The verb "heard" is now represented by the infinitive "hear", and the pronouns "him" and "her" are changed to their nominative forms "he" and "she". Otherwise, the words remain unchanged in their lemma form. The part of speech codes, on the other hand, may at first seem confusing; for example, there are three different codes for the verbs "have", "heard", and "mention".

The part of speech codes used by the Stanford CoreNLP library come from the Penn Treebank Project and contain many more categories compared to those typically taught in primary school grammar courses. For example, **VBN** is the past participle form of a verb, whereas **VB** is the base form of a verb. A table from our annotation shows the entire set of possibilities.

```
> table(token$POS)

-LRB-  -RRB-     ,      :      .      ''     ``     CC     CD     DT     EX
    1      1   573     42    668    294    299    338     87    841     31
   IN     JJ   JJR    JJS     MD     NN    NNP    NNS    PDT    POS    PRP
 1031    500    14      9    161   1101    322    245     11     18    896
 PRP$     RB   RBR    RBS     RP     TO     UH     VB    VBD    VBG    VBN
  289    525    15     11     61    245     16    367    560    117    220
  VBP    VBZ   WDT     WP    WP$    WRB
  183    158    60     70      1     67
```

We see that **JJS**, superlative adjectives, are relatively uncommon, and **IN** tags, prepositions or subordinating conjunction, occur quiet frequently. For a complete description of these tags see the technical report and justification from the Penn Treebank Project [19].

The extended set of parts of speech are quite useful, but many times a smaller set of more familiar options can better serve a particular purpose. The *universal tag-set* has been created and is a language-agnostic part of speech classifier [17]. A mapping from Penn Treebank codes into this smaller tag-set is provided in the **coreNLP** package. A table using the *universal tag-set* reveals a smaller and more familiar list of parts of speech.

```
> ut <- universalTagset(token$POS)
> table(ut)
ut
    .   ADJ   ADP   ADV  CONJ   DET  NOUN   NUM  PRON   PRT  VERB     X
 1878   523  1031   618   338   943  1668    87  1256   324  1766    16
> unique(token$POS[ut == "NOUN"])
[1] "NNP" "NN"  "NNS"
> unique(token$POS[ut == "VERB"])
[1] "VBZ" "VBP" "VBN" "VB"  "VBD" "VBG" "MD"
```

The three subtypes of nouns correspond to plural nouns (**NNS**), proper nouns (**NNS**), and singular nouns (**NN**); there is also a plural proper noun code not seen in this text (**NNPS**). The verb subtypes refer to various broad categories of verb conjugations.

With these universal part of speech codes, we can run some basic analysis on the sentences in our text. First, we count the number of nouns, pronouns, adjectives, and verbs in each sentence using the `tapply` function.

```
> nounCnt <- tapply(ut == "NOUN", token$sentence, sum)
> pronCnt <- tapply(ut == "PRON", token$sentence, sum)
> adjCnt  <- tapply(ut == "ADJ",  token$sentence, sum)
> verbCnt <- tapply(ut == "VERB", token$sentence, sum)
> posDf <- data.frame(nounCnt,pronCnt,adjCnt,verbCnt)
> head(posDf)
  nounCnt pronCnt adjCnt verbCnt
1       3       1      0       1
2       1       3      1       3
3       3       3      0       2
4       3       2      1       3
5       2       1      4       1
6       5       5      2       8
```

9.3 Lemmatization and Part of Speech Tagging

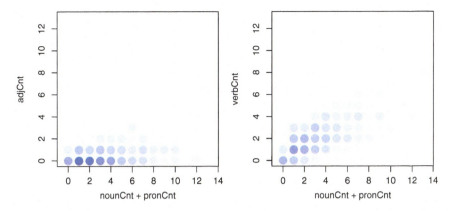

Figure 9.2: Within sentence distribution of universal part of speech tags for "A Scandal in Bohemia".

An interesting stylistic question would be to see the within-sentence distribution of nouns (including pronouns), verbs, and adjectives. Due to the discrete nature of count data, a simple scatter plot will not work well. Instead we take advantage of over-plotting and color opacity to produce an interpretable visual description of this distribution.

```
> plot(nounCnt+pronCnt,adjCnt,pch=19,cex=2,
+      col=rgb(0,0,1,0.02))
```

The output is shown in Fig. 9.2. We see that verbs and nouns are well correlated and roughly appear in equal numbers for short sentences, whereas longer sentences tend to increase in terms of nouns faster than the number of verbs. Adjectives do not follow such a smooth relationship with nouns; regardless of the number of nouns they rarely occur more than two times in a sentence, despite occurring once in almost half of sentences with only one noun.

Part of speech tagging also has the benefit of isolating *function words*, those with primarily grammatical usage such as prepositions and conjunctions, from those words with lexical meaning. Along with the use of lemmatization to collapse various word forms together, we can now gain potentially important contextual information from a text by identifying the most frequently used lemmas from a particular part of speech. The top 25 noun lemmas from our sample text, for example, identify some of the key characters and objects of interest in the story.

```
> index <- which(ut=="NOUN")
> tab <- table(token$lemma[index])
> head(sort(tab,decreasing=TRUE),25)

    Holmes        man photograph    Majesty       hand      woman
        47         31         21         18         17         17
      King     matter      house       door       Irene     minute
        16         15         14         13         13         13
      room     street      Adler       fire     window      Briony
        13         13         12         12         12         11
       eye      Lodge    nothing       time       face       lady
        11         11         11         11         10         10
  Sherlock
        10
```

The third most common word, "photograph", comes from the main objective presented in the story: the recovery of a scandalous photograph. References to the main characters are also present: "Sherlock Holmes" of course, "Majesty" being the royal client wishing to recover the photograph, and "Irene Adler" the subject of the photograph in question.

Knowing beforehand the text in question, we were able to extract the character names from a table of the most common nouns. Identifying facts we already know however is not particularly useful. How might we have better accomplished this using the methods at hand? One option is to use the original Penn Treebank tags to tabulate only the proper nouns.

```
> index <- which(token$POS == "NNP")
> tab <- table(token$lemma[index])
> head(sort(tab,decreasing=TRUE),25)

    Holmes    Majesty       King       Irene      Adler     Briony
        47         18         16         13         12         11
     Lodge   Sherlock        Mr.    Bohemia     Street      Baker
        11         10          8          7          7          6
    Norton     Watson    Godfrey       John        St.     Temple
         6          6          5          4          4          4
    Avenue     Church     Europe     London       Miss     Monica
         3          3          3          3          3          3
 Serpentine
         3
```

The reduced list includes an increased set of characters, while removing many of the non-name nouns from the list. The results are still lacking as the titles and first and last names are not linked together. Some non-names are also present, such as the proper place names "Europe" and "London". In order to resolve these issues we need to discern relationships between pairs of words, rather than working with lemmas individually.

9.4 Dependencies

To this point, we have primarily worked with individual words, tokens, and lemmas. We now approach the subject of sentence *parsing*, where the words within a sentence are assigned a complete linguistic structure linking together all of the

9.4 Dependencies

individual parts. The result of this, known as a parse tree, has a nice graphical structure. In the **coreNLP** package it can be accessed via the `getParse` function, where a character vector with one element per sentence is returned [3]. (We have run all of these code snippets with version 3.5.1 of the Stanford CoreNLP. We know that the next version will use a different names for dependency tags, so the exact output may differ but the general ideas will remain the same.)

```
> parseTree <- getParse(anno)
> length(parseTree)
[1] 668
> cat(parseTree[1])
(ROOT
  (S
    (PP (TO To)
      (NP (NNP Sherlock)  (NNP Holmes)))
    (NP (PRP she))
    (VP (VBZ is)
      (ADVP (RB always))
      (NP (DT THE)  (NN woman)))
    (. .)))
```

The nice graphical description of a particular element requires the function `cat`; it is a base function in R that handles embedded newline characters differently than the more commonly seen `print` function. The resulting graphic combines parsing information with part of speech tags in a pleasing way. However, as just a string, there is little that can be done directly for further analysis.

Fortunately, an alternative representation of the parse structure is also provided in the form of a set of dependencies. These dependencies give the relationships between the pairs of lemmas that when taken together can reconstruct the entire parse tree, much the same way that sets of edges were used to construct larger graphs in Chap. 6. Additionally, dependencies attach each relationship with a code indicating the nature of the relationship. These have the potential to be a powerful tool when cleaning textual data. To access the set of dependencies, the **coreNLP** package provides the `getDependency` function that returns a data frame of relationship pairs.

```
> dep <- getDependency(anno)
> dep[dep$sentence == 1,]
  sentence governor dependent     type governorIdx dependentIdx
1        1     ROOT     woman     root           0            8
2        1   Holmes  Sherlock       nn           3            2
3        1    woman    Holmes  prep_to           8            3
4        1    woman       she    nsubj           8            4
5        1    woman        is      cop           8            5
6        1    woman    always   advmod           8            6
7        1    woman       THE      det           8            7
  govIndex depIndex
1       NA        8
2        3        2
3        8        3
4        8        4
5        8        5
```

```
6        8        6
7        8        7
```

As with the part of speech codes, the dependency type codes can be difficult to interpret without a code book. For a complete list see the *Stanford Typed Dependencies Manual* [4]; the two that we will make explicit use of are **nn**, noun compound modifiers, and **nsubj**, which identifies "a noun phrase, which is syntactic subject of a clause". The latter typically relates a noun and its verb, but may link a noun to another noun (as above) or adjective in the presence of a copular verb. The `govIndex` and `depIndex` point back to rows in the tokens data frame, making linking between the two data types possible.

An alternative visualization of the dependency structure is also provided in the **coreNLP** R package. The syntax takes an annotation object and the id for the sentence of interest as inputs to the `plot` function.

```
> plot(anno,5)
```

The output, shown in Fig. 9.3, shows a compact representation of the sentence's grammatical structure. It is very useful for testing and exploring the output of the part of speech and dependency tagging done by the CoreNLP library.

For another example of how dependency information can be used to understand a textual source, consider identifying the most frequently used verbs that take the action from the pronoun "I" used as the subject of a sentence.

```
> index <- which(token$lemma[dep$depIndex] == "I")
> depSelf <- dep[index,]
> depSelf <- depSelf[depSelf$type == "nsubj",]
> sort(table(depSelf$governor),decreasing=TRUE)[1:10]

heard know found  have   saw am think  call   had  made
    8     8     7     7     6     5     5     4     4     4
```

The analysis here is slightly difficult because "I" may represent the narrator or could be present in a quotation.

Returning to the issue of detecting character names, we can look for dependencies of type **nn**, representing a noun modifying another noun. We extract all dependencies of this type where both related words are proper nouns. Because our story has a small amount of text written in all upper case and the Stanford CoreNLP part of speech tagger labels all of these as proper nouns even when they should not be, we also remove these all upper case words at the same time.

```
> index <- which(dep$type == "nn" &
+                token$POS[dep$govIndex] == "NNP" &
+                token$POS[dep$depIndex] == "NNP" &
+                (toupper(token$token) != token$token)[dep$govIndex] &
+                (toupper(token$token) != token$token)[dep$depIndex])
> nnDep <- dep[index,]
```

9.4 Dependencies

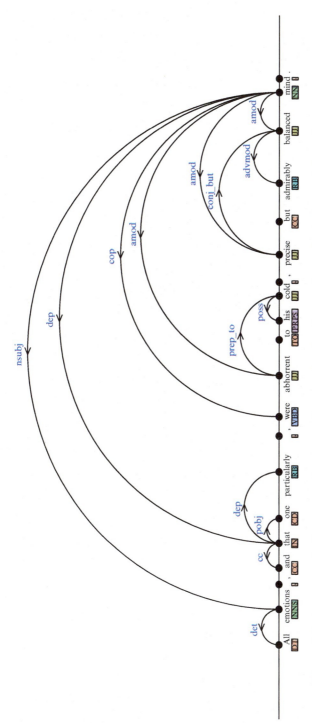

Figure 9.3: An automatically generated sentence diagram showing f, part of speech tagging, and dependency structure.

Putting this together with the part of speech tags that detect proper nouns, we can pull out pairs of modifying proper nouns. When pasted together, these give a much improved set of character names.

```
> pname <- startIndex = endIndex = NULL
> for (g in unique(nnDep$govIndex)) {
+   these <- c(which(nnDep$depIndex == g),
+              which(nnDep$govIndex == g))
+   these <- range(c(nnDep$depIndex[these],nnDep$govIndex[these]))
+   out <- paste(token$token[these[1]:these[2]],collapse=" ")
+   pname <- c(pname, out)
+   startIndex <- c(startIndex, these[1])
+   endIndex <- c(endIndex, these[2])
+ }
> pnames <- data.frame(pname,startIndex,endIndex,
+                     stringsAsFactors=FALSE)
> unique(pnames$pname)
 [1] "Sherlock Holmes"
 [2] "Irene Adler"
 [3] "Baker Street"
 [4] "Mary Jane"
 [5] "Continental Gazetteer"
 [6] "Eglow , Eglonitz"
 [7] "Dr. Watson"
 [8] "Count Von Kramm"
 [9] "Wilhelm Gottsreich Sigismond von Ormstein"
[10] "Grand Duke"
[11] "New Jersey"
[12] "La Scala"
[13] "Prima donna Imperial Opera"
[14] "Crown Prince"
[15] "Clotilde Lothman"
[16] "Briony Lodge"
[17] "Serpentine Avenue"
[18] "St. John"
[19] "Miss Irene Adler"
[20] "Miss Adler"
[21] "Mr. Godfrey Norton"
[22] "Inner Temple"
[23] "Godfrey Norton"
[24] "Regent Street"
[25] "St. Monica"
[26] "Edgeware Road"
[27] "Mrs. Turner"
[28] "Miss Irene"
[29] "Mr. John Hare"
[30] "Mister Sherlock Holmes"
[31] "Mr. Sherlock Holmes"
[32] "Mr. Holmes"
[33] "Charing Cross"
```

One continued deficiency comes from character names with more than two parts, such as "Wilhelm Gottsreich Sigismond von Ormstein". It is possible to determine these from the dependency structure already presented with the incorporation of a slightly more complicated set of code for pasting together proper nouns. Another issue, which cannot be fixed with the tools at hand, is the inclusion of non-person names such as "New Jersey". We will explore how to fix this in the next section, where the more complex logic for longer names will no longer be necessary.

9.5 Named Entity Recognition

The task of automatically detecting and classifying elements of a text into broad semantic categories is known as *named entity recognition*. The named entities recognized by the CoreNLP library are contained in the previously dropped columns of the output from the getToken function [6]. Taking our sample text, we see the following 11 categories picked up by the algorithm ("O" is used for a non-hit).

```
> token <- getToken(anno)
> table(token$NER)

        DATE      DURATION      LOCATION          MISC         MONEY
          69            42            60            21             3
      NUMBER             O       ORDINAL  ORGANIZATION        PERSON
          64          9967             3            29           140
         SET          TIME
           3            47
```

Which kinds of tags were identified as locations? Thankfully, many of the false positives in our character set are picked up by the location tag. See for instance New Jersey and Baker Street.

```
> unique(token$lemma[token$NER=="LOCATION"])
 [1] "Baker"       "Street"       "Odessa"        "Trincomalee"
 [5] "Holland"     "scarlet"      "London"        "Europe"
 [9] "Egria"       "Bohemia"      "Carlsbad"      "Wallenstein"
[13] "England"     "Prague"       "Warsaw"        "New"
[17] "Jersey"      "Scandinavia"  "Langham"       "Briony"
[21] "Lodge"       "Regent"       "St."           "Monica"
[25] "Edgeware"    "Road"         "Serpentine"    "Avenue"
[29] "Darlington"  "Arnsworth"    "Castle"        "Charing"
[33] "Cross"       "Esq."
```

These can be helpful in determining the location or topic of a given story.

Named entity recognition also does an excellent job of identifying, and representing dates and times in a common format. See for instance the parsing of "the twentieth of March, 1888" into the standard ISO 8601 format "1888-03-20".

```
> token[485:490,]
    sentence id      word     lemma CharacterOffsetBegin
485       18  7       the       the                 2471
486       18  8 twentieth twentieth                 2475
487       18  9        of        of                 2485
488       18 10     March     March                 2488
489       18 11         ,         ,                 2493
490       18 12      1888      1888                 2495
    CharacterOffsetEnd POS  NER Speaker NormalizedNER         Timex
```

```
485                2474 DT  DATE         PER0   1888-03-20 1888-03-20
486                2484 NN  DATE         PER0   1888-03-20 1888-03-20
487                2487 IN  DATE         PER0   1888-03-20 1888-03-20
488                2493 NNP DATE         PER0   1888-03-20 1888-03-20
489                2494 ,   DATE         PER0   1888-03-20 1888-03-20
490                2499 CD  DATE         PER0   1888-03-20 1888-03-20
```

Or the string "a quarter past six" into the standardized "T06:15".

```
> token[6991:6994,]
     sentence id     word   lemma CharacterOffsetBegin
6991      435  3        a       a                31136
6992      435  4  quarter quarter                31138
6993      435  5     past    past                31146
6994      435  6      six     six                31151
     CharacterOffsetEnd POS  NER Speaker NormalizedNER  Timex
6991              31137  DT TIME    PER0        T06:15 T06:15
6992              31145  NN TIME    PER0        T06:15 T06:15
6993              31150  IN TIME    PER0        T06:15 T06:15
6994              31154  CD TIME    PER0        T06:15 T06:15
```

Parsing dates and times into a common format is interesting in many contexts. For example, when dealing with non-fiction corpora this method could be used to extract factual information such as dates of birth in an obituary, the time of a recent event in a newspaper article, or the people written about in a set of letters.

The named entity tag that will help the most with our goal of identifying the main characters in our short story, unsurprisingly, is the one indicating persons.

```
> these <- which(token$NER == "PERSON")
> pnames <- pnames[which(pnames$endIndex %in% these),]
> these <- these[-which(these %in% pnames$endIndex)]
> newPnames <- data.frame(pname=token$token[these],
+                         startIndex=these,
+                         endIndex=these,
+                         stringsAsFactors=FALSE)
> pnames <- rbind(pnames,newPnames)
> pnames <- pnames[toupper(pnames$pname) != pnames$pname,]
> length(unique(pnames$pname))
[1] 48
```

The resulting list of characters is a significant improvement over our last attempt, with many false positives removed and longer names reconstructed.

We could also clean up the duplicated names, such as "Holmes". This often occurs when a character is mentioned at some point with only part of their name. We do this by cycling through the list of names and replacing the text of any one that is a strict subset of another.

```
> pnames$pname <- gsub("Mister", "Mr.", pnames$pname)
> for (j in 1:nrow(pnames)) {
matchString = gsub(" ", ".*", pnames$pname[j])
+    these <- grep(matchString,pnames$pname)
+    pnamesSet <- pnames$pname[these]
```

9.6 Coreference

```
+   pnames$pname[j] <- pnamesSet[which.max(nchar(pnamesSet))]
+ }
> unique(pnames$pname)
 [1] "Mr. Sherlock Holmes"
 [2] "Miss Irene Adler"
 [3] "Mary Jane"
 [4] "Dr. Watson"
 [5] "Count Von Kramm"
 [6] "Wilhelm Gottsreich Sigismond von Ormstein"
 [7] "Grand Duke"
 [8] "La Scala"
 [9] "Crown Prince"
[10] "Clotilde Lothman"
[11] "St. John"
[12] "Mr. Godfrey Norton"
[13] "St. Monica"
[14] "Mrs. Turner"
[15] "Mr. John Hare"
[16] "Atkinson"
[17] "Eglow"
[18] "Boswell"
[19] "of"
[20] "Cassel-Felstein"
[21] "Saxe-Meningen"
[22] "Mademoiselle"
[23] "Hankey"
```

The sole remaining error is the inclusion of "La Scala", the famous Milanese opera house. Looking in the original text reveals the name is used in the exclamation "La Scala, hum!". There seems to be no hope of quantitatively removing it with a generic NLP parser without explicitly hard coding the fact that "La Scala" refers to a location rather than a person.

9.6 Coreference

We now have a method for calculating a list of the major characters in a given annotated short story. Our final task is to quantify the relative importance of each of these characters. As a rough measurement, we detect how often each character is directly referenced in the text. It would be possible to simply tabulate and sort the vector pnames. In many cases, this approach would be fine, but it can be improved upon by using one final element of the CoreNLP pipeline called *coreferences* [13].

While the dependency table gives grammatical relationships between words within a sentence, coreferences give semantic relationships between tokens, that may be far away within a given corpus. Specifically, they detect when multiple words refer to the same person or object. For example, in the sentence "Jane was tired. She took a nap.", a coreference algorithm should detect that "Jane" in the first sentence and the pronoun "she" refer to the same person.

Extracting a coreference involves calling the getCoreference function on an annotation object. Note that when no coreferences are detected, this function simply returns a NULL object. The resulting data frame gives all known instances, marked by a unique corefId, of every person or object that has at least two references.

```
> coref <- getCoreference(anno)
> head(coref)
  corefId sentence start end head startIndex endIndex
1       1      620  17  22   21       9668     9672
2       1        1   2   4    3          2        3
3       1        2   5   6    5         14       14
4       1        3   2   3    2         23       23
5       1        4   5   6    5         39       39
6       1        5  12  13   12         61       61
```

Unlike parts of speech or dependencies, the coreference data does not have any specific classification for the type of coreference. The startIndex and endIndex fields refer to rows in the token data frame for convenient mapping to the raw data. Looking at the words associated with corefId equal to 1 reveals the identity of the first entity; it is Sherlock Holmes.

```
> table(token$token[coref$startIndex[coref$corefId == 1]])

    dear      he      He     him himself     his     His
       2      34       7       8       1      29       1
  Holmes       I      me  Mister     Mr.      my      MY
      32      29       6       1       4       5       1
  myself Sherlock SHERLOCK    the     The      We     you
       1       8       1      10       3       1       1
     You    your
       5       1
```

A more methodical method is needed in general to identify the character associated with each id number. To do this we match the endIndex from the coreference data frame to the endIndex from the data frame of character names constructed in the prior section

```
> index <- match(as.numeric(coref$endIndex), pnames$endIndex)
> head(index)
[1] NA  1 NA NA NA NA
```

We then look at which character names are associated with a given coreference id. In the case of multiple matches, we take the most frequently used variant of the name.[7]

```
> temp <- tapply(pnames$pname[index[!is.na(index)]],
+                coref[!is.na(index),1],
+                function(v) {names(rev(sort(table(v))))[1]} )
> perMap <- data.frame(corefId=names(temp),perName=temp)
> perMap
```

---

[7] In this case, coreference id also matched Irene Norton, but our method picked out her more commonly used name variant.

9.6 Coreference

```
    corefId           perName
1         1  Mr. Sherlock Holmes
6         6     Miss Irene Adler
21       21  Mr. Sherlock Holmes
26       26  Mr. Sherlock Holmes
46       46  Mr. Sherlock Holmes
65       65           Dr. Watson
79       79           Mary Jane
171     171           Dr. Watson
195     195      Count Von Kramm
197     197      Count Von Kramm
260     260           Dr. Watson
286     286    Mr. Godfrey Norton
304     304           St. Monica
306     306           St. Monica
315     315        Mr. John Hare
```

Most of the coreference ids are linked to named entities in our list. Upon looking closer at the coreference table, it should not be surprising that the majority of ids consist of only 2–3 references with little context. Also notice that four of the coreference ids (1, 21, 26, and 46) all point to Sherlock Holmes. We have actually been able to improve on the results of the coreference algorithm by merging three of the entity ids! Had we accomplished this using external knowledge or hand tuning it would not be very surprising, but the fact that we were able to improve the coreference detection using purely computational methods is quite exciting. It is also scalable, particularly for those interested in working with a large amount of text.

The final step in determining the number of references to each character comes by summing the number of references in each corefId and merging the three groupings we discovered by character names.

```
> tab <- table(coref[,1])
> index <- match(perMap$corefId, names(tab))
> perMap$count <- tab[index]
> charImport <- sort(tapply(perMap$count, perMap$perName, sum),TRUE)
> charImport
Mr. Sherlock Holmes    Miss Irene Adler  Mr. Godfrey Norton
                248                  38                  23
         St. Monica          Dr. Watson       Mr. John Hare
                 23                  19                   9
    Count Von Kramm           Mary Jane
                  5                   2
```

Unsurprisingly, as we suspected all along, the most important character by reference is Sherlock Holmes. The second and third most important characters on the other hand are quite interesting. One might have expected Watson, but it is Irene Adler and Godfrey Norton. Irene Adler drives the majority of the plot via a scandalous photograph; Godfrey Norton helps to provide the story's ending by marrying Irene and convincing her to no longer hold the King under blackmail.

9.7 Case Study: Sherlock Holmes Main Characters

We have now built an algorithm for extracting character names using the CoreNLP library and verified that the results were reasonable on a single short story. Here we loop over the text from the entire corpus of the 56 short stories featuring Sherlock Holmes. The code may seem a bit daunting, but it consists of the pieces we have already developed (it is by far the longest in the entire text). Note that it may take several hours for this code to run as-is due to the long length of time the annotation process requires; a method that pre-caches the annotations is given in the supplementary materials and may be better for directly following along.

```
> output <- c()
> outputGraphics <- list()
> iter <- 1
> for (f in dir("data/ch09/holmes_anno",full.names=TRUE)) {
+   anno <- readRDS(f)
+   token <- getToken(anno)
+   dep <- getDependency(anno)
+   coref <- getCoreference(anno)
+
+   index <- which(dep$type == "nn" &
+              token$POS[dep$govIndex] == "NNP" &
+              token$POS[dep$depIndex] == "NNP" &
+   nnDep <- dep[index,]
+
+   pname <- startIndex <- endIndex <- NULL
+   for (g in unique(nnDep$govIndex)) {
+     these <- c(which(nnDep$depIndex == g),
+                which(nnDep$govIndex == g))
+     these <- range(c(nnDep$depIndex[these],nnDep$govIndex[these]))
+     index <- these[1]:these[2]
+     words <- token$token[index][token$POS[index] != "." &
+                          token$NER[index] %in%
+   c("O","PERSON")]
+     out <- paste(words,collapse=" ")
+     pname <- c(pname, out)
+     startIndex <- c(startIndex, these[1])
+     endIndex <- c(endIndex, these[2])
+   }
+   pnames <-
+   data.frame(pname,startIndex,endIndex,stringsAsFactors=FALSE)
+
+   these <- which(token$NER == "PERSON")
+   pnames <- pnames[which(pnames$endIndex %in% these),]
+   these <- these[-which(these %in% pnames$endIndex)]
+   newPnames <- data.frame(pname=token$word[these],
+                           startIndex=these,
+                           endIndex=these,
+                           stringsAsFactors=FALSE)
+   pnames <- rbind(pnames,newPnames)
+   pnames <- pnames[toupper(pnames$pname) != pnames$pname,]
+   length(unique(pnames$pname))
+
+   pnames$pname <- gsub("Mister", "Mr.", pnames$pname)
```

9.7 Case Study: Sherlock Holmes Main Characters

```
+   for (j in 1:nrow(pnames)) {
+     matchString <- gsub(" ", ".*", pnames$pname[j])
+     these <- grep(matchString,pnames$pname)
+     pnamesSet <- pnames$pname[these]
+     pnames$pname[j] <- pnamesSet[which.max(nchar(pnamesSet))]
+   }
+
+   index <- match(as.numeric(coref$endIndex), pnames$endIndex)
+   temp <- tapply(pnames$pname[index[!is.na(index)]],
+                  coref[!is.na(index),1],
+                  function(v) {names(rev(sort(table(v))))[1]} )
+   perMap <- data.frame(corefId=names(temp),perName=temp)
+
+   tab <- table(coref[,1])
+   index <- match(perMap$corefId, names(tab))
+   perMap$count <- tab[index]
+   charImport <- sort(tapply(perMap$count, perMap$perName,
+     sum),TRUE)
+   removeThese <- c(grep("Sherlock", names(charImport)),
+                    grep("Holmes", names(charImport)),
+                    grep("Watson", names(charImport)))
+   if (length(removeThese)) charImport <- charImport[-removeThese]
+   output <- c(output, names(charImport)[1])
+
+   crefIds <- perMap$corefId[perMap$perName == names(charImport)[1]]
+   places <- coref$startIndex[coref$corefId %in% crefIds]
+   outputGraphics[[iter]] <- places / nrow(token)
+   iter <- iter + 1
+ }
> output <- gsub(" ,", ",", output)
```

Which gives the following set of 56 characters.

```
> output
 [1] "Irene Adler"                 "Mr. Jabez Wilson"
 [3] "Mr. James Windibank"         "Mr. Charles McCarthy"
 [5] "Lee"                         "Mr. Neville St. Clair"
 [7] "James Ryder"                 "Dr. Grimesby Roylott"
 [9] "Mr. Victor Hatherley"        "Lord Robert St. Simon"
[11] "Miss Mary Holder"            "Mr. Rucastle"
[13] "Mr. John Straker"            "Effie"
[15] "Mr. Hall Pycroft"            "James Armitage"
[17] "Richard Brunton"             "Mr. Alec Cunningham"
[19] "Mrs. Barclay"                "Mr. Blessington"
[21] "Mr. Melas, Harold"           "Mr. Percy Phelps"
[23] "ex-Professor Moriarty"       "Colonel Sebastian Moran"
[25] "Mr. Jonas Oldacre"           "Mr. Abe Slaney"
[27] "Mr. Carruthers"              "Mr. James Wilder"
[29] "Inspector Stanley Hopkins"   "Charles Augustus Milverton"
[31] "Mr. Lestrade"                "Mr. Hilton Soames"
[33] "Stanley Hopkins"             "Mr. Godfrey Staunton"
[35] "Sir Eustace Brackenstall"    "Mr. Eduardo Lucas"
[37] "Miss Sarah"                  "Mr. John Scott Eccles"
[39] "Arthur Cadogan West"         "Mr. Mortimer Tregennis"
[41] "Mrs. Warren"                 "Lady Frances Carfax"
[43] "Inspector, Mr. Culverton Smith" "Mr. Von Bork"
```

```
[45] "Baron Adelbert Gruner"      "Mr. James M. Dodd"
[47] "Billy"                      "Douglas Maberley"
[49] "Mr. Robert Ferguson"        "Mr. Nathan Garrideb"
[51] "Mr. Neil Gibson"            "Mr. Trevor Bennett"
[53] "Mr. Ian Murdoch"            "Leonardo, Griggs"
[55] "Sir Robert Norberton"       "Mr. Josiah Amberley"
```

The results are encouraging and reveal an interesting list of characters (none of which are repeated). Pulling out any particular story tends to reveal a good match between our algorithm and a synopsis of the story. Take, for example, #23 and its introduction of the criminal mastermind Prof. Moriarty from "The Final Problem".

Other than just looking at this list of characters, there is substantial analysis that can also be done with our parsed data. The saved list outputGraphics contains the positions within each story that the given character is mentioned; these are normalized to a scale where position 0 is the first word in the story and position 1 is the last. The entire set of these can be visualized for a representation of when and how often the main character (other than Sherlock Holmes) is referenced in a story.

```
> plot(0,0,col="white",ylim=c(1,56),xlim=c(0,1),axes=FALSE)
> for (j in 1:length(outputGraphics)) {
+   points(outputGraphics[[j]],rep(57-j,length(outputGraphics[[j]])),
+          pch=19, cex=0.4)
+   abline(h=j)
+ }
> text(-.015,1:56,sprintf("%02d",56:1),cex=0.5)
> box()
```

The output is shown in Fig. 9.4. For instance, notice that Irene Adler has relatively few mentions in the first story compared to other characters in later installments. We see various ways of grouping stories based on the character mention patterns; for example, numbers 1–3, 8–10, 22–23, 30–32, and 44–50 all have this main character appearing at the very beginning of the text.

9.8 Other Languages

The Stanford CoreNLP has support for parsing text in languages other than English. Alternative models are currently provided by the Stanford group for Chinese [2], Spanish, German [18], Arabic [7], and French [8]. Other groups have helped to fill in even more languages such as Finnish [10] and Persian [22]. Most of these require an additional download of one or more ".jar" files, that should be downloaded and placed in the same directory where the Stanford CoreNLP files were downloaded. Not all annotators are available for every language, but the tokenizer, sentence splitter, part of speech tagger, and dependency parser are all available for the aforementioned languages. For more details on the ever-expanding set of models see the referenced papers and websites, as well as the documentation in the **coreNLP** package.

9.8 Other Languages

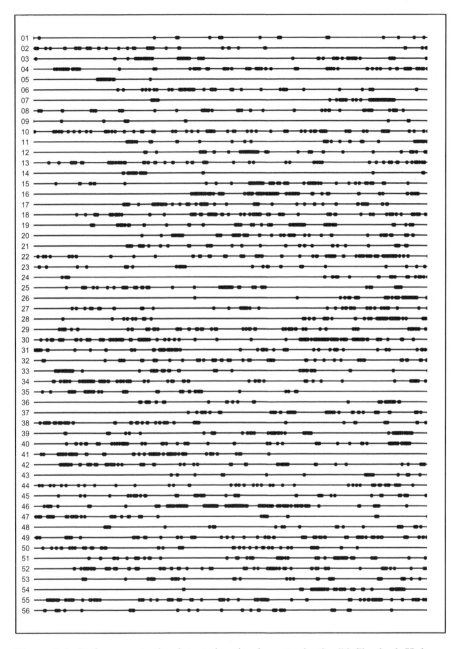

Figure 9.4: References to the detected main character in the 56 Sherlock Holmes short stories. Stories run horizontally, with the start of the text on the far *left* and the end of the text on the far *right*.

The tokenizer and sentence splitter for French (as well as German and Spanish) are included in the base installation of the CoreNLP library. To use the French variant in place of the default English version, a properties file needs to be written specifying the desired annotators and models. For example, we might save the following as "french.properties" as a minimal properties file for tokenizing and sentence splitting on French text:

```
annotators = tokenize, ssplit

tokenize.language = fr
```

With this file in place, we make a call to `initCoreNLP` with an additional `parameterFile` argument indicating the location of the java properties file previously constructed.

```
> initCoreNLP(libLoc="path/to/stanford-corenlp-full-2015-01-29",
+             parameterFile="path/to/french.properties")
```

The functions `annotateString` and `annotateFile` will now use rules based on French for tokenizing input text.

As an example, we have calculated annotations of the French version of Albert Camus's *l'Étranger* using both the default English tokenizer and a French tokenizer as previously described.

```
> getToken(annoEnglish)$token
  [1] "Aujourd"      "'"         "hui"       ","         "maman"
  [6] "est"          "morte"     "."         "Ou"        "peut-être"
 [11] "hier"         ","         "je"        "ne"        "sais"
 [16] "pas"          "."         "J'ai"      "reçu"      "un"
 [21] "télégramme"   "de"        "l'asile"   "."
> getToken(annoFrench)$tokens
  [1] "Aujourd'hui"  ","         "maman"     "est"
  [5] "morte"        "."         "Ou"        "peut-être"
  [9] "hier"         ","         "je"        "ne"
 [13] "sais"         "pas"       "."         "J'"
 [17] "ai"           "reçu"      "un"        "télégramme"
 [21] "de"           "l'"        "asile"     "."
```

Notice that the English version incorrectly separates Aujourd'hui into two tokens, despite it being a single lemma in modern French, but fails to split the contractions J'ai and l'asile into separate tokens. The French variant, however, correctly addresses both of these concerns.

9.9 Conclusions and Extensions

In this section we have quickly covered the majority of the NLP pipeline available from the Stanford CoreNLP library and the primary functions for accessing these from the **coreNLP**. The manuals available from the Stanford NLP website and referenced throughout this chapter provide additional information regarding options and alternative models for fitting various aspects of the pipeline. For example, models exist for extending to a host of other languages such as Chinese and Spanish. We did not touch on the underlying algorithms and theory for how each step in the pipeline is actually being handled. For this, the go-to reference is Jurafsky and Martin's *Speech & Language Processing*, the former being a core member of the group that produced the Stanford CoreNLP library [11]. The text is thorough and quite dense, but requires little in the way of prerequisites and is very accessible.

There are other open source NLP libraries that offer similar functionality to Stanford CoreNLP. Apache OpenNLP, for example, is available and also has a convenient set of wrapper functions available in the package **openNLP** [5]. It is often favored by businesses looking to tweak an existing pipeline and redistribute it due to the less-restrictive licensing of Apache software.

Practice

1. Construct a set of sentences and produce a dependency graph for each. Display all of the parts of speech referenced in the Penn TreeBank part of speech codes.

2. Write a 5–6 sentence paragraph describing, in the first person, one of your best friends. Run an annotation of the paragraph and inspect the coreference data frame. How well did it group all references to your friend to the same id? What minor changes to the text, without changing its meaning to a third party unfamiliar with your friend, might you think would decrease the accuracy of this grouping? Test your hypotheses and evaluate how well you were able to fool the annotator.

3. Using the dependency data frame for each of the 56 short stories, find the most frequently used verb and adjective (make sure to grab the lemmatized version) associated with each main character. Which dependency tags did you use and why for these two tasks?

4. From the named entity recognition tags, calculate the main location or locations where each story takes place. As we did with the character detection algorithm, start with "A Scandal in Bohemia" and work out a general algorithm before cycling over the other 55 texts.

References

[1] Albert Camus. *L'étranger*. Ernst Klett Sprachen, 2005.

[2] Pi-Chuan Chang, Huihsin Tseng, Dan Jurafsky, and Christopher D Manning. Discriminative reordering with chinese grammatical relations features. In *Proceedings of the Third Workshop on Syntax and Structure in Statistical Translation*, pages 51–59. Association for Computational Linguistics, 2009.

[3] Danqi Chen and Christopher D Manning. A fast and accurate dependency parser using neural networks. In *Proceedings of the 2014 Conference on Empirical Methods in Natural Language Processing (EMNLP)*, pages 740–750, 2014.

[4] Marie-Catherine De Marneffe and Christopher D Manning. Stanford typed dependencies manual. *URL http://nlp.stanford.edu/software/ dependencies_manual.pdf*, 2008.

[5] Ingo Feinerer and Kurt Hornik. tm: Text mining package. *R package version 0.5-5., URL http://CRAN.R-project.org/package=tm*, 2011.

[6] Jenny Rose Finkel, Trond Grenager, and Christopher Manning. Incorporating non-local information into information extraction systems by gibbs sampling. In *Proceedings of the 43rd Annual Meeting on Association for Computational Linguistics*, pages 363–370. Association for Computational Linguistics, 2005.

[7] Spence Green and Christopher D Manning. Better arabic parsing: Baselines, evaluations, and analysis. In *Proceedings of the 23rd International Conference on Computational Linguistics*, pages 394–402. Association for Computational Linguistics, 2010.

[8] Spence Green, Marie-Catherine de Marneffe, John Bauer, and Christopher D Manning. Multiword expression identification with tree substitution grammars: A parsing tour de force with french. In *Proceedings of the Conference on Empirical Methods in Natural Language Processing*, pages 725–735. Association for Computational Linguistics, 2011.

[9] Michael Hart. *Project gutenberg*. Project Gutenberg, 1971.

[10] Katri Haverinen, Jenna Nyblom, Timo Viljanen, Veronika Laippala, Samuel Kohonen, Anna Missilä, Stina Ojala, Tapio Salakoski, and Filip Ginter. Building the essential resources for finnish: the turku dependency treebank. *Language Resources and Evaluation*, 48(3): 493–531, 2014.

[11] Dan Jurafsky and James H Martin. *Speech & language processing*. Pearson Education India, 2000.

[12] David Kathman. The question of authorship. *Shakespeare: An Oxford Guide*, pages 620–632, 2003.

[13] Heeyoung Lee, Yves Peirsman, Angel Chang, Nathanael Chambers, Mihai Surdeanu, and Dan Jurafsky. Stanford's multi-pass sieve coreference resolution system at the conll-2011 shared task. In *Proceedings of the Fifteenth Conference on Computational Natural Language Learning: Shared Task*, pages 28–34. Association for Computational Linguistics, 2011.

References

[14] Christopher D Manning, Mihai Surdeanu, John Bauer, Jenny Finkel, Steven J Bethard, and David McClosky. The stanford corenlp natural language processing toolkit. In *Proceedings of 52nd Annual Meeting of the Association for Computational Linguistics: System Demonstrations*, pages 55–60, 2014.

[15] Jean-Baptiste Michel, Yuan Kui Shen, Aviva Presser Aiden, Adrian Veres, Matthew K Gray, Joseph P Pickett, Dale Hoiberg, Dan Clancy, Peter Norvig, Jon Orwant, Steven Pinker, Martin Nowak, and Erez Lieberman Aiden. Quantitative analysis of culture using millions of digitized books. *science*, 331(6014):176–182, 2011.

[16] Claire Cain Miller. Is the professor bossy or brilliant? much depends on gender. *The New York Times*, 2 2015.

[17] Slav Petrov, Dipanjan Das, and Ryan McDonald. A universal part-of-speech tagset. *arXiv preprint arXiv:1104.2086*, 2011.

[18] Anna N Rafferty and Christopher D Manning. Parsing three german treebanks: lexicalized and unlexicalized baselines. In *Proceedings of the Workshop on Parsing German*, pages 40–46. Association for Computational Linguistics, 2008.

[19] Beatrice Santorini. Part-of-speech tagging guidelines for the penn treebank project (3rd revision). 1990.

[20] Benjamin Schmidt. The foreign language of mad men. *The Atlantic*, 3 2012.

[21] Kathryn Schultz. What is distant reading? *The New York Times*, 6 2011.

[22] Mojgan Seraji, Joakim Nivre, et al. Bootstrapping a persian dependency treebank. *Linguistic Issues in Language Technology*, 7(1), 2012.

[23] HS Sichel. On a distribution representing sentence-length in written prose. *Journal of the Royal Statistical Society. Series A (General)*, pages 25–34, 1974.

[24] Kristina Toutanova, Dan Klein, Christopher D Manning, and Yoram Singer. Feature-rich part-of-speech tagging with a cyclic dependency network. In *Proceedings of the 2003 Conference of the North American Chapter of the Association for Computational Linguistics on Human Language Technology-Volume 1*, pages 173–180. Association for Computational Linguistics, 2003.

[25] Michael Wood. *In search of Shakespeare*. Random House, 2005.

Chapter 10
Text Analysis

Abstract In this chapter, several methods for extracting meaning from a collection of parsed textual documents are presented. Examples include information retrieval, topic modeling, and stylometrics. Particular focus is placed on how to use these methods for constructing visualizations of textual corpora and a high-level categorization of some narrative trends.

10.1 Introduction

In the previous chapter we explored methods for converting raw textual data into a sequence of tokens and associating these tokens with various metadata and relationships. The parsed information has already been shown to be effective in the retrieval of factual information (e.g., character names) and a high-level categorization of some narrative trends. We continue with this approach by presenting several techniques for utilizing the output of NLP annotations to explore and visualize a corpus of textual documents.

10.2 Term Frequency: Inverse Document Frequency

A basic task in the field of information retrieval consists of determining the relative importance of each uniquely observed lemma to the context of a given document. Typically, the assessment of importance is done relative to a larger corpus of interest. For example, in a collection of biographical entries, the term "Senator" may be of high importance as one of the primary terms indicating the career of a given individual; it will likely be used frequently in a small set of biographies and very sparingly in the remaining set. However, in a collection of domestic political blogs, the term "Senator" will be used frequently throughout the corpus and (in isolation) offers relatively little important information by which to uniquely categorize a particular blog post. In other words, tf-idf helps us find the lemmas that best uniquely characterize a document.

Determining the relative importance of a lemma to a given document has two distinct use cases. Looking at the most important lemmas to a given document provides an automated way of summarizing the contents of the given document. This can be used for tasks such as document clustering and automated title generation. On the other hand, looking at the documents for which a given lemma is most important provides a simple method for text retrieval and is the basis for many web search engines.

In this section, we present the numerical statistics known as the *term frequency-inverse document frequency* (often shortened to tf-idf) associated with any document and lemma pair from a given text corpus. In order to demonstrate the use of this statistic, we will investigate a collection of 179 Wikipedia articles from pages tagged as coming from philosophers from the sixteenth to the twentieth centuries. Because annotating the corpus takes several hours, we have saved the **coreNLP** annotation objects as serialized R data objects for quick recall.

```
> wikiFiles <- dir("data/ch10/wiki_annotations/", full.names=TRUE)
> wikiNames <- gsub("\\.Rds", "", basename(wikiFiles))
```

With these annotations provided, the first step in determining lemma importance is to pass through the entire corpus of data and construct a table of all the unique lemmas. As the most important meanings, for us, will come from (non-proper) nouns, we tabulate only those lemmas that have Penn TreeBank part of speech codes **NN** and **NNS**. Most of the very common terms, such as pronouns and conjunctions, would be automatically filtered by the tf-idf algorithm, but filtering by part of speech helps to focus the analysis and avoid mostly uninteresting adjectives and verbs from cluttering the results.

```
> lemmas <- c()
> for (f in wikiFiles) {
+   anno <- readRDS(f)
+   token <- getToken(anno)
+   theseLemma <- token$lemma[token$POS %in% c("NNS","NN")]
+   lemmas <- append(lemmas, theseLemma)
+ }
```

Looking at the 50 most frequently occurring lemmas from the encyclopedia entries of our philosophers reveals an unsurprising list. Terms such as "philosophy", "government", "principle", and "theory" appear a high number of times. In the interest of space, we will limit our analysis to these 50 lemmas.

```
> lemmas <- names(sort(table(lemmas),decreasing=TRUE)[1:50])
> lemmas
 [1] "work"       "philosophy" "time"       "year"
 [5] "theory"     "life"       "book"       "idea"
 [9] "world"      "man"        "society"    "state"
[13] "philosopher" "law"       "view"       "people"
[17] "history"    "way"        "part"       "science"
[21] "form"       "death"      "thought"    "study"
[25] "concept"    "child"      "language"   "religion"
```

10.2 Term Frequency: Inverse Document Frequency

```
[29] "nature"      "family"     "power"       "government"
[33] "example"     "system"     "term"        "thing"
[37] "influence"   "essay"      "experience"  "order"
[41] "father"      "principle"  "interest"    "position"
[45] "object"      "friend"     "other"       "student"
[49] "fact"        "war"
```

We now need to construct a *term frequency* matrix from these 50 terms. Each document is associated with a single row of the matrix whereas each lemma is associated with a column of matrix. The entries of the matrix give the number of times each document (row) used each lemma (column). We construct an empty matrix to hold these results.[1]

```
> tf <- matrix(0,nrow=length(wikiFiles),ncol=length(lemmas))
> colnames(tf) <- lemmas
> rownames(tf) <- substr(wikiNames,nchar(wikiNames)-10,
+                         nchar(wikiNames))
```

The documents are cycled over and the counts are filled into the term frequency matrix.

```
> for (j in 1:length(wikiFiles)) {
+   anno <- readRDS(wikiFiles[j])
+   token <- getToken(anno)
+   theseLemma <- token$lemma[token$POS %in% c("NNS","NN")]
+   theseLemma <- theseLemma[theseLemma %in% lemmas]
+   tab <- table(theseLemma)
+   index <- match(lemmas,names(tab))
+   tf[j,!is.na(index)] <- tab[index[!is.na(index)]]
+ }
```

The output reveals, for example, that Machiavelli's page has 29 lemmas equal to "work", whereas Francis Bacon does not have a single reference to the lemma "child".

```
> tf[1:10,seq(1,45,by=5)]
             work life society people form child power thing father
Acyutananda     1    2       0      3    3     1     1     1      2
rdano_Bruno    16    5       0      0    0     1     3     4      0
_Jean_Bodin    27    6       2      4    8     0     8     2      0
Machiavelli    29    8       4      9    4     2    10     6      3
rnon_Sidney     2    2       0      1    1     0     2     1      5
uch_Spinoza    14   12       1      5    0     3     2     8      9
aise_Pascal    19    5       1      2    3     6     1     1     10
_Palatinate     2    4       0      9    0     4     0     0      3
ancis_Bacon     7    5       2      1    1     0     1     1      5
elm_Leibniz    18   11       3      4    6     1     5     2      9
```

A table of the most used terms by document shows the number of documents that reference each word.

---

[1] For the row names of the matrix `tf`, we have used the last ten characters of the Wikipedia filename in order to make the output print better in the width of this book. On your own machine, you may wish to use the entire filename.

```
> sort(table(lemmas[apply(tf,1,which.max)]),decreasing=TRUE)[1:18]
        work philosophy       theory         year         book         life
          45          28           15            9            8            7
     society  government     language        state        child          law
           7           5            5            5            4            4
        time       world          man          war        death         form
           4           4            3            3            2            2
```

Accordingly, a large number of documents have the most references to "work", "philosophy", and "theory". The latter category may be marginally helpful by indicating those philosophers most theory-oriented. Smaller categories such as "child" and "law" give even more contextual information regarding each document, but for the most part these raw counts are of limited use on their own as they fail to account for the relative frequency of each lemma in the corpus as a whole.

To assess how common a lemma is in an entire corpus, we calculate a count of the number of documents that contain the lemma. Note that this is not the number of times the lemma is used in the corpus; it is just the number of documents containing the lemma. It does not distinguish between a document using the lemma 1 or 100 times. Unsurprisingly though, the highest document counts roughly correspond to those lemmas that had the highest counts in the term frequency matrix.

```
> dc <- apply(tf!=0,2,sum)
> sort(dc,decreasing=TRUE)[1:20]
       work         time         year   philosophy         book
        178          175          175          169          169
       life    philosopher       idea         view         part
        167          164          162          161          161
     theory        world        study         form          way
        159          158          156          153          152
     family          man        other      history        death
        149          148          148          147          146
```

Because we want to simultaneously work with the term frequency and document counts, it will be helpful to have these quantities in R objects of the same dimensions. At the moment, dc is only a vector so we use the rep function to construct a larger matrix where every row is the same. We also want to convert raw counts into a *document frequency* matrix, so the matrix elements are also divided by the total number of documents.

```
> df <- matrix(rep(dc,length(wikiFiles)),ncol=length(lemmas),
+               byrow=TRUE)
> head(df[,1:10])
     [,1] [,2] [,3] [,4] [,5] [,6] [,7] [,8] [,9] [,10]
[1,]  178  169  175  175  159  167  169  162  158   148
[2,]  178  169  175  175  159  167  169  162  158   148
[3,]  178  169  175  175  159  167  169  162  158   148
[4,]  178  169  175  175  159  167  169  162  158   148
[5,]  178  169  175  175  159  167  169  162  158   148
[6,]  178  169  175  175  159  167  169  162  158   148
> df = df / length(wikiFiles)
```

10.2 Term Frequency: Inverse Document Frequency

In order to calculate a matrix of lemma importance scores, the term frequency and inverse of the document frequency scores are multiplied together. Often some weighting scheme is also used to help balance the effects of the term and document effects. Here we use a logarithm to transform the document frequency term; this helps to eliminate the appearance of rare words in the output.

```
> impScore <- tf * log(1 / df)
```

Now that we have our importance score, let us look at the first ten philosophers.[2]

```
> impScore[1:10,seq(1,45,by=5)]
              work  life society people  form child power thing father
Acyutananda  0.006 0.139   0.000  0.824 0.471 0.359 0.343 0.297  0.549
rdano_Bruno  0.090 0.347   0.000  0.000 0.000 0.359 1.030 1.188  0.000
_Jean_Bodin  0.151 0.416   0.609  1.099 1.256 0.000 2.746 0.594  0.000
Machiavelli  0.162 0.555   1.218  2.473 0.628 0.718 3.432 1.782  0.824
rnon_Sidney  0.011 0.139   0.000  0.275 0.157 0.000 0.686 0.297  1.374
uch_Spinoza  0.078 0.833   0.305  1.374 0.000 1.077 0.686 2.376  2.473
aise_Pascal  0.106 0.347   0.305  0.549 0.471 2.154 0.343 0.297  2.747
_Palatinate  0.011 0.278   0.000  2.473 0.000 1.436 0.000 0.000  0.824
ancis_Bacon  0.039 0.347   0.609  0.275 0.157 0.000 0.343 0.297  1.374
elm_Leibniz  0.101 0.763   0.914  1.099 0.942 0.359 1.716 0.594  2.473
```

For example, Machiavelli's page has an importance score of 3.432 for "power" but only a score 0.162 for "work", despite the fact that there are almost three times as many references to the "work" lemma. We can see further the effect of tf-idf by looking at the importance scores compared to the raw term frequency counts in our previous table. The two tables further highlight that some very common terms (within the corpus) have decreased in favor of less commonly used terms.

With these importance scores now calculated, we can look at the lemmas with the highest score for each article. A sample from a few prominent pages shows that the tf-idf method has successfully picked up reasonable lemmas to represent some of the major article themes.

```
> sort(impScore["Machiavelli",],decreasing=TRUE)[1:6]
government       power  influence     example   religion      people
     4.984       3.432      3.185       2.949      2.707       2.473
> sort(impScore["oam_Chomsky",],decreasing=TRUE)[1:6]
 language       child    science     society   interest  government
   15.440       3.591      2.514       2.132      1.872       1.869
> sort(impScore["ohn_Paul_II",],decreasing=TRUE)[1:6]
   people       death        war    religion government         man
    7.692       6.725      5.528       4.963      4.361       3.803
> sort(impScore["Jean_Piaget",],decreasing=TRUE)[1:6]
    child      object    concept      theory    thought     example
   47.398      16.860      5.078       3.673      3.473       2.703
```

The entry for Machiavelli reveals lemmas commonly associated with his work: "government", "power", and "influence". Noam Chomsky's work as a linguist

---
[2] We have rounded to three decimal points for readability.

and Jean Piaget's as a developmental psychologist are both highlighted in the selected lemmas. John Paul II is characterized by the events he was involved in (war & government), his area of work (religion), and his death. The reason for the high score for the lemma "people" is slightly less obvious; looking at the original text, this lemma has a high occurrence count due to phrases such as "Polish people" and "200 thousand people attended".

10.3 Topic Models

We have now identified those lemmas within each Wikipedia article that are of particular importance for distinguishing a given document from the bulk of the other articles. The resulting lemmas typically correspond to the topics most closely related to each philosopher's work or life. For example, consider the lemmas "language", "grammar", and "syntax", all of which fall under a broader topic of linguistics. Topics also tend to co-exist in multiple documents. Noam Chomsky, John Searle, and Hilary Putnam may all have articles that fall within a single linguistics category.

A statistical representation of topics within a textual corpus of documents is referred to as *topic models*. Typically, each *topic* is represented by a set of related lemmas; these are often accompanied by weights to indicate the relative prominence of each lemma within a topic. Each document, in turn, is proportionally assigned to each topic. For example, the article about Noam Chomsky may be 90 % in the linguistics category and 10 % in a psychology topic, whereas Hilary Putnam might be split evenly between the linguistics and mathematics topics.

Before discussing the specifics of applying topic models to our corpus of philosopher biographies, it is helpful to roughly sort our collection by the year of birth of each philosopher. Given the named entity recognition algorithm discussed in Sect. 9.5 and that each article mentions the date of birth in the opening sentence, this is a rather manageable task. Cycling through the documents, extracting the first recognized date, and pulling out the year yields a vector `dateSet` of birth years for the corpus.

```
> dateSet <- rep(0L,length(wikiFiles))
> for (j in 1:length(wikiFiles)) {
+   anno <- readRDS(wikiFiles[j])
+   tx <- getToken(anno)$Timex
+   tx <- substr(tx[!is.na(tx)],1,4)
+   tx <- as.numeric(tx)
+   tx <- tx[!is.na(tx)]
+   dateSet[j] <- tx[1]
+ }
```

The set of years can be ordered, and the list of files and names permuted based on them.

```
> wikiFiles <- wikiFiles[order(dateSet)]
> wikiNames <- wikiNames[order(dateSet)]
```

10.3 Topic Models

The result is that our collection is now sorted from oldest to newest philosophers. Clearly this is only a rough proxy for historicizing the data, as the years in which a given person was active in the field may not exactly correspond to their birthdate. However, it does a decent job of sorting the nearly four centuries of philosophers into approximate time buckets.

The majority of topic models assumes that documents are generated according to a *bag of words* model. Here, documents are considered as being simply a collection of words without any additional elements such as word order or grammar. This is the same model we used when building the term frequency matrix in Sect. 10.2. It may seem that the simplicity of this model makes the complex parsing developed in Chap. 9 unnecessary; only the tokenization step seems relevant. However, by using the tags developed by the NLP pipeline, we can selectively decide which lemmas to include in the bag of words. As we did in the term frequency matrix, the bag of words used in our topic model will consist only of lemmas identified as non-proper nouns (Penn TreeBank codes **NNS** and **NN**).

```
> bagOfWords <- rep("",length(wikiFiles))
> for (j in 1:length(wikiFiles)) {
+   anno <- readRDS(wikiFiles[j])
+   token <- getToken(anno)
+   theseLemma <- token$lemma[token$POS %in% c("NNS","NN")]
+   bagOfWords[j] <- paste(theseLemma,collapse=" ")
+ }
```

Topic models are very sensitive to common words such as pronouns, conjunctions, and auxiliary verbs (e.g., be, can have). As we have constructed an entire annotation of our text and conducted part of speech filtering, this will not be an issue in our application. A cruder method for avoiding this without part of speech filtering uses a predefined list of *stop words*, which are automatically filtered out of the topic modeling algorithm. For an example of such a list, see the set of English language stop words built into the open source database software MySql.[3] We mention stop words here, because the R package we are using to fit topic models requires a list of stop words. We construct a temporary file and fill it with the upper and lower case Latin alphabet; every line contains a unique character.

```
> tf <- tempfile()
> writeLines(c(letters,LETTERS),tf)
```

Our make-shift stop word list will help remove a few mis-parsed initials which were incorrectly labeled as non-proper nouns. The temporary file will exist only while the R session is running and will be automatically deleted afterward.

With our list of documents sorted by time, bag of words vector filled, and a temporary file of stop words built, we can now proceed to actually fitting a topic model to our corpus of Wikipedia articles. The model we will use is latent Dirichlet

---
[3]http://dev.mysql.com/doc/refman/5.5/en/fulltext-stopwords.html.

allocation (LDA); the R package used to fit this model is called **mallet** (a wrapper around a Java library by the same name).[4]

To fit a topic model with the **mallet** package, both a mallet instance object and an LDA topic model object must be created [5]. Notice that the LDA object requires prespecifying the number of desired topics; this is a particular feature of the LDA algorithm. Also note that we do not need to construct a term frequency matrix by hand as this step is handled automatically by the R package.

```
> library(mallet)
> instance <- mallet.import(id.array=wikiNames,
+                           text.array=bagOfWords, stoplist.file=tf)
> tm <- MalletLDA(num.topics=9)
Apr 08, 2015 8:20:55 PM cc.mallet.topics.ParallelTopicModel <init>
INFO: Coded LDA: 9 topics, 4 topic bits, 1111 topic mask
```

With these two objects in existence, the instance must then be loaded into the object tm. From here, various tuning parameters may be set (here we use alpha optimization) and the model itself trained and maximized.

```
> tm$loadDocuments(instance)
> tm$setAlphaOptimization(30,50)
> tm$train(200)
> tm$maximize(10)
```

The number of options and their uses when applying a topic model to a corpus of text using the **mallet** package is quite extensive. The original documentation should be consulted for more specific details; the options shown in the code snippet above should be a good starting point for a reasonable size corpus of text.

With the topic model fit to the corpus of data, we now extract three separate result objects: a matrix of topics, a matrix of words, and a vector of the topic vocabulary.

```
> topics <- mallet.doc.topics(tm, smoothed=TRUE, normalized=TRUE)
> words <- mallet.topic.words(tm, smoothed=TRUE, normalized=TRUE)
> vocab <- tm$getVocabulary()
```

We have chosen to receive smoothed and normalized versions of the data. Smoothing is typically preferred for most applications as it helps to eliminate extreme or noisy values from words with low counts. Normalization turns the topic values into percentages; adding together the normalized topic values for every document will always equal 1. We recommend normalized counts for exploratory data analysis tasks such as ours. Un-normalized counts, which give the raw number of word frequencies, may be useful for predictive modeling tasks. Looking at the dimensions of these objects gives a clue as to the exact information contained in the output.

---

[4]The precise mathematic formulation of LDA is fairly involved and we will not give a full specification here. For a more detailed description, see the original LDA paper [1].

10.3 Topic Models

```
> dim(topics)
[1] 179   9
> dim(words)
[1]     9 12123
> length(vocab)
[1] 12123
```

The matrix `topics` contains a row for each document and column for the nine topics. The entries give the topic distribution for each document as a percentage; each row sums to exactly 1. The matrix `words` contains a column for each unique lemma in the bag of words model and the nine rows to each topic. The entries correspond to the probability of a randomly selected lemma from a given topic being equal to the corresponding word; again, all of the rows sum to 1. Finally, the vector `vocab` is a character vector indicating the lemmas which correspond to the columns in the matrix `words`.

With these results in hand, a natural first step is to look at the top few words within each of the nine topics. The top five words in each topic can be displayed by ordering the elements of the matrix `words` over each row.[5]

```
> t(apply(words,1,function(v) vocab[order(v,decreasing=TRUE)[1:5]]))
     [,1]         [,2]          [,3]        [,4]       [,5]
[1,] "government" "time"        "man"       "nation"   "law"
[2,] "year"       "life"        "time"      "death"    "family"
[3,] "society"    "state"       "power"     "idea"     "class"
[4,] "world"      "life"        "man"       "idea"     "self"
[5,] "work"       "philosophy"  "book"      "theory"   "philosopher"
[6,] "theory"     "mathematics" "logic"     "set"      "number"
[7,] "culture"    "poem"        "poet"      "critic"   "writer"
[8,] "man"        "race"        "time"      "religion" "life"
[9,] "object"     "meaning"     "language"  "word"     "world"
```

The interpretation of the output from an LDA model is left to the user and this is where familiarity with your corpus is key. Some of the categories here seem fairly easy to understand in terms of broad interpretable categories. The sixth topic applies to any of the philosophers working in mathematics where the sub-fields of logic and set theory are prevalent, while the first topic appears to capture political philosophy and politics. In the second topic, generic terms of a biographical nature are presented, and the third topic is a collection of terms relating to the social sciences (sociology, mostly). It will be helpful to construct a labeling of these topics for use in visualizations. One approach is to paste together the top three to five words in each topic. We will instead hand-construct the labels as follows:

```
> topicNames <- c("politics","biography","social-science",
+                 "existentialism","philosophy","logic",
+                 "poetry","culture","language")
```

---

[5] Note that the output of each topic model will be slightly different, even if using the same text and parameters. The supplementary materials has a copy of the object tm, which exactly replicates the results in this text.

It is important to keep in mind that these were determined by hand and should not be considered a definitive description of the topics.

One way to visualize the structure of the topics constructed in a LDA algorithm is to graphically represent the matrix `words`. As this matrix has a large number of columns, it is best to consider a subset of these. We will pick out the top 50 most prevalent lemmas in the bag of words model.

```
> index <- order(apply(words,2,max),decreasing=TRUE)[1:50]
> set <- unique(as.character(apply(words,1,function(v)
+                 vocab[order(v,decreasing=TRUE)[1:5]])))
> index <- match(set,vocab)
> mat <- round(t(words[,index]),3)
> mat <- mat / max(mat)
```

The resulting matrix can be visualized by using circle of various sizes to represent the probability of the word in a document from one of the nine topics. We will be looking at the probability of the top-50 words in each topic.

```
> plot(0,0,col="white",ylim=c(-1,nrow(mat)),xlim=c(-2,ncol(mat)))
> for(i in 1:nrow(mat)) lines(x=c(1,ncol(mat)),y=c(i,i))
> for(i in 1:ncol(mat)) lines(x=c(i,i),y=c(1,nrow(mat)))
> points(col(mat), nrow(mat) - row(mat) + 1, pch=19,cex=mat*3,
+        col=rainbow(ncol(mat),alpha=0.33)[col(mat)])
> text(0.5, nrow(mat):1, vocab[index], adj=c(1,0.5),cex=0.7)
> text(1:ncol(mat), -0.75, topicNames, adj=c(0.5,0),cex=0.7,srt=60)
```

The result is shown in Fig. 10.1. Notice that most of the top words are concentrated in only a single topic. Some of the more common terms such as "idea" and "estate" are spread across multiple topics. Interestingly, there does not seem to be two topics that share a large number of lemmas; this indicates that the LDA algorithm did a decent job of finding distinct topics within the text corpus.

A similar diagram can be constructed for the matrix `topics` to visualize the topic distribution across the corpus.[6] The resulting plot is shown in Fig. 10.2.

```
> mat = topics / max(topics)
> plot(0,0,col="white",ylim=c(-1,nrow(mat)),xlim=c(-2,ncol(mat)))
> for(i in 1:nrow(mat)) lines(x=c(1,ncol(mat)),y=c(i,i))
> for(i in 1:ncol(mat)) lines(x=c(i,i),y=c(1,nrow(mat)))
> points(col(mat), nrow(mat) - row(mat) + 1, pch=19,cex=mat*3,
+        col=rainbow(ncol(mat),alpha=0.33)[col(mat)])
> text(0.5, nrow(mat):1, vocab[index], adj=c(1,0.5),cex=0.7)
> text(1:ncol(mat), -0.75, topicNames, adj=c(0.5,0),cex=0.7,srt=60)
```

In contrast to the distribution of words over topics, the distribution of topics over documents is not nearly as parsimonious. Nearly every document has a noticeable distribution over at least two topics; some have as many as five detectable topics. Many of the distributions confirm our prior knowledge of the corpus—the classifi-

---

[6] The code snippet here will produce a single plot with all of the documents in one column. Running it selectively over rows of the matrix mat (i.e., 1:60, 61:120, and 121:179) was used to produce the actual figure shown in the text.

cation of the poet Fondane in the poetry topic, Mao into the biography and politics topics, and John Searle into linguistics. In contrast, the grouping of the nineteenth century biologist Ernst Haeckel, Italian philosopher Julius Evola, and Romanian historian Mircea Eliade into the topic "culture" may not have been easily picked out based on prior knowledge. Reading their pages after the fact shows many interesting similarities between these men. It is these latent connections that are often an exciting new area of scholarly inquiry.

As a result of sorting the documents by time, we also see that the distribution of topics slowly changes over time. This phenomenon, known as *topic drift*, is well known to occur in many corpora [3, 8]. For example, the "politics" topic is prominent in the few dozen articles but drops off significantly over the remainder of the corpus. Why this shift? The drop off of this category may represent a changing focus away from political philosophy in the nineteenth and twentieth centuries. It may also have been caused by the rise of a separate field of political science in the late nineteenth century. These are all just speculation but importantly show some forms of inquiry made possible by topic modeling.

Another method for visualizing the output of a topic model is by conducting dimensionality reduction on the matrix `topics`. Taking the first three principal components of the matrix (as covered in Sect. 8.4) allows up to explore the distribution of the corpus over all of the topics.

```
> pc <- prcomp(topics,scale.=TRUE)
> docsSC <- scale(topics,center=pc$center,scale=pc$scale)
> topicSC <-
    scale(diag(ncol(topics)),center=pc$center,scale=pc$scale)
> docsPC <- docsSC %*% pc$rotation
> topicPC <- topicSC %*% pc$rotation
```

Notice that we also manually determined the location of documents that are entirely contained in each of the nine topics. The location of these are stored in the matrix `topicPC` and shown together with the actual documents in Fig. 10.3. A selected set of documents are labeled with the corresponding philosopher's names. For example, Kierkegaard is shown as being in-between existentialism and generic philosophy, whereas Gödel is pulled toward the logic topic. The figure is useful for understanding the correlation structure of the topic themselves. The mathematical fields of logic and language are close in all three principal components; a similar relationship holds between social science and politics.

10.4 Stylometric Analysis

Term frequency matrices and topic models seek to systematically represent the content of textual documents. *Stylometry* compliments these approaches by characterizing writing style. It is often employed to study persistent patterns in a particular author's writing over time and, for example, plays a major role in authorship detection. Stylometrics may also study more localized elements of style pertaining to a particular work.

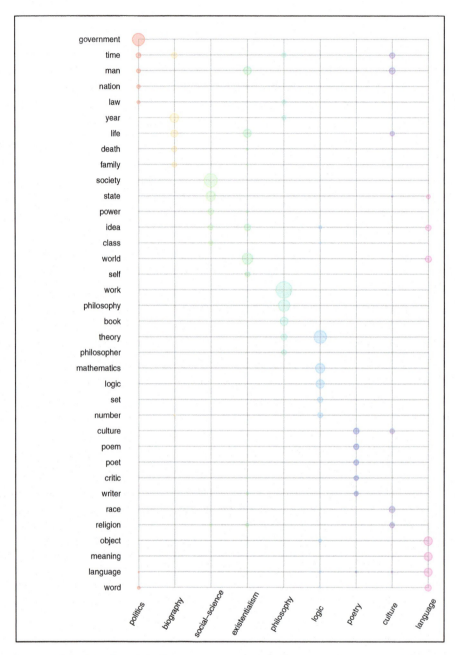

Figure 10.1: Distribution of lemma frequencies within topics learned via LDA on the Wikipedia corpus of philosophers from the sixteenth to the twentieth centuries.

10.4 Stylometric Analysis

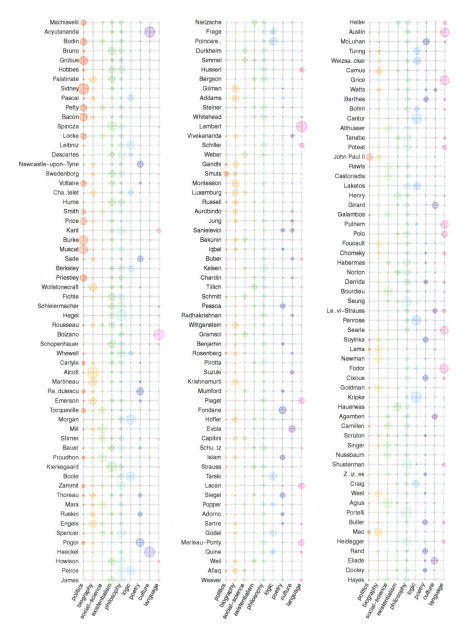

Figure 10.2: Distribution of topics within documents learned via LDA on the Wikipedia corpus of philosophers from the sixteenth to the twentieth centuries.

Topic modeling has as a small set of canonical methods (PLSI, LSA, LDA), by which most analyses start, all of which generally employ a bag of words model of text. There is no corresponding feature set for stylometric analysis; a large set of features and methods employed depend on the application and goals of the analysis. We will explore two examples of stylometric feature sets (part of speech bigrams and function words), both by way of a *principal component analysis* that was covered in Sect. 8.4. The first example uses document-level characteristics and the second uses block-wise characteristics.

The Wikipedia corpus we used for topic modeling does not make a good corpus for stylometric analysis as the tone is intentionally uniform and the number of authors (and their exact contribution) is hard to discern. We instead use a collection of 26 novels from Project Gutenberg from 4 authors: Mark Twain, Charles Dickens, Nathaniel Hawthorne, and Sir Arthur Conan Doyle. As before, we have pre-annotated these documents in this corpus using the **coreNLP** package in order to speed up the process of analyzing the documents.

The distribution of parts of speech, such as what proportion of words are verbs, is a well-known stylistic feature. On its own, however, the part of speech distribution is not typically variant enough across authors to differentiate style. A solution to this is to look at subsequent pairs of parts of speech; for example, how often verbs immediately follow nouns. Known as part of speech *bigrams*, these features often have far more fluctuation between various writers.[7] In order to explore bigrams, a set of speech tags must be applied. One could use the raw Penn TreeBank part of speech codes, though this results in a total set of about $40^2 = 1600$ possible bigrams (many of which are fairly rare). We instead use the universal tag-set mappings covered in Sect. 9.3 to reduce the number of part of speech pairs to $12^2 = 144$.

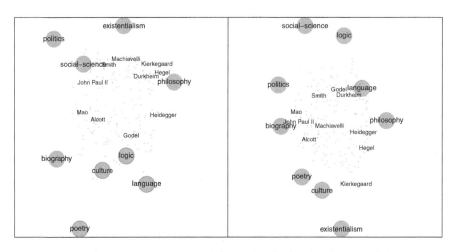

Figure 10.3: Principal components of the topic distribution in the Wikipedia corpus of philosophers from the sixteenth to the twentieth centuries. The larger topic data points correspond to the theoretical location of a document which was entirely contained in one topic.

---

[7] Generally, the term *bigram* can refer to a sequence of any two object types such as words, letters, or morpheme. More generally, the term N-gram refers to a sequence of N objects.

10.4 Stylometric Analysis

The first step in applying part of speech bigrams to the Gutenberg corpus involves constructing a 26 by 144 matrix of counts, with one row per text and one column per part of speech pair. We use the `expand.grid` function to conveniently construct all combinations of the 12 parts of speech in the universal tag-set.

```
> gutenFiles = c("pg76.Rds", "pg74.Rds", "pg1837.Rds", "pg102.Rds",
+   "pg7193.Rds", "pg98.Rds", "pg1400.Rds", "pg730.Rds",
+   "pg766.Rds", "pg883.Rds", "pg19337.Rds", "pg653.Rds",
+   "pg33.Rds", "pg13707.Rds", "pg77.Rds", "pg2081.Rds",
+   "pg976.Rds", "pg9255.Rds", "pg513.Rds", "pg2852.Rds",
+   "pg244.Rds", "pg2097.Rds", "pg3289.Rds", "pg139.Rds",
+   "pg126.Rds", "pg7964.Rds")
> gutenFiles = paste0("../data/ch10/gutenbergClean_annotations/",
+   gutenFiles)
> gutenNames = c(rep("Mark Twain",5),rep("Charles Dickens",7),
+       rep("Nathaniel Hawthorne",7),rep("Sir Arthur Conan Doyle",7))
> cols = c(rep("#DB9D85",5),rep("#86B875",7),
+           rep("#4CB9CC",7), rep("#CD99D8",7))
```

We now loop over the corpus of documents extracting the counts of the part of speech bigrams and saving the counts in the matrix `pos2gram`.[8]

```
> for (j in 1:length(gutenFiles)) {
+   anno <- readRDS(gutenFiles[j])
+   ut <- universalTagset(getToken(anno)$POS)
+   ut <- paste(ut[-length(ut)],ut[-1],sep="-")
+   tab <- table(ut)
+   index <- match(colnames(pos2gram),names(tab))
+   count <- tab[index[!is.na(index)]]
+   total <- sum(tab[index[!is.na(index)]])
+   pos2gram[j,!is.na(index)] <- count / total
+ }
```

The resulting matrix can be decomposed into its principal components in order to visualize the resulting data in a small number of dimensions.

```
> pc <- prcomp(pos2gram)
> pos2gramPC <- scale(pos2gram, center=pc$center, scale=pc$scale)
+               %*% pc$rotation
> centroid <- apply(pos2gramPC,2,
+                   function(v) tapply(v, gutenNames, mean))
```

The author centroids are also calculated in order to plot the author's names on the resulting visualization. A scatter plot of the results are shown in Fig. 10.4. The first three principal components do a very good job of separating the four authors. In fact, the first component separates Nathaniel Hawthorne from the others, the second separates Sir Arthur Conan Doyle, and the third separates Mark Twain from Charles Dickens.

While it is often difficult to determine a lot of interpretable information from principal components, it still sometimes reveals interesting information. In our case, notice, for example, the prominence of bigrams involving punctuation.

---

[8] We normalize these counts by the total number of bigrams in order to not inflate the counts in the longer texts.

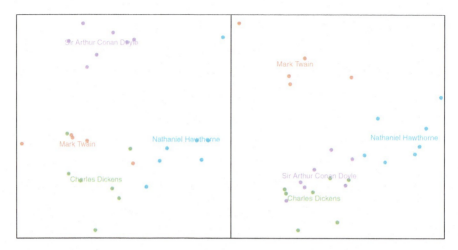

Figure 10.4: Scatter plot of the principal components from an analysis of part of speech bigrams from 26 novels from 4 different authors. The first three principal components are plotted.

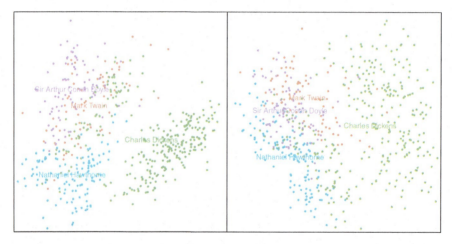

Figure 10.5: Scatter plot of the principal components from an analysis of the top 50 lemmas from 26 novels from 4 different authors. The first three principal components are plotted against 5000 word blocks of text.

```
> pc$rotation <- round(pc$rotation,3)
> head(pc$rotation[,1][order(abs(pc$rotation[,1]),decreasing=TRUE)])
PRON-VERB   ADJ-NOUN          .-.    ADP-DET   NOUN-ADP    DET-ADJ
   -0.529      0.404       -0.293      0.282      0.266      0.231
> head(pc$rotation[,2][order(abs(pc$rotation[,2]),decreasing=TRUE)])
   NOUN-.     .-CONJ    PRON-VERB     .-VERB   NOUN-ADP    ADP-DET
   -0.425     -0.324        0.289     -0.278      0.273      0.260
```

10.4 Stylometric Analysis

```
> head(pc$rotation[,3][order(abs(pc$rotation[,3]),decreasing=TRUE)])
      .-.    .-VERB ADP-PRON NOUN-VERB    NOUN-.  CONJ-VERB
   -0.610    -0.329   -0.252     0.243    -0.240      0.216
```

The double punctuation bigram, ".-.", may for instance occur when a quotation mark ends a sentence. It is not surprising that this would distinguish between authors writing various works of fiction.

It is also possible to build stylometric features by looking at the actual words, rather than parts of speech, used within a corpus. However, unlike with topic modeling, we will use raw counts of the most common lemmas (such as conjunctions, punctuation, and pronouns). There is evidence that the frequency of these is fairly consistent across mediums and over time for a given author [7].

Rather than studying the 26 texts individually, we split each text into 5000 word-blocks.[9] To start, we fill a matrix of lemmas with 5000 rows and a column for each block by cycling over the corpus of texts.

```
> lemma <- auth <- NULL
> for (j in 1:length(gutenFiles)) {
+   anno <- readRDS(gutenFiles[j])
+   temp <- getToken(anno)$token
+   temp <- matrix(temp,nrow=5000)
+   temp <- temp[,-ncol(temp),drop=FALSE]
+   lemma <- cbind(lemma, temp)
+   auth <- c(auth, rep(gutenNames[j],ncol(temp)))
+ }
```

We then determine the top 50 lemmas from this entire set, which will make up the final feature set.

```
> lemmaSet <- names(sort(table(lemma),decreasing=TRUE))[1:50]
> lemmaSet
 [1] ","      "the"    "."      "be"     "and"    "he"     "of"     "a"
 [9] "I"      "to"     "in"     "have"   "it"     "that"   "you"    "'"
[17] "she"    "''"     "``"     "with"   "not"    "\""     "as"     "they"
[25] ";"      "say"    "for"    "my"     "!"      "at"     "we"     "--"
[33] "do"     "but"    "on"     "?"      "'s"     "so"     "this"   "which"
[41] "by"     "all"    "there"  "would"  "if"     "no"     "from"   "what"
[49] "when"   "go"
```

Notice the prevalence of punctuation, conjunctions, articles, pronouns, and determiners in this list. As one particular side-effect, the average number of sentences in a block can be calculated by counting the number of periods, question marks, and exclamation marks.[10]

Using the set of top words contained in lemmaSet, we build a matrix of word counts from the 571 equally sized blocks of words.

---

[9]The final, incomplete block is ignored.

[10]It may seem that these counts would incorrectly include other uses of these marks, such as abbreviations like "Dr." and "Mr.". However, in these cases the tokenizer will not separate the period from the remainder of the word. These symbols are only defined as separate lemmas when they define sentence boundaries (the one caveat being that this would include sentences found within long embedded quotes).

```
> mat <- cbind(match(lemma, lemmaSet),as.numeric(col(lemmaSet)))
> mat <- mat[!is.na(mat[,1]),]
> tab <- table(mat[,2],mat[,1])
```

A scatter plot based on the first three principal components of the matrix `auth` is shown in Fig. 10.5. The separation between blocks of text from Charles Dickens and the remainder of the set is very good; Nathaniel Hawthorne is also fairly well separated. Mark Twain and Sir Arthur Conan Doyle overlap considerably and on the whole are difficult to distinguish with this particular feature set. However, comparing to the previous analysis with part of speech bigrams is not entirely fair as it is easier to separate the entire text compared to just a smaller segment.

Overall, stylometrics offers an approach to exploring writing styles. We have shown just a few ways this form of analysis can be applied. Depending on the object of study and interests, the way one approaches stylometrics changes and is also why it is a powerful method for representing and interpreting textual documents.

10.5 Further Methods and Extensions

We have briefly looked at three applications of the text annotations developed in Chap. 9. Many extensions and tweaks exist for these methods. A hierarchical variant to the standard LDA algorithm that adaptively learns the number of topics has been developed [10]. It has become fairly popular and often yields better results than the fixed topic model, particularly for large copora. There is also great deal of mathematical depth in the LDA algorithm that was glossed over here. A good introduction to this and the importance of properly tuning the model and understanding the output is given by Kurt Hornik and Bettina Grün [2].

There are also many other examples of tasks in text analysis, several of which are popular in humanities applications. Examples include *sentiment analysis* [6], *concept mining* [4], and *document clustering* [9]. A good text for exploring these and other applications is *Fundamentals of Predictive Text Mining* [11]. Text mining is a very active field in computer science, with recent journal articles a great reference for the latest techniques. The *Transactions on Speech and Language Processing* jointly published by the IEEE and ACM is a good starting point.[11]

Practice

1. We started tf-idf analysis by filtering on the non-proper nouns. What happens when all the unique lemmas are included in the importance matrix? In particular, how are very common terms such as conjunctions handled?

2. Try using an unfiltered input to the LDA analysis. What happens in this case? Try again where part of speech tagging is still used, but both verbs and nouns are included.

---

[11] http://tslp.acm.org/.

3. Using the original set of filtered lemmas, run the LDA algorithm with just four topics. Can you determine good names for these topics? Try running the algorithm multiple times; do the topics remain constant after each run?

4. Run the bigram part of speech analysis as 5000 word chunks. How well does this analysis separate the four authors?

5. Using the block-wise method, construct a feature set that counts the number of tokens (raw words, not their lemmas) with 1, 2, 3, ... characters (you can cap it at 16). Run another analysis using the counts of words that are used only once in the block of text, twice, thrice, ... (this can be capped at 16 as well; hint: use `table(table(...))`). How well do these separate the authors?

References

[1] David M Blei, Andrew Y Ng, and Michael I Jordan. Latent dirichlet allocation. *the Journal of machine Learning research*, 3: 993–1022, 2003.

[2] Kurt Hornik and Bettina Grün. topicmodels: An r package for fitting topic models. *Journal of Statistical Software*, 40(13): 1–30, 2011.

[3] Dan Knights, Michael C Mozer, and Nicolas Nicolov. Detecting topic drift with compound topic models. In *ICWSM*, 2009.

[4] Maheshkumar H Kolekar, Kannappan Palaniappan, Somnath Sengupta, and Gunasekaran Seetharaman. Semantic concept mining based on hierarchical event detection for soccer video indexing. *Journal of multimedia*, 4(5):298–312, 2009.

[5] David Mimno. *mallet: A wrapper around the Java machine learning tool MALLET*, 2013. URL http://CRAN.R-project.org/package=mallet. R package version 1.0.

[6] Bo Pang and Lillian Lee. Opinion mining and sentiment analysis. *Foundations and trends in information retrieval*, 2 (1–2):1–135, 2008.

[7] Roger D Peng and Nicolas W Hengartner. Quantitative analysis of literary styles. *The American Statistician*, 56(3):175–185, 2002.

[8] Kevin Dela Rosa, Rushin Shah, Bo Lin, Anatole Gershman, and Robert Frederking. Topical clustering of tweets. *Proceedings of the ACM SIGIR: SWSM*, 2011.

[9] Michael Steinbach, George Karypis, Vipin Kumar, et al. A comparison of document clustering techniques. In *KDD workshop on text mining*, volume 400, pages 525–526. Boston, MA, 2000.

[10] Yee Whye Teh, Michael I Jordan, Matthew J Beal, and David M Blei. Hierarchical dirichlet processes. *Journal of the american statistical association*, 101 (476), 2006.

[11] Sholom M Weiss, Nitin Indurkhya, and Tong Zhang. *Fundamentals of predictive text mining*. Springer Science & Business Media, 2010.

Part III
Appendix

Chapter 11
R Packages

Abstract In this chapter, methods for installing the R packages and third-party libraries needed for the examples in this text are given. Several common issues are addressed and resources for additional help are supplied.

11.1 Installing from Within R

One of the R programming language's greatest strengths is the large set of open source user-contributed packages. These add additional functionality to the base language ranging from one off implementations of new cutting edge methods, to large general purpose suites of functions for various application domains. R packages are available on a number of sites, GitHub, for example, being a popular first stop of those under active development. The majority of stable packages are eventually published in The Comprehensive R Archive Network (CRAN), located at cran.r-project.org. As of mid-2015 nearly 7000 packages were available for download through CRAN.

The R language provides a method for automatically downloading and installing user-contributed packages.[1] For example, the following downloads the package **RColorBrewer** from CRAN and installs it onto a user's machine:

```
> install.packages("RColorBrewer")
```

Because the CRAN repository is mirrored across the world, this command may (depending on your operating system and default settings) open a pop-up window or terminal dialogue asking users to choose which mirror they would like to download from. The choice should not effect the results, though picking a relatively proximal location will help to reduce download speeds and network load.

---

[1] Depending on your installation, such as RStudio or the R console, other methods may also be available. We will stick to the one method which should be available on all R setups.

When installing the first package, the following question may pop up in the R session:

```
Would you like to use a personal library instead?   (y/n)
```

This message implies that the user does not have the correct permissions to install packages into the same location where R itself is installed. By typing "y" (yes), R will setup a separate user-writable location in which to install packages; this should not require any additional steps, and the installed packages can be loaded exactly as if they were installed into the same location as the base R.

One useful option to the `install.packages` command is the `type` parameter. It can be set to `source`, `mac.binary`, `mac.binary.mavericks`, and `win.binary`.[2] Attempting to install packages with the default value of type is the best first choice, but manually switching to a binary version (if not the default) may fix any problems that initially result from the default. For example, the **jpeg** package is known to cause problems when installing from source. On Mac OSX 10.9, this can be avoided by the following:

```
> install.packages("jpeg", type="mac.binary.mavericks")
```

Windows users will find that the type is generally set to the binary version by default, so this is unlikely to be a source of problems. For Mac Users the default depends on the method of installation. Binaries are not supplied for Linux, though many distributions provide packages with difficult installations as binaries through their individual repositories.[3]

We have tried to keep the number of package required within this text to a minimum. The following ten packages can be installed directly via from CRAN without any additional dependencies or system requirements.

```
RColorBrewer         png    (*)
igraph               sp
maptools             jpeg   (*)
abind                rgdal  (*)
colorspace           rgeos  (*)
```

Stars denote packages which may require manually setting `type` to binary. Additionally, the package **snippets** can be downloaded with a slightly modified version of the command:

```
> install.packages("snippets",,"http://rforge.net/")
```

It also has no external system dependencies, and only requires special treatment as it is currently not loaded onto CRAN from the alternative repository RForge.

Three additional packages are used in the text, and the process for setting them up is described in the following sections.

---

[2] These may change slightly over time with new versions of Windows and/or Mac OSX. Check with `?install.packages` for those available within your version of R.

[3] Typically via commands such as: `apt-get`, `yum`, or `rpm`.

11.2 rJava

The **rJava** package provides an essential link between R and the Java programming language. It is required in order to run the packages **coreNLP** and **mallet**, which are central to the text parsing and analysis shown in Chaps. 9 and 10. It requires having the Java language installed and accessible from within R, but otherwise is downloadable via CRAN by the typical `install.packages` command. For details on how to install Java, see `https://java.com/download`.

Two common issues that seem to arise when installing or loading **rJava** are the following:

- On Windows, both R and Java should either both be 32-bit or both be 64-bit. Mixing the two types can cause errors.

- Sometimes **rJava** package cannot find the Java program.
  ```
  > Sys.setenv(JAVA_HOME='C:\\Program Files\\Java\\jre7')
  ```

- In other cases, a number of issues have been solved by first clearing the JAVA_HOME variable prior to loading the library.
  ```
  Sys.setenv(JAVA_HOME="")
  ```
  This seems to fix a number of cross-platform issues, so we suggest it before asking for additional help.

If problems persist following this solution, try searching for your problem on `http://stackoverflow.com/` or via the R help mailing list.

After successfully installing **rJava**, the packages **mallet** and **coreNLP** can be installed from CRAN without any additional dependencies.

11.3 coreNLP

The **coreNLP** package provides wrappers and helper functions for calling the Stanford CoreNLP library. Its usage is described in detail throughout Chap. 9 and used as text preprocessor in Chap. 10. Once **rJava** has been installed, the **coreNLP** package can also be installed from CRAN as usual. However, due to the size of the Stanford CoreNLP library the required Java files must be downloaded separately. This can be done manually by visiting `http://nlp.stanford.edu/software/corenlp.shtml`, or by calling the following from the package:

```
> library(coreNLP)
> downloadCoreNLP()
```

The `downloadCoreNLP` function also provides methods for grabbing language-specific models for parsing non-English text.

11.4 sessionInfo

For the purpose of debugging problems, the following is the session info command for the version of R and contributed packages used to create all of the output and graphics within this book.

```
> sessionInfo()
R version 3.2.0 (2015-04-16)
Platform: x86_64-apple-darwin14.3.0 (64-bit)
Running under: OS X 10.10.3 (Yosemite)

locale:
[1] en_US.UTF-8/en_US.UTF-8/en_US.UTF-8/C/en_US.UTF-8/en_US.UTF-8

attached base packages:
[1] stats     graphics  grDevices utils     datasets  methods
[7] base

other attached packages:
 [1] mallet_1.0         rJava_0.9-6        abind_1.4-3
 [4] jpeg_0.1-8         rgeos_0.3-8        rgdal_0.9-3
 [7] snippets_0.1-0     maptools_0.8-36    sp_1.1-0
[10] RColorBrewer_1.1-2 igraph_0.7.1       colorspace_1.2-6
[13] coreNLP_0.3

loaded via a namespace (and not attached):
[1] Rcpp_0.11.6      lattice_0.20-31 XML_3.98-1.1
[4] png_0.1-7        grid_3.2.0      plyr_1.8.2
[7] foreign_0.8-63   plotrix_3.5-12
```

There is no need to exactly mimic this setup; it is provided only as a guide for assistance in any troubleshooting when issues arise following along with the code snippets in this text.

Chapter 12
100 Basic Programming Exercises

Abstract In this chapter, short programming exercises based on the material from Chaps. 2 to 5 are presented.

The following questions should be solvable using material directly presented in the respective chapters, with two notable exceptions. We did not introduce the concept of user-generated functions or how to capture answers to questions from the terminal. These were not directly applicable to the flow of the introductory chapters, but make for great building blocks for interesting programming questions. The following code snippet can be used as a template for how to do both:

```
> ask <- function() {
>   z <- readline("enter your name: ")
>   print(paste("Hello ", z, "!", sep=""))
> }
> ask()
```

When running the last line, R will ask for your name. After hitting "enter", the message will be displayed. Notice that the result from `readline` is always a character vector. If the result should be a number it must be explicitly converted.

```
> ask <- function() {
>   z <- readline("enter a number: ")
>   z <- as.numeric(z)
>   return(z + 1)
> }
> ask()
```

The other expectation is the use of the `if` statement throughout questions in Chaps. 2 and 3, even though it was not formally introduced until Sect. 4.6. The `if` statement evaluates the statement after it only if the argument is true. For example, the following prints only one of the two statement:

```
> if (1 > 2) print("one is larger than two")
> if (1 < 2) print("one is less than two")
[1] "one is less than two"
```

Using this construct for questions the earlier chapters allowed us to significantly widen their scope and extent without overly complicating the material.

Chapter 2

1. Ask for a positive number and return a vector of all the numbers between 1 and the input.

2. Ask for a number and return a vector of all the even numbers between 1 and the input.

3. Ask for a positive integer n. Return the sum: $1 + 1/2 + 1/3 + 1/4 + \cdots + 1/n$.

4. Ask for the total of a bill and return the amount of a 15 % tip. The `round` function is useful for cleaning up the result to an even penny.

5. Ask for a user's birth year and print the age they will turn this year. You can write the current year directly without trying to determine it externally (it is possible to determine the current year, but was not covered in Chap. 2).

6. Write a function which asks for a number and determines if it is a whole number (or not). Print a message displaying the result using `print`.

7. The factorial of an integer is the product of all the positive integers less than or equal to it. For example, the factorial of 4 is equal to $4 * 3 * 2 * 1 = 24$. There is a function `factorial` in base R for calculating these. Ask for a number and return the factorial, without using the R function. Hint: The function `prod` may be helpful.

8. Ask the user for a number between 1 and 10 and return the corresponding simple ordinal number. For example, 1 should be 1st, 2 should be 2nd, and 4 should be 4th. Hint: You should not write 10 separate if statements. Notice that the numbers 4–10 all have the same ending of "th".

9. Repeat the previous question, but allow the user to input any whole, positive number. Hint: Keep the input as a character vector and make use of the `nchar` and `substr` functions.

10. There is a character vector available in base R called `state.abb` giving the two digit postal abbreviations for the 50 US States. Write a function which asks for an abbreviation and returns TRUE if it is an abbreviation and FALSE otherwise.

11. Repeat the previous question, but allow for cases where the user inputs a different capitalization. For example, "CA", "Ca", and "ca" should all return as TRUE.

12. R provides another vector of state names as a vector called `state.name`. The elements line up with the abbreviations; for example, element 33 of the abbreviations is "NC" and element 33 of the names is "North Carolina". Write a function which asks for an abbreviation and returns the corresponding state name. If there is none, return the string "error".

13. Finally, write a function which asks for either a state name or state abbreviation. When given an abbreviation, it returns the state name, and when given a name it returns the state abbreviation. If there is no match to either it returns the string "error".

14. The object `state.x77` is a matrix that gives several summary statistics for each of the 50 US States from 1977. Calculate the number of high school graduates in each state, and sort from highest to lowest.

15. Calculate the number of high school graduate per square mile in each state.

16. Ask the user to provide a state abbreviation, and return the number of high school graduates in that state in 1977.

17. Now, print a vector of the state names from the highest illiteracy rate to the lowest illiteracy rate. Hint: The state names are given as `rownames`.

18. Construct a data frame with ten rows and three columns: `Illiteracy`, `Life_expectancy`, `Murder`, and `HS_grad`. Each column gives the names of the worst 10 state names. Hint: some measures are good when they are high and others are good when the are low. You will need to take account of these.

19. Using vector notation, print the state names which are in both the top 10 for illiteracy and top 10 for murder rates in 1977.

20. There are several other small datasets contained within the base installation of R. One of these is the Titanic dataset, accessed by the object `Titanic`. The format is a bit strange at first, but can be converted to a data frame with the following code:

```
ti <- as.data.frame(Titanic)
```

It has a row for each combination of Class, Sex, Age, and Survival flag, along with a frequency count (see ?Titanic for more information). Write a function which asks the user to input a Class category (either "1st", "2nd", "3rd", or "Crew") and prints the **total** survival and death counts for that category.

21. Take the titanic dataset and again ask the user to select a class. Write the subset of the data from this class and save it as a comma separated value file named "titanicOutput.csv" in the current working directory. Print to the user the full path of the created file.

22. Ask the user for the working directory where the previous command was run. Set the working directory to this location, read the titanic dataset into R and return it.

23. Repeat the previous question, but instead print the passenger Class for which the file "titanicOutput.csv" was saved.

24. R provides another dataset called WorldPhones giving the number of telephones in seven world regions, in thousands, for the years 1951, 1956, 1957, 1958, 1959, 1960, and 1961. Calculate the percentage change in number of phones for each region between 1951 and 1961. Use vector notation, do not do each region by hand! Hint: Percentage change is (new value − old value)/old value.

25. Ask the user for a year between 1951 and 1961. Return the number of phones in Europe for the year closest, but not after, the input year.

Chapter 3

26. The dataset iris is a very well-known statistical data from the 1930s. It gives several measurements of iris sepal and petal lengths (in centimeters) for three species. Construct a table of sepal length rounded to the nearest centimeter versus Species.

27. Construct the same table, but rounded to the nearest half centimeter.

28. Plot a histogram of the sepal length for the entire iris dataset.

29. Replicate the previous histogram, but manually specify the break points for the histogram and add a custom title and axis labels.

30. Plot three histograms showing the sepal length separately for each species. Make **sure** the histograms use the same break points for each plot (Hint: use the same as manually set in the previous question). Add helpful titles for the plots, and make sure to set R to display three plots at once.

31. Calculate the deciles of the petal length for the entire iris dataset.

32. Construct a table showing the number of samples from each species with petal length in the top 30 % of the dataset. How well does this help categorize the dataset by species?

33. Now bin the iris dataset into deciles based on the petal length. Produce a table by species. How well does this categorize the dataset by species?

34. We can get a very rough estimate of the petal area by multiplying the petal length and width. Calculate this area, bin the dataset into deciles on area, and compute table of the petal length deciles against the area deciles. How similar do these measurements seem?

35. Without using a for loop, construct a vector with the median petal length for each species. Add appropriate names to the output.

36. Repeat the previous question using a for loop.

37. Finally, repeat again using `tapply`.

38. As in a previous question, write a function which asks the user for a state abbreviation and returns the state name. However, this time, put the question in a for loop so the user can decode three straight state abbreviations.

39. The command `break` immediately exits a for loop; it is often used inside of an `if` statement. Redo the previous question, but break out of the loop when a non-matching abbreviation is given. You can increase the number of iterations to something large (say, 100), as a user can always get out of the function by giving a non-abbreviation.

40. Now, reverse the process so that the function returns when an abbreviation is found but asks again if it is not.

41. Using a for loop, print the sum $1 + 1/2 + 1/3 + 1/4 + \cdots + 1/n$ for all n equal to 1 through 100.

42. Now calculate the sum for all 100 values of n using a single function call.

43. Ask the user for their year of birth and print out the age they turned for every year between then and now.

44. The dataset `InsectSprays` shows the count of insects after applying one of six different insect repellents. Construct a two-row three-column grid of histograms, on the same scale, showing the number of insects from each spray. Do this using a for loop rather than coding each plot by hand.

45. Repeat the same two by three plot, but now remove the margins, axes, and labels. Replace these by adding the spray identifier (a single letter) to the plot with the `text` command.

46. Calculate the median insect count for each spray.

47. Using the `WorldPhones` dataset, calculate the total number of phones used in each year using a for loop.

48. Calculate the total number of phones used in each year using a single apply function.

49. Calculate the percentage of phones that were in Europe over the years in question.

50. Convert the entire WorldPhones matrix to percentages; in other words, each row should sum to 100.

Chapter 4

51. Produce a scatter plot of sepal length versus petal length in the iris dataset.

52. Add color to the scatter plot of sepal length versus petal length to distinguish the three iris species. Use solid dots to highlight the colors.

53. Using the previous plot as a starting point, change the size of the points based on the sepal width. Hint: A good way to get nice sizes is to divide the sepal width by the median width.

54. Change the plot to use the text of the species type instead of dots. You can remove the sizing based on sepal width so that all of the text is of the same size; however, it may help to make all the text points smaller than the default to reduce overplotting.

55. Add a vertical and horizontal median to the scatter plot of sepal length versus petal length.

56. Add *by group* vertical and horizontal medians to the scatter plot of sepal length versus petal length. There should be three vertical and three horizontal lines. Color the lines and points based on species, and make the lines dashed rather than solid.

57. Reconstruct the scatter plot of sepal length versus petal length with species colors. Add text to show the medians of the three groups. Test out different sizes for the points and text to make nice looking plot.

58. Construct a plot of petal length versus sepal width. The plot has two large clusters of points (in the upper left and lower right) and one outlier in the bottom left. Construct a coloring for these three groups. Produce a side by side plot showing petal length versus sepal width next to sepal length versus petal length. Use the new color scheme for both.

59. Create a scatter plot matrix (pairs plot) from the four numerical variables in the iris dataset. You should reduce the margins to fit the entire plot on the screen but do not need to directly replicate all of the tweaks from Sect. 4.6.

60. Change the custom scatter plot matrix to have a histogram on the diagonal axis.

61. Take the `InsectRepelant` dataset and produce a single line plot of the data. It will be easiest going forward to do this by (1) plotting the data with a white color, and (2) making a single call to the `lines` function.

62. The first row of the `InsectRepelant` dataset has a count of 10. Add to the plot a stack of solid points to represent this count between the coordinates (1,1) and (1,10).

63. Now, replicate this for every row of data on a plot. Do not include the line as it will no longer be needed. You can do this in several ways, though the most straightforward is as a loop over the rows of the dataset. Hint: You may need to create a special case for the two rows with a count of zero.

64. Duplicate the previous plot, but use the spray type as a text object (it is a single letter between A and F) in place of the dots).

65. Add vertical bars to separate the groups. Do not do this manually, but use vectors to plot all the lines at once.

66. Using dots again instead of letters replicate the plot such that one dot represents three counts. Do not plot any remainder, so a count of 5 should have only one dot. Hint: The `floor` function will be helpful; it removes the fractional part of a number.

67. Now, redo the plot such that the fractional part of the remainder is represented by a smaller dot. So a remainder of 0.33 gets a dot with `cex=0.33` and a remainder of 0.66 gets a dot with `cex=0.66`.

68. The object `AirPassengers` is a dataset which gives the number of international airline passengers by month for 12 years of data. It is stored by default in an atypical format but can be converted to a matrix easily:

```
ap <- matrix(as.numeric(AirPassengers),ncol=12)
rownames(ap) <- month.abb
colnames(ap) <- 1949:1960
```

Calculate the total flyers for each year, and then calculate the total number of flyers over each month. Are there any noticeable patterns?

69. Construct a line plot of the number of fliers for 1949. Use custom axes to label the months.

70. Construct a graphic with line plots for every year. Add a text label to the data point for July to label the years. Hint: Use `range(ap)` to determine the limits of the y-axis to capture all of the data.

71. Produce a scatter plot of the 1949 data against the 1950 data. Use `text` to label the points. Remember to offset the labels from the points.

72. Produce a new dataset which shows the month percentage of flights for each year. In other words, each column should sum to 100. Save this as `scaledAp`.

73. Create a new line chart showing these standardized values for each year over the months.

74. Create an empty plot with x and y ranges from 1 to 12. Create a dot at each coordinate (i, j) to represent the value in the 12 by 12 matrix `ap`. Use relative sizes to show the value. Construct useful custom axes (use the option `las=2` to make the axes look nicer).

75. Recreate the plot using the `scaledAp` data. Color points blue if they are less than $100/12$ and red if they are greater than $100/12$ (we use this cut-off as it represents a typical month).

Chapter 5

76. The dataset `ChickWeight` contains several time series showing the weight of young chickens feed one of four different diets. Produce a series of line plots using categorical colors. Use the **colorspace** package for the colors.

77. Remove the five chicks with incomplete data. Normalize the weights of each chick such that each weighs 0 on the first day and 1 on the last day.

78. Construct a matrix with one row for each chick showing the growth rate, (new weight−old weight/old weight) for each day. This will have 11 columns and a row for each chick.

79. Plot the chick ids against the growth rates.

80. Change labels from the previous plot into text commands giving the day in time for a random sample set of 3 days selected for each chick.

81. Repeat the previous plot with solid dots, where a sequential palette is used to indicate time.

82. Create and place a legend decoding the colors from the previous plot. You will have to increase the size of the plot and perhaps make the legend smaller than the default to fit everything. What do you notice about typical growth rates from this plot now?

83. Take `AirPassengers` dataset and plot the 1949 counts against the 1950 counts, using a categorical palette to distinguish the four seasons of the data.

84. Redo the previous plot using a sequential heat palette to show the months and include a legend to explain the colors.

12 100 Basic Programming Exercises

85. Plot two randomly chosen numeric variables from the iris dataset.

86. A previous question asked to plot the sepal length versus petal length for the iris data, where each point is labeled with text giving the plant species. Redo this plot using subsampling to reduce the over plotting. Use a color palette to select the colors for the plot.

87. Now, redo the plot of sepal length versus petal length using a sequential color palette to display sepal width, using five buckets for the bins.

88. Add a helpful legend for the colors in the previous plot to describe the coloring of the points.

89. Reconstruct the `scaledAp` data, but this time subtract the $100/12$ from every entry. Create a histogram of the results. The average value should be zero, but the median of the scaled results will be negative.

90. Create a divergent palette with 21 bins from the `scaledAp`. Recall that this requires two sets of bins. Use this to plot the entire dataset as a single time series; add a line through the data points to improve readability.

91. Edit the previous line plot to have a legend off to the right of the entire plot, and add custom x-axis labels showing the years.

92. Write a for loop that cycles over the numbers 1–100. For each iteration of the loop, if the number is divisible by 3, print "fizz" to the console, and if divisible by 5, print "buzz". Otherwise print the number itself. (This is a well-known intro interview question for new programmers called FizzBuzz).

93. Repeat FizzBuzz using a vector in place of a loop. The return value will be a character vector.

94. Create a function which asks the user for how many letters they would like their password to be and then generates a random string of letters/numbers of that length as a random password. Hint: R has the objects `letter` and `LETTERS` built in a default object.

95. Sample 1000 points from the set containing just 1 and -1. Calculate the cumulative sum of this sample. This simulates a mathematical model known as a random walk.

96. Plot the cumulative sum of the random walk over time as a line plot. Run it several times to see different random outputs. What does the plot remind you of?

97. R provides the function `Sys.sleep`, which causes the program to wait for a given number of seconds before proceeding. Combine this with a short time period (0.1 seconds is a good first guess) to animate the previous plot by waiting in-between drawing each line segment.

98. Calculate 10,000 separate random walks, saving the 500th and 1000th step from each. Take the result and create a scatter plot of the results; use a color with an alpha channel to reduce the effects of over plotting. What patterns do you see in the plot?

99. Calculate side-by-side histograms of the 500th and 1000th positions from the previous simulation. What patterns do you notice here?

100. Write a function to simulate the game "rock-scissors-paper". You should ask the user to select one of these by name, generate a random response, and indicate who won.

Chapter 13
100 Basic Programming Solutions

Abstract Code snippets showing possible solutions to the exercises presented in Chap. 12 are presented in this chapter.

These are examples of how to solve the problems presented in Chap. 12, but they are by no means the only way of solving them. These snippets were written to use as limited a set of functions as possible, and more elegant solutions often exist. They should by no means be studied as the "right" way to solve the problems; in many cases, they are far from that.

Chapter 2

Solution to Question #1

```
ask <- function() {
  num <- readline("enter a number: ")
  num <- as.numeric(num)
  return(1:num)
}
```

Solution to Question #2

```
ask <- function() {
  num <- readline("enter a number: ")
  num <- as.numeric(num)
  ans <- seq(2, num, by=2)
  return(ans)
}
```

Solution to Question #3

```
ask <- function() {
  num <- readline("enter a number: ")
```

```
  num <- as.numeric(num)
  ans <- sum(1 / (1:num))
  return(ans)
}
```

Solution to Question #4

```
ask <- function() {
  num <- readline("bill amount: ")
  num <- as.numeric(num)
  num <- round(num * 0.15,2)
  return(num)
}
```

Solution to Question #5

```
ask <- function() {
  num <- readline("birth year: ")
  num <- as.numeric(num)
  ans <- 2015 - num # change 2015 to the current year
  print("You turned (or are turning)" ans, "years old this year")
}
```

Solution to Question #6

```
ask <- function() {
  num <- readline("enter a number: ")
  num <- as.numeric(num)
  if (num == round(num)) print("Whole number")
  if (num != round(num)) print("Not a whole number")
}
```

Solution to Question #7

```
ask <- function() {
  num <- as.numeric(readline("enter a number: "))
  return(prod(num:1))
}
```

Solution to Question #8

```
ask <- function() {
  num = as.numeric(readline("enter a number between 1 and 10: "))

  if (num == 1) ans <- paste(num, "st", sep="")
  if (num == 2) ans <- paste(num, "nd", sep="")
  if (num == 3) ans <- paste(num, "rd", sep="")
  if (num > 3)  ans <- paste(num, "th", sep="")

  return(ans)
}
```

13 100 Basic Programming Solutions

Solution to Question #9

```
ask <- function() {
  num <- readline("enter a number between 1 and 10: ")
  lastNum <- as.numeric(substr(num, nchar(num), nchar(num)))

  if (lastNum == 1) ans <- paste(num, "st", sep="")
  if (lastNum == 2) ans <- paste(num, "nd", sep="")
  if (lastNum == 3) ans <- paste(num, "rd", sep="")
  if (lastNum > 3)  ans <- paste(num, "th", sep="")

  return(ans)
}
```

Solution to Question #10

```
ask <- function() {
  abb <- as.numeric(readline("enter an abbreviation: "))
  ans <- abb %in% state.abb
  return(ans)
}
```

Solution to Question #11

```
ask <- function() {
  abb <- readline("enter an abbreviation: ")
  abb <- toupper(abb) # because state.abb is all upper case
  ans <- abb %in% state.abb
  return(ans)
}
```

Solution to Question #12

```
ask <- function() {
  abb <- readline("enter an abbreviation: ")
  ans <- state.name[abb == state.abb]
  if (length(ans) == 0) ans = "error"
  return(ans)
}
```

Solution to Question #13

```
ask <- function() {
  abb = readline("enter an abbreviation or state name: ")

  if (any(abb == state.abb)) {
    ans <- state.name[abb == state.abb]
  } else if (any(abb == state.name)) {
    ans <- state.abb[abb == state.name]
  } else {
    ans <- "error"
  }

  return(ans)
}
```

Solution to Question #14

```
ans <- sort(state.x77[,1] * state.x77[,6])
```

Solution to Question #15

```
ans <- sort(state.x77[,6] / state.x77[,8])
```

Solution to Question #16

```
ask <- function() {
  abb <- readline("enter an abbreviation: ")
  index = which(abb == state.abb)
  ans <- state.x77[index,1] * state.x77[index,6]
  return(ans)
}
```

Solution to Question #17

```
ans1 <- rownames(state.x77)[order(state.x77[,3], decreasing=TRUE)]
ans1 <- rownames(state.x77)[order(state.x77[,"Illiteracy"],
                            decreasing=TRUE)]
```

Solution to Question #18

```
index <- order(state.x77[,3], decreasing=TRUE)[1:10]
Illiteracy <- rownames(state.x77)[index]

index <- order(state.x77[,4])[1:10]
Life_expectancy <- rownames(state.x77)[index]

index <- order(state.x77[,5], decreasing=TRUE)[1:10]
Murder <- rownames(state.x77)[index]

index <- order(state.x77[,6])[1:10]
HS_grad <- rownames(state.x77)[index]

ans = data.frame(Illiteracy, Life_expectancy, Murder, HS_grad,
                 stringsAsFactors=FALSE)
```

Solution to Question #19

```
oldAns <- ans # from previous question
ans <- oldAns$Illiteracy[which(oldAns$Illiteracy %in% oldAns$Murder)]
```

Solution to Question #20

```
ti <- as.data.frame(Titanic)
ask <- function() {
  cl <- readline("enter Class ('1st', '2nd', '3rd' or 'Crew'): ")

  tiSubset <- ti[ti$Class == cl,]
  deaths <- sum(tiSubset$Freq[tiSubset$Survived == "No"])
```

13 100 Basic Programming Solutions   197

```
  survived <- sum(tiSubset$Freq[tiSubset$Survived == "Yes"])

  print(paste("Total deaths", deaths))
  print(paste("Total survived", survived))
}
```

Solution to Question #21

```
ti <- as.data.frame(Titanic)
ask <- function() {
  cl <- readline("enter Class ('1st', '2nd', '3rd' or 'Crew'): ")

  tiSubset <- ti[ti$Class == cl,]
  write.csv(tiSubset, "titanicOutput.csv")

  print(paste("Saved output to ", getwd(), "/titanicOutput.csv",
      sep=""))
}
```

Solution to Question #22

```
ask <- function() {
  wd <- readline("directory of saved titanic data: ")

  setwd(wd)
  tiInput <- read.csv("titanicOutput.csv", as.is=TRUE)

  return(tiInput)
}
```

Solution to Question #23

```
ask <- function() {
  wd <- readline("directory of saved titanic data: ")

  setwd(wd)
  tiInput <- read.csv("titanicOutput.csv", as.is=TRUE)

  print(paste("You saved data from the Class:", tiInput$Class[1]))
}
```

Solution to Question #24

```
ans <- (WorldPhones[7,] - WorldPhones[1,]) / WorldPhones[1,]
```

Solution to Question #25

```
ask <- function() {
  year <- as.numeric(readline("enter a year between 1951 and 1961:
      "))
  allYears <- as.numeric(rownames(WorldPhones))
  index <- which(allYears <= year)
  index <- index[length(index)]
```

```
  ans <- WorldPhones[index,2] * 1000
  return(ans)
}
```

Chapter 3

Solution to Question #26

```
ans <- table(round(iris$Sepal.Length), iris$Species)
```

Solution to Question #27

```
ans <- table(round(iris$Sepal.Length*2)/2, iris$Species)
```

Solution to Question #28

```
hist(iris$Sepal.Length)
```

Solution to Question #29

```
hist(iris$Sepal.Length, breaks=seq(4,8,by=0.5),
     xlab="Sepal Length",
     ylab="Count",
     main="Distribution of Sepal Length for the Iris Dataset")
```

Solution to Question #30

```
par(mfrow=c(1,3))
hist(iris$Sepal.Length[iris$Species == "setosa"],
     breaks=seq(4,8,by=0.5),
     xlab="Sepal Length",
     ylab="Count",
     main="Sepal Length for species setosa")
hist(iris$Sepal.Length[iris$Species == "versicolor"],
     breaks=seq(4,8,by=0.5),
     xlab="Sepal Length",
     ylab="Count",
     main="Sepal Length for species versicolor")
hist(iris$Sepal.Length[iris$Species == "virginica"],
     breaks=seq(4,8,by=0.5),
     xlab="Sepal Length",
     ylab="Count",
     main="Sepal Length for species virginica")
```

Solution to Question #31

```
ans <- quantile(iris$Petal.Length,prob=seq(0,1,length.out=11))
```

Solution to Question #32

```
breakPoints <- quantile(iris$Petal.Length,prob=0.7)
ans <- table(iris$Species, breakPoints > iris$Petal.Length)
```

13 100 Basic Programming Solutions   199

Solution to Question #33

```
breakPoints <- quantile(iris$Petal.Length,
                        prob=seq(0,1,length.out=11),
                        names=FALSE)
bin <- cut(iris$Petal.Length, breakPoints,labels=FALSE,
           include.lowest=TRUE)
ans <- table(iris$Species, bin)
```

Solution to Question #34

```
breakPoints <- quantile(iris$Petal.Length,
                        prob=seq(0,1,length.out=11),
                        names=FALSE)
binLength <- cut(iris$Petal.Length, breakPoints,labels=FALSE,
           include.lowest=TRUE)

area <- iris$Petal.Length * iris$Petal.Width
breakPoints <- quantile(area,
                        prob=seq(0,1,length.out=11),
                        names=FALSE)
binArea <- cut(area, breakPoints,labels=FALSE,
           include.lowest=TRUE)

table(binLength, binArea)
```

Solution to Question #35

```
ans <- rep(0, length=3)
ans[1] <- quantile(iris$Petal.Length[iris$Species == "setosa"],
                   probs=0.5)
ans[2] <- quantile(iris$Petal.Length[iris$Species == "versicolor"],
                   probs=0.5)
ans[3] <- quantile(iris$Petal.Length[iris$Species == "virginica"],
                   probs=0.5)
names(ans) <- c("setosa", "versicolor", "virginica")
```

Solution to Question #36

```
species <- unique(iris$Species)
ans <- rep(0, length=3)
for (i in 1:3) {
  ans[i] <- quantile(iris$Petal.Length[iris$Species == species[i]],
                   probs=0.5)
}
names(ans) <- c("setosa", "versicolor", "virginica")
```

Solution to Question #37

```
tapply(iris$Petal.Length, iris$Species, quantile, probs=0.5)
```

Solution to Question #38

```
ask <- function() {
  for (i in 1:3) {
    abb = readline("enter an abbreviation: ")
    ans <- state.name[abb == state.abb]
    if (length(ans) == 0) ans = "error"
    print(ans)
  }
}
```

Solution to Question #39

```
ask <- function() {
  for (i in 1:100) {
    abb = readline("enter an abbreviation: ")
    ans <- state.name[abb == state.abb]
    if (length(ans) == 0) break
    print(ans)
  }
}
```

Solution to Question #40

```
ask <- function() {
  for (i in 1:100) {
    abb = readline("enter an abbreviation: ")
    ans <- state.name[abb == state.abb]
    if (length(ans) != 0) break
    print("No match found!")
  }
  return(ans)
}
```

Solution to Question #41

```
for (i in 1:100) {
  print(sum(1 / (1:i)))
}
```

Solution to Question #42

```
ans <- cumsum(1 / (1:100))
```

Solution to Question #43

```
ask <- function() {
  num <- readline("birth year: ")
  num <- as.numeric(num)
  age <- 2015 - num # change 2015 to the current year

  for (i in 1:age) {
    print(paste("You turned", i, "years old in", 2015-age+i))
  }
}
```

Solution to Question #44

```
sprays <- unique(InsectSprays$spray)
par(mfrow=c(2,3))
for (j in 1:length(sprays)) {
  hist(InsectSprays$count, breaks=seq(0,30,by=5))
}
```

Solution to Question #45

```
sprays <- unique(InsectSprays$spray)
par(mfrow=c(2,3))
par(mar=c(0,0,0,0))
for (j in 1:length(sprays)) {
  hist(InsectSprays$count, breaks=seq(0,30,by=5),
       axes=FALSE,xlab="",ylab="",main="")
  box()
  text(20,25,paste("Spray='",sprays[j],"'",sep=""))
}
```

Solution to Question #46

```
ans <- tapply(InsectSprays$count, InsectSprays$spray,
              quantile, probs=0.5)
```

Solution to Question #47

```
ans <- rep(NA, nrow(WorldPhones))
for (i in 1:nrow(WorldPhones)) {
  ans[i] = sum(WorldPhones[i,])
}
```

Solution to Question #48

```
ans <- apply(WorldPhones, 1, sum)
```

Solution to Question #49

```
ans <- 100 * WorldPhones[,2] / apply(WorldPhones, 1, sum)
```

Solution to Question #50

```
ans <- 100 * WorldPhones / apply(WorldPhones, 1, sum)
```

Chapter 4

Solution to Question #51

```
plot(iris$Sepal.Length,iris$Petal.Length)
```

Solution to Question #52

```
species <- unique(iris$Species)
colVals <- c("red", "green", "blue")
cols <- colVals[match(iris$Species, species)]
plot(iris$Sepal.Length,iris$Petal.Length, col=cols, pch=19)
```

Solution to Question #53

```
species <- unique(iris$Species)
colVals <- c("red", "green", "blue")
cols <- colVals[match(iris$Species, species)]
sizes <- iris$Sepal.Width / quantile(iris$Sepal.Width, probs=0.5)
plot(iris$Sepal.Length,iris$Petal.Length, col=cols,
     pch=19, cex=sizes)
```

Solution to Question #54

```
species <- unique(iris$Species)
colVals <- c("red", "green", "blue")
cols <- colVals[match(iris$Species, species)]
plot(iris$Sepal.Length,iris$Petal.Length, col="white",
     pch=19, cex=sizes)
text(iris$Sepal.Length,iris$Petal.Length, iris$Species,
     col=cols, cex=0.5)
```

Solution to Question #55

```
plot(iris$Sepal.Length,iris$Petal.Length)
abline(v=quantile(iris$Sepal.Length,probs=0.5))
abline(h=quantile(iris$Petal.Length,probs=0.5))
```

Solution to Question #56

```
colVals <- c("red", "green", "blue")
cols <- colVals[match(iris$Species, species)]
plot(iris$Sepal.Length,iris$Petal.Length,
     col=cols, pch=19, cex=sizes)

vals <- tapply(iris$Sepal.Length, iris$Species, quantile,probs=0.5)
abline(v=vals, col=colVals, lty="dashed")
vals <- tapply(iris$Petal.Length, iris$Species, quantile,probs=0.5)
abline(h=vals, col=colVals, lty="dashed")
```

13 100 Basic Programming Solutions   203

Solution to Question #57

```
species <- unique(iris$Species)
colVals <- c("red", "green", "blue")
cols <- colVals[match(iris$Species, species)]
plot(iris$Sepal.Length,iris$Petal.Length, col=cols, pch=19)

xval <- tapply(iris$Sepal.Length, iris$Species, quantile,probs=0.5)
yval <- tapply(iris$Petal.Length, iris$Species, quantile,probs=0.5)

text(xval, yval, species, cex=1.5)
```

Solution to Question #58

```
plot(iris$Petal.Length,iris$Sepal.Width)
groups = rep(2L,nrow(iris))
groups[iris$Petal.Length < 2] = 1L
groups[iris$Petal.Length < 2 & iris$Sepal.Width < 2.5] = 3L

par(mfrow=c(1,2))
colVals <- c("red", "green", "blue")
plot(iris$Petal.Length,iris$Sepal.Width, col=colVals[groups], pch=19)
plot(iris$Sepal.Length,iris$Petal.Length, col=colVals[groups],
     pch=19)
```

Solution to Question #59

```
par(mfrow=c(4,4))
par(mar=c(1,1,1,1))
par(oma=c(2,2,2,2))

for (i in 1:4) {
  for (j in 1:4) {
    plot(iris[,i], iris[,j], pch=19, cex=0.5)
  }
}
```

Solution to Question #60

```
par(mfrow=c(4,4))
par(mar=c(1,1,1,1))
par(oma=c(2,2,2,2))

for (i in 1:4) {
  for (j in 1:4) {
    if (i != j) plot(iris[,i], iris[,j], pch=19, cex=0.5)
    if (i == j) hist(iris[,i], main="")
  }
}
```

Solution to Question #61

```
plot(InsectSprays$count,col="white")
lines(InsectSprays$count)
```

Solution to Question #62

```
plot(InsectSprays$count,col="white")
lines(InsectSprays$count)
points(rep(1,10),1:10,pch=19)
```

Solution to Question #63

```
plot(InsectSprays$count,col="white")

for (i in 1:nrow(InsectSprays)) {
  thisCount = InsectSprays$count[i]
  if (thisCount > 0) points(rep(i,thisCount),1:thisCount,pch=19)
}
```

Solution to Question #64

```
plot(InsectSprays$count,col="white")

for (i in 1:nrow(InsectSprays)) {
  thisCount = InsectSprays$count[i]
  thisSpray = InsectSprays$spray[i]
  if (thisCount > 0) text(rep(i,thisCount),1:thisCount,thisSpray)
}
```

Solution to Question #65

```
plot(InsectSprays$count,col="white")

for (i in 1:nrow(InsectSprays)) {
  thisCount = InsectSprays$count[i]
  thisSpray = InsectSprays$spray[i]
  if (thisCount > 0) text(rep(i,thisCount),1:thisCount,thisSpray)
}

abline(v=seq(0.5,72.5,by=12))
```

Solution to Question #66

```
plot(floor(InsectSprays$count/3),col="white")

for (i in 1:nrow(InsectSprays)) {
  thisCount = floor(InsectSprays$count/3)[i]
  thisSpray = InsectSprays$spray[i]
  if (thisCount > 0) points(rep(i,thisCount),1:thisCount,pch=19)
}
```

Solution to Question #67

```
plot(floor(InsectSprays$count/3),col="white")

for (i in 1:nrow(InsectSprays)) {
  thisCount = floor(InsectSprays$count/3)[i]
  thisSpray = InsectSprays$spray[i]
  if (thisCount > 0) points(rep(i,thisCount),1:thisCount,pch=19)
  fracPart = (InsectSprays$count/3)[i] -
      floor(InsectSprays$count/3)[i]
  points(i,thisCount+1,pch=19,cex=fracPart)
}
```

Solution to Question #68

```
ans <- apply(ap, 1, sum)
ans <- apply(ap, 2, sum)
```

Solution to Question #69

```
plot(1:12, ap[,1], col="white", axes=FALSE)
axis(2)
axis(1, at=1:12, rownames(ap))
lines(1:12, ap[,1])
```

Solution to Question #70

```
plot(1:12, ap[,1], col="white", axes=FALSE, ylim=range(ap))
axis(2)
axis(1, at=1:12, rownames(ap))
for (j in 1:nrow(ap))
  lines(1:12, ap[,j])

text(rep(7,12),ap[7,],colnames(ap), cex=0.5)
```

Solution to Question #71

```
plot(ap[,1], ap[,2], pch=19, ylim=c(100,180))
text(ap[,1], ap[,2]+5, rownames(ap))
```

Solution to Question #72

```
# As a for loop
scaledAp <- ap
for (j in 1:12) {
  scaledAp[,j] <- 100 * scaledAp[,j] / sum(scaledAp[,j])
}

# Matrix math version
scaledAp <- t(t(ap) / apply(ap,2,sum)) * 100
```

Solution to Question #73

```
plot(1:12, scaledAp[,1], col="white", axes=FALSE,
     ylim=range(scaledAp))
axis(2)
axis(1, at=1:12, rownames(scaledAp))
for (j in 1:nrow(scaledAp))
  lines(1:12, scaledAp[,j])

text(rep(7,12),scaledAp[7,],colnames(scaledAp), cex=0.5)
```

Solution to Question #74

```
plot(0,0,xlim=c(1,12),ylim=c(1,12), col="white",
     axes=FALSE, main="", xlab="", ylab="")
box()
axis(1,at=1:12,colnames(ap), las=2)
axis(2,at=1:12,rownames(ap), las=2)

for (i in 1:12) {
  points(rep(i,12), 1:12, cex = ap[,i] / mean(ap), pch=19)
}
```

Solution to Question #75

```
plot(0,0,xlim=c(1,12),ylim=c(1,12), col="white",
     axes=FALSE, main="", xlab="", ylab="")
box()
axis(1,at=1:12,colnames(scaledAp), las=2)
axis(2,at=1:12,rownames(scaledAp), las=2)

cols = matrix("blue", nrow=12, ncol=12)
cols[scaledAp > 1/12 * 100] <- "red"

for (i in 1:12) {
  points(rep(i,12), 1:12, cex = scaledAp[,i] / mean(scaledAp),
         pch=19,col=cols[,i])
}
```

Chapter 5

Solution to Question #76

```
library(colorspace)
cols <- rainbow_hcl(4)
plot(0,0,col="white",xlim=range(ChickWeight$Time),
     ylim=range(ChickWeight$weight), xlab="Time",
     ylab="Weight")

for (j in unique(ChickWeight$Chick)) {
```

13 100 Basic Programming Solutions   207

```
  index <- which(ChickWeight$Chick == j)
  lines(ChickWeight$Time[index],
        ChickWeight$weight[index],
        col=cols[ChickWeight$Diet[index][1]],
        lwd=3)
}
```

Solution to Question #77

```
cw <- ChickWeight[-which(ChickWeight$Chick %in% c(44,8,18,16,15)),]
for (j in unique(cw$Chick)) {
  index <- which(cw$Chick == j)
  cw$weight[index] = cw$weight[index] - cw$weight[index][1]
  cw$weight[index] = cw$weight[index] / cw$weight[index][12]
}

cols <- rainbow_hcl(4)
plot(0,0,col="white",xlim=range(cw$Time),
     ylim=range(cw$weight), xlab="Time",
     ylab="Weight")

for (j in unique(cw$Chick)) {
  index <- which(cw$Chick == j)
  lines(cw$Time[index],
        cw$weight[index],
        col=cols[cw$Diet[index][1]],
        lwd=3)
}
```

Solution to Question #78

```
cw <- ChickWeight[-which(ChickWeight$Chick %in% c(44,8,18,16,15)),]
ans <- matrix(NA, ncol=11, nrow=length(unique(cw$Chick)))
for (j in 1:nrow(ans)) {
  index <- which(cw$Chick == unique(cw$Chick)[j])
  ans[j,] <- (cw$weight[index][-1] - cw$weight[index][-12]) /
             cw$weight[index][-12]
}
```

Solution to Question #79

```
cols <- rainbow_hcl(4)
plot(0,0,col="white",xlim=c(1,nrow(ans)), ylim=range(ans))
for (j in 1:length(unique(cw$Chick))) {
  points(rep(j,11), ans[j,])
}
```

Solution to Question #80

```
cols <- rainbow_hcl(4)
plot(0,0,col="white",xlim=c(1,nrow(ans)), ylim=range(ans))
for (j in 1:length(unique(cw$Chick))) {
  index <- sample(1:11,3)
  text(rep(j,3), ans[j,index], seq(0,20,by=2)[index])
}
```

Solution to Question #81

```
cols <- sequential_hcl(11)
plot(0,0,col="white",xlim=c(1,nrow(ans)), ylim=range(ans))
for (j in 1:length(unique(cw$Chick))) {
  points(rep(j,11), ans[j,], pch=19, col=cols)
}
```

Solution to Question #82

```
cols <- rev(sequential_hcl(11))
plot(0,0,col="white",xlim=c(1,nrow(ans)), ylim=c(-0.15,0.7))
for (j in 1:length(unique(cw$Chick))) {
  points(rep(j,11), ans[j,], pch=19, col=cols)
}

legendText <- paste("growth between days ", seq(0,20,by=2), " to ",
                   c(seq(2,20,by=2),21),sep="")
legend("topright", legend=legendText, col=cols, pch=19, cex=0.6,
       bg=grey(0.9))
```

Solution to Question #83

```
cols <- rainbow_hcl(4)
cols <- rep(cols, each=3)
plot(ap[,1], ap[,2], col=cols, pch=19)
```

Solution to Question #84

```
cols <- heat_hcl(12)
plot(ap[,1], ap[,2], col=cols, pch=19)
legend("topleft", legend=rownames(ap), col=cols, pch=19)
```

Solution to Question #85

```
plot(iris[,sample(1:4,2)])
```

Solution to Question #86

```
species <- unique(iris$Species)
colVals <- rainbow_hcl(3, alpha=0.2)
cols <- colVals[match(iris$Species, species)]
colVals <- rainbow_hcl(3, alpha=0.8)
colsText <- colVals[match(iris$Species, species)]
```

```
index <- sample(1:nrow(iris), 45)
plot(iris$Sepal.Length,iris$Petal.Length, col=cols,
     pch=19)
text(iris$Sepal.Length[index],iris$Petal.Length[index],
     iris$Species[index], col=colsText[index], cex=0.5)
```

Solution to Question #87

```
breakPoints <- quantile(iris$Sepal.Width,
                        prob=seq(0,1,length.out=6),
                        names=FALSE)
bin <- cut(iris$Sepal.Width, breakPoints,labels=FALSE,
           include.lowest=TRUE)
colVals <- rev(sequential_hcl(6))
cols <- colVals[bin]

plot(iris$Sepal.Length,iris$Petal.Length, col=cols,
     pch=19)
```

Solution to Question #88

```
legendText <- paste(breakPoints[-6], " to ", breakPoints[-1],sep="")
legend("bottomright", legend=legendText, col=colVals, pch=19,
    cex=0.6,
       bg=grey(0.9))
```

Solution to Question #89

```
scaledAp <- t(t(ap) / apply(ap,2,sum)) * 100
scaledAp <- scaledAp - 100/12
hist(scaledAp)
```

Solution to Question #90

```
bpUpper <- quantile(scaledAp[scaledAp > 0], seq(0,1,by=0.1))
bpLower <- quantile(scaledAp[scaledAp < 0], seq(0,1,by=0.1))
breakPoints <- c(bpLower, bpUpper)
colVals <- diverge_hsv(21)

bin <- cut(scaledAp, breakPoints,labels=FALSE,
           include.lowest=TRUE)
plot(as.numeric(scaledAp), col=colVals[bin], pch=19)
lines(as.numeric(scaledAp),col=grey(0.2))
```

Solution to Question #91

```
par(mar=c(5.1, 4.1, 4.1, 10))
plot(as.numeric(scaledAp), col=colVals[bin], pch=19,
     axes=FALSE, xlab="", ylab="")
lines(as.numeric(scaledAp),col=grey(0.2))
box()
axis(1, at=seq(0,12*12,by=12), 1949:1961)
```

```
legendText <- paste(round(breakPoints[-22],2), " to ",
                    round(breakPoints[-1],2),sep="")
legend(160, 2, cex=0.5, legend=rev(legendText), pch=19,
        col=rev(colVals), xpd=TRUE)
```

Solution to Question #92

```
for (i in 1:100) {
  if (i %% 3 == 0) print("fizz")
  else if (i %% 5 == 0) print("buzz")
  else print(i)
}
```

Solution to Question #93

```
input <- 1:100
ans <- as.character(input)
ans[input %% 3 == 0] <- "fizz"
ans[input %% 5 == 0] <- "buzz"
```

Solution to Question #94

```
ask <- function() {
  z <- readline("how long should the password be: ")
  z <- as.numeric(z)
  z <- sample(c(letters,LETTERS,0:9), z, replace=TRUE)
  return(paste(z, collapse=""))
}
```

Solution to Question #95

```
x <- sample(c(-1,1), 1000, replace=TRUE)
ans <- cumsum(x)
```

Solution to Question #96

```
x <- sample(c(-1,1), 1000, replace=TRUE)
ans <- cumsum(x)
plot(ans, type="l")
```

Solution to Question #97

```
x <- sample(c(-1,1), 1000, replace=TRUE)
ans <- cumsum(x)

plot(ans, type="l", col="white")
for (j in 1:999) {
  lines(c(j,j+1), c(ans[j], ans[j]+1))
  Sys.sleep(0.1)
}
```

Solution to Question #98

```
N <- 10000
x500 <- rep(NA, N)
x1000 <- rep(NA, N)
for (i in 1:N) {
  x <- sample(c(-1,1), 1000, replace=TRUE)
  x <- cumsum(x)
  x500[i] = x[500]
  x1000[i] = x[1000]
}
```

Solution to Question #99

```
par(mfrow=c(1,2))
breaks <- seq(-150, 150, by=10)
hist(x500, breaks=breaks)
hist(x1000, breaks=breaks)
```

Solution to Question #100

```
opts <- c("rock", "scissors", "paper")
ask <- function() {
  user <- readline("rock, scissors, or paper: ")
  index <- which(opts == user)
  
  if (length(index) == 0) return("invalid response")
  
  computer <- sample(opts, 1L)
  
  if (computer == "rock") {
    if (user == "rock") return("you tie")
    if (user == "scissors") return("you lose")
    if (user == "paper") return("you win")
  }
  if (computer == "scissors") {
    if (user == "rock") return("you win")
    if (user == "scissors") return("you tie")
    if (user == "paper") return("you lose")
  }
  if (computer == "paper") {
    if (user == "rock") return("you lose")
    if (user == "scissors") return("you win")
    if (user == "paper") return("you tie")
  }
}
```

Printed by Printforce, the Netherlands